From Mainframe to Workstations

From Mainframe to Workstations

Offloading Application Development

Mark A. Butterline

QED Publishing Group
Boston • London • Toronto

P.O. Box 82-181
Wellesley, MA 02181

QED Publishing Group is a division of QED Information Sciences, Inc.

Library of Congress Catalog Number: 92-12411
International Standard Book Number: 0-89435-420-5

Printed in the United States of America
92 93 94 10 9 8 7 6 5 4 3 2 1

Library of Congress Cataloging-in-Publication Data

Butterline, Mark A..
From mainframe to workstations: offloading application development / Mark A. Butterline.
Includes bibliographical references and index.
ISBN 0-89435-420-5
1. Computer software—Development. 2. Application software.
I. Title.
QA76.76.D47B88 1992
005.2'2—dc20 92-12411
CIP

To my wife (and editor) Marianne

Contents

List of Figures xi
Introduction xiii

***CHAPTER 1. IS OFFLOADING RIGHT FOR ME?* 1**

The Prerequisites 2
Analyzing User Needs 3
Development Cycle Issues 11
Functional Role Issues 15
Cultural and Organizational Implications 18
Offloaded Development as Part of a Larger Strategy 19
Keeping Expectations Realistic 21
Summary 22
References 23

***CHAPTER 2. THE BENEFITS OF AN OFFLOADED DEVELOPMENT ENVIRONMENT* 25**

Improved Productivity 25
Improved Quality 29
Decreased Mainframe Usage 30
Access to Nonmainframe Production Platforms 32

Bonus Benefits 33
Calculating Benefits 36
Benefits Worksheet 37
Summary 40
References 40

CHAPTER 3. THE COSTS OF AN OFFLOADED DEVELOPMENT ENVIRONMENT 43
Hardware 43
Software 48
Planning and Installation 51
Training 52
Operation, Administration, and Maintenance (OA&M) 53
Learning Curve 54
Summary 57
References 58

CHAPTER 4. PLANNING CONSIDERATIONS 59
The Pitfalls 59
Avoiding the Pitfalls 60
Landing Upper-Management Support 62
Selecting the Support Team 63
Recruiting the Initial Users 66
Training 66
Summary 69

CHAPTER 5. SELECTING PC WORKSTATION SOFTWARE TOOLS 71
Selection Criteria 72
Tools in the Marketplace 84
Supplemental Offloaded Development Environment Tools 118
Summary 120
References 120

CHAPTER 6. DETERMINING THE WORKSTATION OPERATING ENVIRONMENT 121
Workstation Operating System 121
Memory Management Systems 126
Workstation Hardware 128
Summary 130

CHAPTER 7. CONNECTING IT ALL TOGETHER 133
Offloaded Development Environment Architecture 133
Local Area Network (LAN)/Server Hardware and Software Selection 151
Selection of Mainframe Communication Methods and Facilities 159
Other Communication Links 174
Integrated Offloaded Development Environment Packages 176
Summary 179

CHAPTER 8. SETTING UP AND OPERATING AN OFFLOADED DEVELOPMENT ENVIRONMENT 181
Testing Components 181
Ordering Components 190
Laying Out the Hardware (Floor Plan) 193
Laying Out the Hardware (Cubical Layout) 194
Installation 196
Rollout Plans 198
The Four Stages of User Involvement 200
Defining Local Procedures 201
"Hand Holding" 208
Summary 210

CHAPTER 9. SECURING THE OFFLOADED DEVELOPMENT ENVIRONMENT 211
PC Workstation Security 211
LAN/Server Security 215

Source Code Control 217
Summary 221
References 222

CHAPTER 10. EXPANDING AN OFFLOADED DEVELOPMENT ENVIRONMENT 223
Adding New Tools 223
Adding New Users 224
Joining Forces: Connecting to Other Groups 224
How to Link Offloaded Development Environments 227
Summary 228

CHAPTER 11. MEASURING THE EFFECTS OF AN OFFLOADED DEVELOPMENT ENVIRONMENT 229
Measuring Effects on Productivity 229
Measuring Effects on Mainframe Usage 232
Measuring Effects on Quality 236
Conclusion 237
Sample Survey for Offloaded Development Environment Users 238
Sample Survey for Project Leaders/MIS of Offloaded Development Environment Users 240
Summary 241
References 241

CHAPTER 12. THE FUTURE 243
PC Hardware 243
Software Tools 243
PC Workstation Operating Systems 245
Summary 245

APPENDIX A: SAMPLE ROLLOUT PLAN 247

APPENDIX B: GLOSSARY 251

APPENDIX C: TRADEMARKS 255

INDEX 265

List of Figures and Tables

Figure *Page*

2-1. Effect of system response time on user response time. 26

2-2. Effect of system response time on user transaction rate. 27

5-1. SPF/PC primary option menu. 85

5-2. SPF/PC edit option. 86

5-3. Micro Focus COBOL/2 workbench (mainframe development environment) signon screen. 89

5-4. Micro Focus editor. 90

5-5. Micro Focus Checker. 92

5-6. Micro Focus editor (after finding error with Micro Focus Checker). 93

5-7. Micro Focus Animator. 94

5-8. Realia editor (RED). 98

5-9. Realia RealDBUG. 99

5-10. Realia RealDBUG (view value). 100

7-1. Traditional single-tier mainframe development environment. 137

7-2. Channel attached, single-tier mainframe development environment. 140

Figure		*Page*
7-3.	Two-tier development environment.	142
7-4.	2.5-tier development environment.	146
7-5.	Three-tier development environment.	149
7-6.	3270 emulation.	161
7-7.	3270 emulation with protocol converter.	162
7-8.	3274/6 controller emulation.	163
7-9.	Centralized server-based emulation.	166
7-10.	Decentralized server-based emulation.	167
8-1.	Example of test plan worksheet.	187
8-2.	Improper positioning.	195
8-3.	Proper positioning.	196
8-4.	Minutes of user meeting.	209
9-1.	User deterrence.	217
11-1.	File server utilization vs. mainframe utilization.	234

Table		*Page*
1-1.	Importance of development tools.	4
2-1.	Impact of office automation.	35
2-2.	Effect of unpaid overtime.	37
2-3.	Savings comparison per developer.	38
2-4.	Cost comparison per project (10 developers for 6 months).	39
3-1.	Sample cost worksheet.	55
5-1.	PC workstation software tool selection criteria.	73
6-1.	Intel CPUs.	129
8-1.	Items that may be able to be moved to high DOS memory.	184
8-2.	PC workstation file extensions.	203

Introduction

Moving application development activities from the mainframe to the PC workstation will be the single most important technology change that most commercial DP shops will have to address in the 1990s. The two main reasons for this are the following:

1. The power of the PC-based development tools (e.g., compilers, debuggers, DBMS tools, TP monitor tools, CASE tools) will greatly exceed the power of their traditional mainframe counterparts.
2. The economics of PC-based mainframe application development will become irresistible. Currently, productivity increases of 30% to 40% are achievable with an outlay of $10,000 to $20,000 per developer.

This book is intended to aid those who will be determining the appropriateness of offloaded development for their organizations and subsequently justifying, designing, assembling, and operating an offloaded development environment. This book outlines all the issues and options that implementors and administrators of offloaded development must address. It also offers advice on avoiding the pitfalls that befell many of the early pioneers in this field, including the author.

To all those considering making the move to an offloaded development environment, the author offers the following advice:

1. Do not underestimate the effort involved in moving mainframe programmers to PC-based environments. The large number of design decisions that must be made, coupled with the wide range

of components that must be integrated and the all too numerous vendors that must be dealt with make implementing an offloaded development environment a very challenging and time-consuming task.

2. Offloaded development is not a substitute for good development practices or competent management. DP shops that lack either of these things should address these problems first.

3. Always keep an eye on the ultimate goal of offloaded development, namely improved competitiveness through reduced costs and improved quality. These goals should manifest themselves in terms of the reduced need for technical staff and the reengineering of existing applications into even more powerful and valuable systems. Don't let yourself, or your shop, become so bogged down in the details of setting up a complex offloaded development environment that you forget the reasons you undertook this effort in the first place. It is up to you to extract the benefits of offloaded development!

This book provides practical information on every aspect of offloaded development, giving readers the best possible chance of successfully making the move to a PC-based environment. Good luck.

Mark A. Butterline

1

Is Offloading Right for Me?

In an effort to improve the cost effectiveness of application development organizations, many businesses and institutions have pursued, and continue to pursue, a wide variety of options and ideas. The most extreme of these ideas have included moving programming functions offshore (to Eastern Europe or the Far East) and purchasing entire system development companies. One idea that has gained a lot of momentum in recent years — and is not nearly as drastic as those mentioned above — is offloading mainframe development to workstations (usually PCs or PC/LAN systems). The main reasons cited by most DP shops for making the move to PC-based development environments are the following:

1. The need to improve productivity.
2. The need to improve quality.
3. The need to reduce mainframe costs.
4. The need to keep current with changes in technology.

This book will examine these reasons in depth. It also will answer questions concerning the design and implementation of an offloaded development environment and will provide advice on avoiding the major pitfalls that one may encounter when offloading mainframe development to PC workstations.

However, before the "how to" can be addressed, the "whether to" must first be determined. This chapter explores the major issues that must be considered when determining if offloading is right for you. It will provide information on the following: the prerequisites to offloading development; the analysis of user needs; the impact of offloaded development on current functional roles; and the impact of the development cycle on the effectiveness of the offloaded development environment. In addition, this chapter will discuss offloading development as part of a larger strategy to improve productivity and quality. Some advice for keeping user and management expectations realistic is also included.

THE PREREQUISITES

Before a group of mainframe developers can ask themselves if offloading development activities to PC workstations is right for their situation, they must meet certain prerequisites. The following prerequisites are concepts that most commercial DP shops have hopefully embraced years before reaching the point of offloading development.

1. *Effective code control on the mainframe.* If there is no effective scheme for preventing one developer from modifying a piece of code that another developer is also working on, then offloading development activities from a single computer to multiple computers will only lead to a more confusing situation.

2. *Use of structured programming techniques.* Structured programming is a basic concept in commercial data processing. Given the amount of resources spent on maintaining existing applications, structured programming is an absolute essential. However, if a shop is considering offloading their development activities, and they are not using structured programming techniques, about the only thing that can be hoped for is the faster generation of unstructured code.

3. *Effective test environment.* Not having an effective test environment shows a lack of commitment to producing high-quality data systems. By offloading application development activities from a mainframe to multiple smaller computers, with all their associated control issues, developers will be thrust into an environment that will make it even more difficult to set up an effective test environment.

4. *Standard development practices.* About the most important thing to have when developing a large application is good front-end analysis (i.e., data and function analysis). Good front-end analysis contributes more to productivity and quality than offloading

mainframe development. While offloaded development environments provide for the use of PC-based CASE tools that support front-end analysis, trained, knowledgable analysts are required to make proper use of these tools. Lack of sound development practices such as these will doom all large projects, whether developed in an offloaded environment or not.

5. *Strong management.* Strong management is recognized as a prerequisite to building jet aircraft, nuclear power plants, and oil refineries because it is essential to the assembly of the tens of thousands of working parts that must all function together. The same is true when it comes to building large application systems, perhaps even more so because some systems have millions of working parts. Strong management is especially needed to control and focus efforts when introducing a complex offloaded development environment to an already complicated environment.

ANALYZING USER NEEDS

In this section the analysis of user needs is broken into two parts. The first is a general examination of the types of mainframe tools and how they are used by developers. The second is a set of specific questions that potential users must answer. A sample survey is included.

Mainframe Tools and How They Are Used

When analyzing the needs of potential users for an offloaded development environment, the most important question is "What tools are being used on the mainframe?" This is because offloading mainframe development is mostly a question of mainframe emulation on smaller computers.

Information on a wide range of tools must be collected. From the beginning, it should be assumed that 100% duplication of the mainframe development environment will not be achieved. This is okay because some types of tools are more important than other types (e.g., compilers are more important than debuggers), and high degrees of compatibility need only be attained for the most important tools.

Table 1-1 shows the relative importance of various types of development tools. Of course, there may be some differences depending on the individual situation. When collecting information on user needs, be sure these areas are addressed.

Table 1-1. Importance of development tools.

Critical	Compilers/Run Time Environments TP Monitors DBMSs/Run Time Environments
Very Important	Exec Language Interpreter (JCL) Code Generators (Lower CASE) Upper CASE Tools Change Management Release Management
Important	Editors Debuggers Utilities (SyncSort, COMPAREX) Report Writers Statistical Packages
Good to Have	Playback Test Tools Test Data Generation Diagramming Tools Word Processors Spreadsheets

Another question that is almost as important as what tools are being used on the mainframe is *how* they are being used. In some situations where a team is using a mainframe compiler that is fully supported on a PC workstation (e.g., IBM OS/VS COBOL) they might be using a DBMS that is not (e.g., Model 204). If the number of modules that contained calls to the unsupported DBMS were small, use of an offloaded development environment may still be possible. Thus, many standard development practices that developers should be following in their mainframe environments really pay off when considering a move to an offloaded development environment. These are the most important practices.

1. *Isolation of I/O.* Having calls to DBMSs and TP monitors isolated from the system logic not only gives development groups extra flexibility in the selection of system software, it also simplifies the conversion of programs from mainframe to offloaded development environments. Keeping calls to DBMSs and TP monitors relegated to a small number of I/O modules decreases the number of potential trouble spots.

2. *Use of mainstream tools.* Use of obscure languages, DBMSs, TP monitors, and so on, not only makes it difficult for management to find and retain knowledgable staff, it ignores the reality that software vendors usually do not pay attention to these areas. It is a lot easier to find PC-based COBOL tools than it is to find PC-based PL/I tools.

3. *Discouraging the use of interlanguage calls.* Interlanguage calls (e.g., a COBOL program calls a subroutine written in PL/I) are never simple to implement, even in the world of IBM mainframes. This is why they are strongly discouraged in most DP shops. Offloaded development environments are no exception to this. Trying to get a program written in one language, supported by one vendor's package, to call a program written in another language, supported by a different vendor's package, is usually extremely difficult if not impossible in the PC workstation environment.

4. *Use of common modules.* In addition to improving developer productivity and the quality of the systems being produced, extensive use of common modules will greatly assist the transition from mainframe to offloaded development. This occurs for two reasons. First, it is easier to identify the key modules of the existing mainframe system. This is important when checking for compatibility problems between mainframe and workstation-based tools. Second, use of common modules means there will be fewer modules to keep track of and move around.

Initial Survey Areas

As mentioned above, certain questions need to be asked of potential users to decide who should become real users and how their offloaded development environment should be configured. The following areas should be identified.

1. *Tool usage levels.* The measurement of mainframe tool usage will show what areas will need the most attention when it comes time to select PC workstation counterparts. The version, or release number, of the mainframe tools also should be collected if this is an open question. In addition to helping to select workstation tools, these measurements, when performed both before and after deployment, are a gauge of the effectiveness of the environment.

2. *Function of potential users.* The job of the potential user needs to be identified (e.g., programmer, analyst, system tester), as some functions are better suited to offloading than others. This area will be addressed in greater detail later in the chapter.

3. *Type of systems being developed.* It is important to know whether the users will be working on permanent systems that will be enhanced or maintained or whether they will be working on "throw-away" or ad-hoc systems. This will affect the potential cost effectiveness of the offloaded development environment.

4. *Development life cycle position.* Whether a potential user's project is in the development, enhancement, or maintenance part of the development life cycle will affect his or her selection as offloaded development environment user. This is because of the effect on the environment's cost effectiveness and/or deployment timing. A more in-depth discussion on this topic is covered in the next section.

5. *Expected work levels.* How much future work is expected for a potential user, and its nature, are important considerations when planning an offloaded development environment. Potential users that anticipate low work levels (e.g., repair maintenance work only) probably should not be selected. Users on projects that need large-scale enhancement on a regular schedule are among the best candidates.

6. *Identify critical system components.* If converting the developer(s) of an existing system, it is important to identify which system components or modules must be fully functional in the offloaded development environment, for example, that all critical modules can reproduce the same results with the PC workstation's debugger tool as on the mainframe. This information will be needed by the people who will select the workstation tools for the offloaded environment.

7. *Identify interlanguage calls (and other crazy interfaces).* This is basically the same situation as in the above item. The idea is to catch all insurmountable obstacles to the effective use of an offloaded development environment before any large commitment of resources is made.

The following is an example of an initial offloaded development environment survey whose questions correspond to the above list. In addition to questions that pertain to the decision whether to move to an offloaded development environment or not (questions 1 through 7), there are also questions that reveal baseline information necessary to measure the effectiveness of the environment once it is installed (questions 8 through 10). They are included in this survey as a convenience and are discussed in more detail below. It should be noted that this survey is intended only as a sample, as question content will vary from group to group.

8. *Computer usage levels.* The measurement of computer usage levels is important in gauging the cost effectiveness of the offloaded development environment. Mainframe charges (i.e., TSO, hard disk usage, etc.) should be studied, both before and after the introduction of offloaded development. Users also should give percentage estimates of the amount of time spent on mainframes, minis (servers), and PC workstations before and after conversion. This will serve as a verification check against the mainframe chargeback reports.

9. *Job satisfaction.* An area that management usually has some interest in is employee job satisfaction. This should be measured both before and after conversion to the offloaded development environment.

10. *Knowledge levels.* Knowledge levels of offloaded development environment tools, hardware, and operating systems should be measured both before and after conversion. The "before" information will help identify the areas where training is needed and the "after" numbers will indicate how much the user's skill sets have expanded.

Sample Initial Offloaded Development Survey

Name: ____

1. Rate your current level of usage of the following:

   Scale: H - High
   M - Medium
   L - Low
   NA - Not Applicable/None

   A. Operating Systems

   ____ MVS
   ____ VM
   ____ UNIX
   ____ MS-DOS
   ____ Other (specify: ____________)

B. Languages

____ COBOL
____ C
____ C++
____ PL/I
____ FORTRAN
____ IBM 370 Assembler
____ Easytrieve Plus
____ SPSS
____ SAS
____ RAMIS
____ FOCUS
____ APS/MVS
____ Other (specify: ____________)

C. DBMS

____ DB2
____ IMS
____ IDMS
____ Oracle
____ INFORMIX
____ VSAM
____ Flat Files
____ Other (specify: ____________)

D. TP Monitors

____ CICS
____ IMS(DC)
____ IDMS(DC)
____ Other (specify: ____________)

E. Mainframe Utilities/Tools

____ ISPF
____ File-AID/DATA-XPERT
____ Librarian/Panvalet
____ SyncSort
____ COMPAREX
____ Other (specify: ____________)

F. UNIX Utilities/Tools

____ StarGROUP (LAN package)
____ PMX/StarMAIL (LAN based e-mail)

G. MS-DOS Utilities/Tools

____ SPF/PC
____ Word Perfect
____ Microsoft Word
____ Lotus 1-2-3
____ Microsoft EXCEL
____ DBASE
____ RELAY GOLD
____ ATTMail Access Plus (e-mail)
____ Microsoft WINDOWS
____ Other (specify: ____________)

2. Indicate your main function(s).
(Check all that apply.)

____ Programmer
____ Analyst
____ Programmer/Analyst
____ System Tester
____ Production Support
____ Project Leader
____ IS Manager

3. Indicate the types of applications that you develop.
(Check all that apply.)

____ Single use systems (e.g., ad-hoc reporting, "throw-away" systems)
____ Permanent systems (i.e., systems that will be maintained or enhanced)

4. Where in the development cycle is your application?
(Check the stage that best fits.)

____ Initial development
____ Continuing development (i.e., adding enhancements)
____ Repair maintenance (i.e., fixing problems as they are discovered)

5. Over the next year, what percentage of your time will be spent in these stages of the development cycle?

____ New development
____ Continuing development (i.e., adding enhancements)
____ Repair maintenance (i.e., fixing problems as they are discovered)

____
100%

6. Identify the important modules in your application system. Important modules are those that are frequently worked on or are called by many other parts of the system.

____

____

____

____

____

____

7. Describe any interlanguage calls that are in, or planned for, your application system. Also describe any unusual interface needs that your system has (e.g., IDMS-UNIX interface).

____

____

____

____

____

____

8. How much time do you spend on these platforms?

Mainframe (MVS, VM)	____ hours per week
Minis and Super-Micros (UNIX)	____ hours per week
PCs (MS-DOS, OS/2)	____ hours per week
Other (specify: ____________)	____ hours per week

9. Indicate your current level of job satisfaction. (Check one.)

____ Very Satisfied

____ Satisfied

____ Neutral

____ Unsatisfied

____ Very Unsatisfied

10. Indicate your level of knowledge of these workstation-based tools.

Scale: H - High
M - Medium
L - Low
N - None

____ Micro Focus COBOL/2 Workbench
____ Realia COBOL
____ XDB-Workbench for DB2
____ Micro Focus IMS Workbench
____ RealIMS
____ Micro Focus CICS Workbench
____ RealCICS
____ EXCELERATOR
____ APS/PC
____ TELON/PWS
____ PVCS
____ Endevor

DEVELOPMENT CYCLE ISSUES

The impact of offloaded development on groups in different stages of the development cycle (e.g., initial development, maintenance) varies greatly. Impact also varies depending on the type of applications being developed (e.g., permanent, throw-away).

New Development

The impact of offloaded development environments on new systems development varies depending on the type of system being developed. Groups developing permanent systems (i.e., systems that will be maintained or updated after delivery) will usually find more benefit than those developing throw-away or ad-hoc reporting systems. This is because straight new development will usually involve long periods of coding, testing, and repeated compilations as opposed to throw-away or ad-hoc report development that might involve more code reuse, less testing, and fewer compilations.

The impact of offloading new development work can be divided into three main areas.

1. *Productivity.* A major benefit of working on single-user PC workstations is subsecond response time for trivial commands

(e.g., editing, file handling). Typically this means that instead of waiting 3, 5, or 10 seconds when hitting the carriage return on a terminal, the response time is only a fraction of a second. While this may sound trivial, subsecond response time can have a large impact on productivity. This is because the concentration of the user of a subsecond environment is not interrupted as often as that of someone who is using a multisecond response time environment. In other words, when a subsecond user hits a carriage return and waits only a fraction of a second for his entry to be processed, he has no time to start thinking about what to have for lunch. He does not waste time reestablishing concentration on the problem at hand because he did not lose it in the first place. This particular aspect of subsecond response time was studied at IBM [1,2,3,4] and other companies. In these studies programmers used dumb terminals that were channel-attached to MVS mainframes. This meant the users had subsecond response for trivial commands, such as ISPF edit commands, but not for compiles. The impact on programmers' productivity was a decrease of the necessary programmer resources to build applications by 30% to 50%. This had a significant impact on project delivery times as well as employee morale.

Another element of productivity is improvements attributable to use of more powerful tools. For example, in COBOL debugging and unit testing, full screen display (e.g., Micro Focus Animator) is generally regarded as superior to single-line display (e.g., IBM TESTCOB). In this situation, a 50% productivity improvement for this part of the development cycle is possible. Of course, large productivity improvements can be found in situations where tools previously did not exist on the mainframe (e.g., Micro Focus Checker — an interactive compiler that is linked to a full screen editor).

A final consideration is the degree of interactivity. In most mainframe environments, when a command is entered an entire screen of data is sent between the computer and terminal. This is not the case with PCs, and this leads to a great increase in human/computer interactivity. In addition, peripherals such as mice can also speed up activities.

2. *Quality.* As with productivity, the quality of applications developed in the subsecond response time environment of single-user PC workstations is significant. This is due to the effects of workstation testing tools versus those on the mainframe. Most applications developed for large businesses involve the use of DBMSs,

and sometimes TP monitors. Doing significant unit, string, and system testing usually involves working against a single-test database. Single-test databases are used because it is usually not a trivial matter to set up a test database, regardless of size (it usually involves going to a DBA). When testing, the programmers or testers find themselves in the position of wanting to test a module or system thoroughly but not at the risk of crashing or extensively damaging the test database or TP monitor region. This could interfere with someone else's work and/or take a long time to fix or restore from a backup. Thus, testing is difficult, time consuming, and not as complete as it could be.

In a workstation environment, developers can create their own test databases or TP monitor test regions without assistance from others. They also can test more thoroughly because damaged databases are easily replaced, sometimes with just a single copy command. PC-based testing also can involve the execution of code that is difficult or nearly impossible to test in the mainframe environment (e.g., sudden and unexpected database unavailability). Another benefit of subsecond response time in the area of testing is the fact that since it is easier and faster, more testing can, and usually does, take place.

3. *Costs.* Costs, and cost savings, play a large part in any decision to go to an offloaded development environment. The costs for an offloaded development environment can range anywhere from \$2,500 to \$20,000 or more per user. Typical costs will be in the range of \$12,000 to \$18,000 (see Chapter 3 for more information). These costs are offset in two major ways. The first and most important is productivity. Successful offloaded development environments should encounter productivity improvements of at least 30% (i.e., if a project had \$100,000 in labor costs before deployment on an offloaded development environment, it should only have labor charges of \$70,000 after converting over; see Chapter 2 for more information). In large companies this would mean a per person productivity increase worth \$30,000 per year (i.e., 2,000 billable hours per year × \$50 per hour × 30% savings). This, of course, assumes that there is extra work waiting to be performed by the developer.

   The other major cost saving is reduced mainframe charges. In many large companies MVS TSO charges exceed \$1,000 per month per developer for those actively doing new development work.

These charges are usually attributable to CPU or I/O intensive activities such as compiling and testing. Coding and editing functions are usually inexpensive. In successful offloaded development environments, a large number of compilations and tests are carried out on PC workstations. In new development environments, where programs are repeatedly compiled and then dynamically tested many times, this can account for 80% to 90% of developer TSO charges. Obviously, for environments where mainframe-based production runs are also performed by the developer (e.g., ad-hoc reporting) the percentage would be less.

Thus, the high-level numbers for an offloaded development environment are as follows:

Costs: ~ $15,000 per developer (including hardware, software, support)

+ ~ $3,000 per developer per year (ongoing support)

Benefits: ~ $30,000 per developer per year (productivity improvement)

+ ~ $10,000 per developer per year (reduced mainframe charges)

Maintenance

The benefits of an offloaded development environment can be numerous and make adapting that environment a very attractive option. Maintenance projects, however, are a little trickier.

Whether or not a project in the maintenance part of the development cycle should consider moving to an offloaded development environment depends mostly on how much it resembles a new development project. Projects that handle a large quantity of changes and enhancements on a regular basis should see nearly the same benefits that a new development project sees. Projects that involve only small-scale changes or enhancements, or just repair maintenance, will usually not be able to cost justify the conversion to an offloaded environment. This is because changing just a few lines of code in a module cannot support the time or trouble of downloading it to a PC workstation, making and testing the change, and then uploading. It would be easier to just do the change on the mainframe.

It should be noted that a project that was originally developed in an offloaded development environment probably should continue to be supported in the same environment, unless the level of changes or repairs is extremely low.

FUNCTIONAL ROLE ISSUES

The impact of offloaded development on the various functional roles found in a large commercial DP shop varies depending on a number of criteria. The most important of these is workstation tool availability, whether it is a COBOL debugger, data analysis tool, or project management system. The other criteria are the value of improved communications between various functions and the economies of scale. These criteria are used when examining the impact of offloaded development environments on the following functions:

1. *Programmers.* As discussed earlier in the chapter, large chunks of programmer function can be moved to an offloaded development environment. These include coding, editing, syntax checking/compiling, unit testing, and some string and system testing. Use of lower CASE tools (e.g., code generators) in conjunction with upper CASE tools can be very effective here. In general, programmers are usually the main beneficiary of converting to an offloaded development environment.

2. *Analysts.* Almost all upper CASE tools (i.e., tools used for data or function analysis) are PC-based and thus are natural candidates for inclusion in an offloaded development environment. Upper CASE tools that work closely with lower CASE tools used by programmers are especially desirable. The main caveat here is that there are many people in commercial DP that are passing themselves off as analysts when they have not completed any formal curriculum of analyst training. In some large companies, the number of qualified analysts is no more than 2% or 3% of the number of people identifying themselves as analysts. Obviously, analyst professionalization is something that needs to be addressed. This is important to note because only qualified analysts can take full advantage of upper CASE tools. To unqualified people, upper CASE tools will be no more than high-priced drawing tools.

3. *Programmer/analysts.* The same applies to programmers and analysts. Together, the above three functions have the most to gain from offloaded development.

4. *System testers.* System testers can gain some significant benefits from the offloaded development environment. Most of these benefits have to do with being able to use a more secure and robust set of tools than would normally be available on the mainframe. As described earlier, the main tools are PC workstation versions of mainframe DBMSs and TP monitors (see Chapter 5). They allow users to do more rigorous or damaging tests than would be practical in a multi-user situation. These environments also give the individual the tools necessary to set up test databases or regions without the assistance of other personnel. This reduced need to interface with other personnel, of course, improves the productivity of the experienced tester.

   A type of tool that can prove useful in regression testing is the keystroke capture/playback tool. When used in conjunction with a file/database comparison utility, keystroke capture/playback tools give testers the ability to construct highly mechanized regression test systems. These systems do involve some considerable effort in set up and maintenance, but they can reduce the time needed to certify new releases of application systems in addition to improving the integrity of the certification.

   Keystroke capture/playback tools come in both PC workstation and server versions (e.g., CA-TRAPS, AT&T PC ESCORT on the PC workstation, and AT&T ESCORT for UNIX servers). Depending on the size of the files or quantity of TP screens involved in a regression test, PC workstation, server, or mainframe-based file comparison utilities would be used (e.g., 'fc' command in MS-DOS, 'diff' command in UNIX, COMPAREX on IBM mainframes).

   In addition to these rather sophisticated tools, word processors can be very handy, as system testing usually involves large amounts of paperwork generation.

5. *Production.* Personnel involved in running production probably will experience the smallest benefit from the offloaded development environment. Obviously, this is because running production usually means accessing the mainframe directly. However, certain aspects of the offloaded development environment can assist the user involved in production. The first area is word processing. Like the

system tester, the production person is usually involved in the creation and processing of large amounts of paperwork. PC-based word processors can improve productivity and effectiveness here. The second area is electronic mail. Although not mentioned previously, all users of an offloaded development environment should have access to an e-mail system. For the production person this can be of particular importance because of the need for very good communications between the production person and his or her suppliers (i.e., programmers, system testers) and clients (i.e., end users).

Another consideration when deciding to deploy an offloaded development environment is that including production personnel does not involve as many expenses when compared with programmers or analysts. This is due to the fact that production personnel do not need expensive software development packages or significant amounts of "hand holding" from support personnel.

6. *Project management.* It seems that most IS managers these days have standalone PCs to assist them with budgeting matters, memo writing, and communications (i.e., spreadsheets, word processors, and e-mail packages). However, such folks can benefit from being connected into the offloaded development environment that is used by their employees. Some of the more important uses of an offloaded development environment for IS managers include the following:

   a. Improved communications. The effectiveness of e-mail systems is in direct proportion to its economies of scale. The more people on the system that you need to communicate with, the more it is used and the more valuable the e-mail system becomes.

   b. Sharing of documents and spreadsheets. This can be made easier and faster through use of shared directories on the LAN on an offloaded development environment.

   c. Project planning/scheduling. The use of project management tools (e.g., TIMELINE, VIEWPOINT) can be made more effective with the use of an environment where both the manager and the managed can have equal access to planning information. This, again, is accomplished via the offloaded development environment's LAN.

7. *Project leaders.* Since the project leader functions tend to consist of a combination of other functions (e.g., system testing, project management, programming, analysis), they can benefit from the offloaded development environment in the same ways that single-function users can. The main danger with this is that a project leader can be spread a little too thin with each of the different types of tools. Therefore, it is usually a good idea to take a phased approach to introducing the project leader to the full offloaded development environment.

CULTURAL AND ORGANIZATIONAL IMPLICATIONS

The impact of offloaded development on the culture and organizational structure of a DP shop can, in some circumstances, be very significant. Thus, the management of groups that will be introducing offloaded development technology should be aware of the possible implications and plan accordingly. Some of the major impacts can include the following:

1. *Threat to hierarchical management structure.* With the availability of networked PC workstations on a large scale, the bringing together of teams of developers to accomplish specific tasks is usually easier than in the mainframe-only environment. This can be attributed to the use of e-mail/groupware and greater flexibility in the deployment and use of hardware and software tools. When technical boundaries are less of a problem to the assembling of development teams, organizational boundaries or hindrances become more obvious and may therefore become targets for change.

2. *Management has more on its plate.* Most managers of mainframe-based DP shops are not used to dealing with large-scale hardware issues or network management. In the old mainframe-only environment, these things were usually handled by the same people who operated and maintained the mainframes. Therefore, management reaction to the possible introduction of offloaded development may be one that underestimates the effort and complexity involved or, worse still, one of hostility.

3. *Conflicts between liberal and conservative proponents of new technology.* In the mainframe-only environment the decision to deploy and use new technology was usually made by folks other than the application developers, usually by some sort of central support group. In an offloaded development environment the positions are reversed and the development groups have to decide what to embrace. This

can result in tension between liberal and conservative proponents of new technology. What management must do in these situations is play devil's advocate against the majority. If a majority of a development team wants to pursue the introduction of new hardware and software aggressively, management should ask for a closer examination of the viability of the proposed new tools. If the majority is overly conservative, then management needs to provide extra encouragement to pursue new technology.

4. *Restructuring of support and administration functions.* With the deployment of offloaded development technology, more administrative and support functions will need to be moved to the application development groups themselves. Management who regards support groups as a bunch of people in headquarters who say "What?" and "I don't know" a lot may be reluctant to commit resources to the group.
5. *Competition between business and technical needs.* When setting up an offloaded development environment, it is very important to put the users to work on it immediately after their training is completed. Organizations that are overly focused on meeting short-term customer needs, even at the expense of their short-term technical needs, will have significant problems in getting over the initial learning curve. A proper balance between business and technical needs should be instilled in the users before they convert to offloaded development.
6. *Changes in chargeback for internal support.* In many large companies there is an MIS department that operates and maintains mainframes and networks and provides a central organization for technical support and standards. In most cases the funding for all this is included in the mainframe usage rates. However, with more computing being done on PC workstations, servers, and LANs, the traditional funding method starts to dry up. Management needs to address this question and either find additional funding sources or scale back support.

OFFLOADED DEVELOPMENT AS PART OF A LARGER STRATEGY

Today's large commercial DP shops face many more competitive challenges than they did 10 years ago. Some of these challenges include competition from outside developers/integrators (e.g., EDS), competition from internal groups within a company, and the recognition that small teams of developers are generally more effective than large teams of developers, even when addressing very large projects. This, of course, has led some large DP shops to launch comprehensive efforts to "clean up" their organizations. The smart organizations are addressing many different types of improvements in addition to the use of offloaded development environments. These improvements include the following:

1. *Better systems analysis.* This means a couple of things. The most important is competent data and functional analysis, along with the creation of high-quality logical specifications. Upper CASE tools can help here, but they are no substitute for highly qualified personnel who have received comprehensive training in analysis techniques and methods.

2. *Better management.* Many IS managers don't seem to realize that they are in charge of teams that are building machines (i.e., systems) with hundreds of thousands, even millions, of working parts. This implies tight management and significant use of measurements.

3. *Improved productivity and quality.* Getting the job done faster and better can be extremely important, especially when one considers that application systems are now being used to gain strategic advantage over competitors (e.g., Beneton's inventory control and order system). Offloaded development environments can help quite a bit here, but they are not the whole story. Attention paid to improving quality via more measurements, better design, and more extensive testing is very important.

4. *Education levels.* Given the brains (or imagination) required in the building of today's strategically important systems, education levels are becoming more and more important. In the old days (i.e., the 70s and 80s), when payroll systems or other kinds of back room operations were being mechanized, DP shops didn't need a lot of highly educated "rocket scientists" to build application systems. Now, however, companies need people who can understand very complex business situations and high technology. University graduates (i.e., bachelors, masters, and doctorates) are usually the kind of people who can better understand what is needed. This is not because they have been specifically trained to address these issues but because they usually have some experience in figuring out complex problems.

Thus, offloaded development environments should be regarded as just one part of an overall strategy to improve a commercial DP shop's effectiveness. In fact, in some situations (e.g., improving systems analysis), offloaded development environments will take a back seat, in both importance and cost effectiveness, to other parts of a strategy.

KEEPING EXPECTATIONS REALISTIC

In trying to answer the question of whether offloaded development is right for a particular group or not, we have examined a large amount of screening criteria. This screening, along with thorough planning, is the key to successfully implementing an offloaded development environment. However, one aspect that still needs to be addressed is how to keep expectations realistic.

In today's world of application development tools, the spotlight is usually on PC-based tools. This, of course, is not surprising given the power and flexibility associated with computers dedicated to serving single users. These capabilities include multi-MIP processors, in combination with high-resolution color graphics and dedicated peripherals, such as hard/floppy disks and mice. Given this environment, many vendors have come out with some very "sexy" tools that a lot of people in commercial DP shops are eager to get their hands on.

This attractiveness can, of course, be a positive thing, in that it makes it easy to stimulate interest in potential users. It can, however, provoke too much excitement, in that overly optimistic expectations can be created. This is especially true for some IS managers, especially those who have not personally developed software applications for a long time. It should be noted that this situation does not often apply to programmers because they usually will not become wildly enthusiastic about a tool or set of tools until they understand exactly how to use the tools to do their jobs. This takes time for training and experimentation.

This overexcitement can be due to a number of things — the desire to find a quick fix to productivity and quality problems, or possibly the desire to make a simple decision to buy a tool rather than tackle tough management problems. Whatever the reason, it is important for management (and to a lesser extent the application developers) to understand that moving to an offloaded development environment takes a long time (six months to a year). Dedication to achieving a highly productive environment in the long term is necessary. Management that cannot sustain such an effort should avoid conversion to an offloaded development environment.

SUMMARY

To determine if an offloaded development environment is right for your organization it is imperative to take into account what type of systems your developers are building and how this development is being accomplished. Using a survey, such as the sample survey in this chapter, to solicit information from all developers in your organization can be very valuable. Another area that must be explored when deciding if offloading mainframe development to a PC-based environment would be beneficial is your organization's current position in the development cycle. If your shop is developing new applications or making significant enhancements to existing applications, then offloading development will most likely be justified because of the improvements in the areas of developer productivity, program quality, and mainframe usage charges. If, however, your shop is primarily working on application maintenance or on the development of throw-away applications, then the cost of moving to a PC-based environment may be difficult to justify.

The degree to which each person in your organization will benefit from the use of a PC-based development environment also will depend on the functional role that he or she is performing. Programmers, analysts, and programmer-analysts are usually the main beneficiaries of offloaded development. System testers, project managers, and project leaders also can take advantage of the new environment, but their gains may not, by themselves, justify the initial costs of offloading.

Offloaded development environments should be regarded as just one part of an overall strategy to improve a DP shop's effectiveness. Other improvements that can and should be made include better systems analysis, better management, and improved productivity and quality through the use of better measurements, improved software design, and more extensive testing.

Finally, keeping expectations realistic is very important because moving to an offloaded development environment takes a long time, usually six months to a year. A long-term commitment to achieving a highly productive development environment is necessary.

REFERENCES

1. Doherty, W. J., and R. P. Kelisky. 1979. Managing VM/CMS systems for user effectiveness. *IBM Systems Journal*. Volume 18, Number 1. 143–163.
2. Thadhani, A. J. 1981. Interactive user productivity. *IBM Systems Journal*. Volume 20, Number 4. 407–423.
3. Thadhani, A. J. 1984. Factors affecting programmer productivity during application development. *IBM Systems Journal*.Volume 23, Number 1. 19–35.
4. Lambert, G. N. 1984. A comparative study of system response time on program developer productivity. *IBM Systems Journal*. Volume 23, Number 1. 36–43.

2

The Benefits of an Offloaded Development Environment

As cited in Chapter 1, most DP shops make the move to offloaded development environments to improve productivity, to improve quality, to reduce mainframe costs, and to keep current with new technology, including nonmainframe production platforms. This chapter will examine these benefits in depth. In addition, this chapter will address the issue of "bonus" benefits. Bonus benefits refer to those that on their own would not justify the cost involved in offloading development but which are certainly useful extras to have once the necessity of offloading has been established. Also included at the end of this chapter is a section on calculating benefits, including some sample worksheets. These worksheets and the worksheet at the end of Chapter 3 will help determine if offloading is right for you.

IMPROVED PRODUCTIVITY

Improved productivity in an offloaded development environment is primarily attributable to subsecond response time. Subsecond response time refers to system response times of less than one second, and its importance has been studied and documented in a number of DP shops.

In 1979, Doherty and Kelisky of IBM[1] observed that system response time had a direct impact on user response time (i.e., the time taken to decide on the next system request and then enter it). The longer the system's response time, the longer the user's response time (see Figure 2-1). Doherty and Kelisky, along with Thadhani[2,3] and Lambert,[4] both of IBM, attributed the longer user response time to the ineffectiveness of the short-term memory buffer within the developer's mind. That is, when a developer performs a computer-based task, she works out a sequence of commands that she will use to accomplish the task rather than just determining what the next command should be at run time. This sequence of commands is stored in a short-term memory buffer. If system response time is very short, less than one second, the developer proceeds through the sequence with minimal delay (the only delay would be the time it takes to type a keyboard entry or move and click a mouse). However, when the system response time is long (greater than one second), the developer often becomes distracted and has to rethink the planned sequence of commands. Thus, decreased system response time leads to decreased user response time and, as observed in the IBM studies, an increase in the rate of developer transactions (see Figure 2-2).

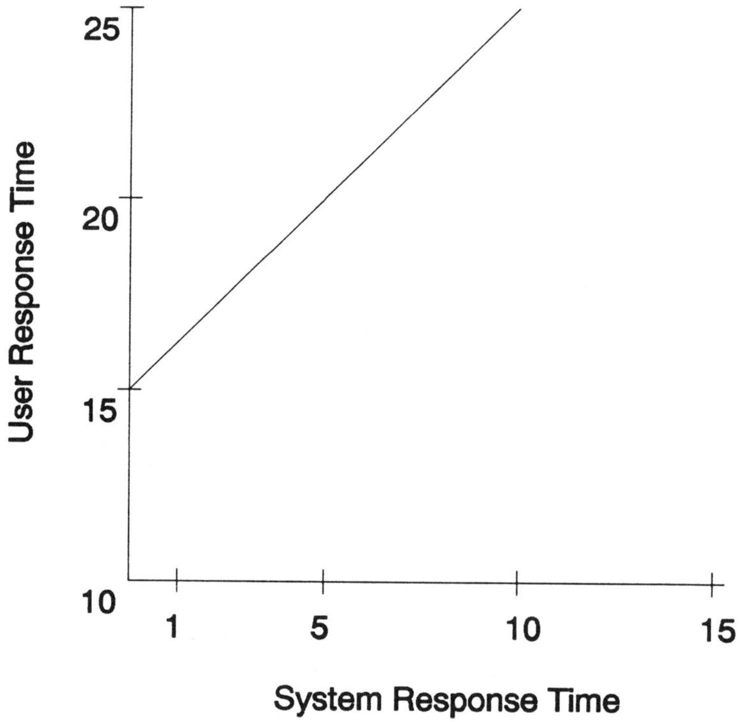

Figure 2-1. Effect of system response time on user response time.

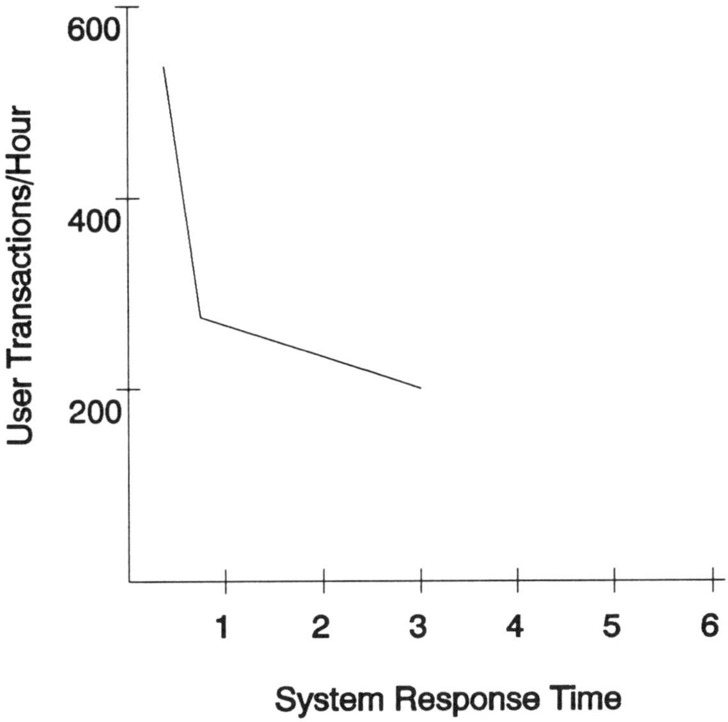

Figure 2-2. Effect of system response time on user transaction rate.

While it is evident at this point that subsecond response time leads to an increase in developer transactions, the important question becomes "Does this increase in developer transactions lead to real productivity increases?" In the IBM studies, and in a study conducted at AT&T,[5] this proved to be the case. Below is a brief description of some of the studies conducted and their findings.

The Thadhani Experiment

In Thadhani's experiment, mainframe developers were given a mainframe computer with utilization kept intentionally low. This yielded average response times of less than 0.2 seconds for human intensive activities (e.g., editing and browsing). The developers involved in the test spent 20 to 25 hours per week at their terminals doing work.

Around 90% to 95% of the terminal time was spent doing human-intensive activities. The rest of the time was spent doing computer-intensive activities (e.g., compiling, printing). The developers reported that the time they spent designing, coding, and unit testing was reduced by between 37% and 50%.

The Lambert Study

In Lambert's study, a team of developers had an environment similar to Thadhani's but with an average response time of 0.84 seconds for human-intensive activities. The experiment also consisted of a control team working in a standard multisecond response time environment with average response times for human-intensive activities greater than 2 seconds. Overall, the study team experienced a significant increase in work productivity yielding a savings of 37% in the overall effort versus the control team.

The AT&T Study

In the AT&T study, teams of developers were provided with an offloaded development environment consisting of Micro Focus COBOL-IMS Workbench with SPF/PC and an early version of AT&T's Application Development Workgroup/COBOL (see Chapters 5 and 7 for more information on these packages). The developers used AT-class PCs and were connected via StarLAN to a 3B2 super-microcomputer server that was connected to a mainframe. The first team, which had a significant local function point database prior to the test, yielded a 29% savings in total project effort (i.e., billable hours). This was despite the fact that the team had to perform more manual function analysis activities than they normally were used to. The second team did not have a local baseline, so they compared their results against an average of function point postmortems of similar COBOL-IMS projects implemented in AT&T within the previous two years. The result was a 37% decrease in total project effort.

Thus, subsecond response time in both mainframe-only and offloaded development environments appears to yield significant productivity increases. However, it is important to note that the improved rate of productivity experienced in the studies may not be entirely accounted for by the availability of subsecond response time. For example, in Lambert's study the developers worked together in a project office rather than being scattered over a large floor of developers. This made communications easier. In the AT&T study the developers were using an entirely different tool set. For debugging and unit testing, the full-screen Micro Focus Animator was used instead of the single line display tool TESTCOB. Productivity increases were probably also derived from situations where tools that did not exist on the mainframe were used, such as Micro Focus Checker (i.e., a full-screen interactive compiler that is linked to a full-screen editor).

Other factors that also may have contributed were the following:

1. Use of high-performance developers versus average-performance developers.
2. Differing characteristics of the applications that were developed.
3. Use of function points to measure productivity.
4. The "Hawthorne effect" — the fact that a group of workers is being studied, rather than the experimental factors that are being manipulated, causes them to react.

Thus, subsecond response time is a large part of the offloaded development environment's productivity gain, but there is more to be considered.

IMPROVED QUALITY

One major concern when moving to a subsecond response time environment is the possibility of a decline in the quality of the systems from the reduction in user "think time" or the faster data entry. Fortunately, this does not occur. In Lambert's study, there was no statistically significant difference in the number of discovered errors between the study group using subsecond response time and the control group with multisecond response time. As with IBM, the groups at AT&T that measured system quality showed no significant difference in the number of errors.

One explanation for these results may be that any decrease in quality due to reduced think time or faster data entry was offset by other positive factors. For example, if the developer's short-term memory buffers were not disrupted as often in the subsecond response time environment, the quality of the sequence of activities stored in the buffers may have been higher than it would have been in a multisecond response time environment. Another explanation may be that more testing is performed. This was indicated in several user comments in the AT&T study. They said that because they had more time and because testing could be done faster, more testing was being done.

While subsecond response time can impact the quality of the applications developed under offloaded development, implementors should plan to obtain the most significant improvements from the use of offloaded development tools. Some tools, especially upper CASE tools, can have a tremendous impact on quality. For more information see the following chapters on tool selection and impact.

DECREASED MAINFRAME USAGE

After considering productivity and quality, the most important benefit of an offloaded development environment is reduced mainframe use. In the previously discussed Lambert study, the project developed in the mainframe-based subsecond response time environment showed a 40% increase in the rate at which TSO resources were being used. Overall, however, there was no increase in the amount of mainframe resources used per module developed. This is because the 40% increase in the rate of TSO usage was almost entirely offset by the 37% improvement in productivity.

In the AT&T study of offloaded development environments with subsecond response time, a savings of 85% in module development TSO costs was realized. This savings was mostly due to offloaded compiling, unit testing, and debugging (i.e., computer-intensive activities) and to a lesser extent offloaded coding and editing (i.e., human-intensive activities). Because computer-intensive activities usually take very little clock time when compared with human-intensive activities, the reduction in cost associated with them is generally underestimated by the users. For example, when the programmers in the AT&T study were surveyed on how much they thought they reduced their mainframe charges, they significantly underestimated their mainframe cost savings. Specifically, programmers in the study estimated their mainframe cost savings at 67% versus the real cost savings of 85%. The real savings number was derived from actual mainframe chargeback bills.

However, when trying to predict what the effect of an offloaded development environment will be on a mainframe's usage, it's important to note that it will vary from project to project depending on a number of factors, including the following:

1. *Programmer work habits.* Many program development methodologies state that there should be a significant amount of desk checking of code before compiling and dynamic testing takes place. This practice not only saves time in the testing stage, it saves computing resources. The problem here is that few programmers work this way and prefer to speed through the coding stage and go straight to the compiling and dynamic testing stages. If an organization of programmers were extremely well disciplined and doing large amounts of desk checking, the benefits of the offloaded development environment in the area of mainframe usage would be limited because the amount of resources that could possibly be saved would be much smaller.

2. *Type and amount of dynamic testing.* Offloaded development environments have variable impacts on mainframe costs because of the differing impact on different types of dynamic testing. If an offloaded development environment has a reasonably complete set of tools, unit testing should be supported entirely on the PC workstations. With the arrival of JCL emulators (e.g., Proximity's ProxMVS) and emulations of some of the more common mainframe utilities (e.g., Micro Focus MVSSORT in place of SyncSort), string testing of multistep procedures also can be performed on the PC workstation. Volume testing and system testing are another matter. With the present power of PC workstations, it simply is not practical to volume-test programs that invoke many thousands of database calls on the PC workstation. This kind of testing must still be performed on the mainframe. System testing also must be performed on the mainframe, or whatever production platform will be used, as this is part of the definition of system testing. In summary, if an offloaded development environment is well equipped, the mainframe costs associated with unit and string testing can be eliminated. However, the mainframe costs associated with system testing, and most cases of extensive and expensive volume testing, will not be reduced.

3. *Time spent online.* This is somewhat related to programmer work habits, in that the amount of time spent actually using a mainframe computer will impact how much user time can be offloaded from the mainframe to the PC workstation. If a programmer spends very little time on a mainframe to begin with, she is not going to significantly reduce mainframe charges by moving most of her online activities to a PC workstation. The reasons for a limited amount of online time can include desk checking (as

outlined above), attendance at meetings, lack of immediate access to mainframe terminals, and extensive travel requirements.

Thus, the impact of offloaded development on mainframe usage can be immense in some, but not all, situations.

ACCESS TO NONMAINFRAME PRODUCTION PLATFORMS

Access to nonmainframe production platforms (i.e., UNIX, MS-DOS, OS/2, and client/server) is another benefit of offloaded development. Many of the same reasons for offloading development apply to offloading production.

1. The need to leverage existing COBOL skills.
2. The need to leverage existing libraries of COBOL code.
3. The high degree of portability of COBOL across platforms (i.e., UNIX (System V, BSD, AIX, XENIX), MS-DOS, OS/2).
4. The large selection of powerful COBOL tools available on the above platforms.

Not surprisingly, many of the same benefits for developers in the offloaded development environment are shared by end users on the nonmainframe production platforms. Some of the major benefits include the following:

1. Subsecond response time for end users. The same reasons that make subsecond response time beneficial for developers (e.g., uninterrupted short-term memory) will, in many situations, make it beneficial for end users as well.
2. The availability of graphical and/or mouse-driven interfaces.
3. The reduction in mainframe chargeback.

Thus, offloading small or medium-sized systems to smaller platforms can provide a number of significant benefits. It should be noted though that it can be very difficult to decide at what point a system should be located on the mainframe, the PC, or both (i.e., client/server). There are no obvious formulas to decide what path to take in all situations. Needless to say, extreme caution should be observed when dealing with large or critical applications.

BONUS BENEFITS

The main reason to introduce an offloaded development environment into a DP shop is to improve its system development by giving application developers a more powerful development platform. However, once the platform is installed, additional uses may be found. One of these is the mechanization of office/administrative functions for the developers, as well as their management and other support personnel. This mechanization usually goes by the name of office automation (OA) or group productivity software (groupware).

OA became popular in the 1970s when vendors, such as Wang, offered word processor systems that utilized proprietary hardware and software platforms. Usually they consisted of dumb terminals attached to a minicomputer running a small number of programs or processes, all supplied by a single vendor. When PCs and LANs came along in the 1980s, OA functions were moved to these platforms and given the new name, groupware. One difference has been that groupware packages have usually been provided on a single-function basis, with the customer left to assemble the desired environment. In the early 1990s, though, some Microsoft Windows-based environments have been introduced that tie together a number of groupware facilities into a single environment. These include Hewlett Packard's NewWave and NCR's Cooperation. Another difference is that the number of mechanized office support functions has grown. The list now includes the following:

1. *Word processing/publishing.* The original OA function has now been supplemented with publishing capabilities via such packages as Xerox's Ventura. So, in addition to the faster creation of memos, published documents — newsletters, sales brochures, and user manuals — can be produced.

2. *Electronic mail.* Electronic mail, or e-mail, provides a very quick and cheap way to communicate in an intraoffice environment. When a LAN is linked to other LANs, via bridges/routers or an outside e-mail service (e.g., AT&T Mail, AT&T Easylink, MCI Mail), effective interoffice communication is also possible. Many top-level executives of major technology companies, such as Gates of Microsoft[6] and Kahn of Borland,[7] make large use of e-mail, sometimes sending and receiving a hundred messages a day. The advantage for these executives and their companies is that it

flattens their organization. Everyone has access to everyone else. E-mail systems can also support other functions, such as electronic directories, which list user's addresses and functions, and electronic shared folders that provide subscribers with daily organization or company bulletins. Functions like these are very useful as a way of keeping employees who work in very narrow areas from developing acute cases of "tunnel vision."

3. *Project planning.* Planning software allows groups to link up personnel, equipment, and facilities with the individual steps that make up a project. This kind of software can check resource availability, make assignments, and count the costs of projects.

4. *Spreadsheets and financial planning.* From a group point of view, spreadsheets on LANs can be very useful for developing budgets that require input from large numbers of people. Beyond basic spreadsheets, some financial packages can assist users with financial analysis and forecasting.

5. *Graphics.* Graphics software allows unsophisticated users to make professional-looking graphics.

6. *Calendars.* LAN-based calendar systems allow for easier scheduling of meetings because these systems allow the caller of a meeting to check the availability of attendees without having to contact them directly.

7. *FAX interface.* In addition to e-mail, another form of electronic communication that can be included on an OA/groupware platform is software that allows for the transmission and reception of FAX images without a FAX machine.

8. *Electronic meetings.* Electronic meetings, or e-meetings, are starting to attract attention in the general press.[8] E-meetings are basically brainstorming sessions where participants input their ideas via keyboard rather than meet face to face. This, of course, is done anonymously and provides a way for users to challenge authority and to hear new or offbeat ideas. It also gives more soft-spoken folks a chance to be heard. One package that supports this activity is GroupSystems by Ventana Corporation. While the number of companies who have used these systems is small, the results have been impressive. IBM claims GroupSystems has made their meetings 60% more efficient, and Bell South claims that they have not found any situation where people meet that this concept has not proved incredibly useful.

9. *Image storage.* In addition to the storage, movement, and display of text, graphical images also can be stored, moved, and displayed. Both still and moving images can be worked with. All this will likely be integrated into e-mail and e-meeting systems in the near future.

Despite the mechanization of the above functions, some in the industry have claimed that investment in OA has yielded little or no positive impact on office worker productivity. This concern has been spelled out in a number of reports by Roach of Morgan Stanley[9–15] and several articles in *Fortune*,[16] *Business Week*,[17,18] and other publications.

The problem with these reports is that they rely on rather precise measurements of office worker output. Unfortunately, there are no natural units of output for office workers, as there are for factory workers. That is, if you think it's tough to measure programmer productivity, try measuring the productivity of an executive secretary or a middle manager.

While OA has met with some opposition, it has its share of proponents as well. Panko of Hawaii[19] points out that it is very difficult to measure office worker productivity in most industries. However, he also notes that in the industries where there are some established measurements, the impact of OA has been very positive. For example, in commercial banking — an industry with a high percentage of office workers — productivity has increased 3.3% per year from 1980 to 1987. In the communication industry, which also has a high percentage of office workers, the improvement has been even higher, 4.3% per year from 1973 to 1979 and 3.9% per year from 1979 to 1985. In these industries Panko notes that OA investment is significantly higher than in other industries (see Table 2-1).

Table 2-1. Impact of office automation.

Industry	Amount of OA investment times national average	Productivity improvement rate per year	Time period
Commercial Banking	2.2	3.3%	1980–1987
Communications	4.3	4.3%	1973–1979
Communications	4.3	3.9%	1979–1985

Thus, levels of OA investment may have a lot to do with productivity impact. Each organization must look at their own particular situation and determine what is the right amount of investment for themselves.

CALCULATING BENEFITS

Since employers pay the costs of setting up and operating offloaded development environments, they are most keenly interested in the impact of the environment. This impact can be felt at different levels of the business, but the most important is the impact at the strategic level. From the time when commercial DP started to the 1980s, most DP projects involved the mechanization of back room, or clerical, operations. However, in the 1980s some companies started using computer systems to gain strategic advantage over their competition. These systems allowed companies to respond to market changes in such a timely manner that their competitors were placed at a significant disadvantage. One of the best publicized examples of this was Beneton's worldwide order processing system that tells its factories what products need to be made on a daily basis. This system allowed Beneton to increase greatly their revenues, despite the fact that they were operating in a shrinking market. Thus, any improvement that can help employers, or companies, deliver a strategic system faster can significantly impact the revenue and future of the whole company. When back room, or clerical, operations are the systems being mechanized, then the above-mentioned productivity and quality factors will not have an impact on revenue, but they may have a significant impact on expenses.

One anomaly, documented by Capers Jones,[20] that can distort the impact of an offloaded development environment is the effect of unpaid overtime. In the United States most programmers are not unionized and are considered "exempt" professionals (i.e., exempt from the laws that state workers must be paid for the overtime they work). This means that if a productivity improvement, such as an offloaded development environment, allowed programmers to go home on time and not work weekends but did not allow for any additional work during regular hours, the employer would see no immediate benefit if the overtime had been unpaid (see Table 2-2).

Table 2-2. Effect of unpaid overtime.

	Programmer with offloaded development environment and 30% productivity gain	**Programmer without offloaded development environment and no productivity gain**
Hours worked per week	40	52
Hours paid per week	40	40
Net benefit to programmer	12 hours free time	0
Net benefit to employers	0	0

In the above case the productivity improvement would need to exceed 30% for the employer to save on compensated programmer work time. It should be stated, though, that employers who use this argument to reject efforts to improve productivity probably will have to confront problems in other areas (e.g., employee turnover, technological obsolescence).

Another major expense savings that employers may observe is the postponing or cancellation of mainframe upgrades. In the IBM world, this kind of savings can easily amount to many hundreds of thousands of dollars. Very successful offloaded development operations may even be able to reduce the number of mainframes.

Thus, the overall benefits of offloaded development can have a significant impact on both revenues and expenses (see Table 2-3).

BENEFITS WORKSHEET

Quantifiable benefits for offloaded development environments can be broken down into two views, savings comparison per developer and cost comparison per project. Worksheets for each of these views are shown in Tables 2-3 and 2-4.

Table 2-3. Savings comparison per developer.

Item	With Offloaded Environment	Without Offloaded Environment
Billable hours/year (40 hours × 52 weeks × 80%)	1,664	1,664
Productivity improvement rate	30%	0%
Bill rate per hour	$50	$50
Productivity savings per year	$24,960	$0
Mainframe charges/year ($1,000/month × 12 months)	$12,000	$12,000
Mainframe usage reduction rate	75%	0%
Mainframe usage savings per year	$9,000	$0
Terminal & controller usage charges/year ($100/month × 12 months)	$1,200	$1,200
Terminal & controller usage reduction	100%	0%
Terminal & controller savings per year	$1,200	$0
Total savings per year	$35,160	$0

Table 2-4. Cost comparison per project (10 developers for 6 months).

Item	With Offloaded Environment	Without Offloaded Environment
Billable hours (40 hours × 26 weeks × 80% × 10 developers)	8,320	8,320
Productivity effect (100% – 30% improvement rate)	70%	100%
Bill rate per hour	$50	$50
Labor charges	$291,200	$416,000
Normal mainframe charges ($1,000/month × 6 months × 10 developers)	$60,000	$60,000
Mainframe usage rate (100% – 75% reduction)	25%	100%
Net mainframe usage charges	$15,000	$60,000
Terminal & controller usage charges ($100/month × 6 months × 10 developers)	$0	$6,000
Total project costs	$306,200	$482,000

SUMMARY

The main benefits of using an offloaded development environment are the following:

1 *Improved productivity (usually in the range of 30% to 40%).* Productivity gains mostly due to the effects of subsecond response time.

2. *Improved quality.* Quality gains are primarily attributable to the use of CASE tools, although more and better dynamic testing (i.e., unit and string testing) can also be a factor.

3. *Decreased mainframe usage.* The amount of mainframe usage reductions will depend on individual circumstances. Anything up to 85% is possible.

Other benefits of using an offloaded development environment can include the following:

1. *Access to office automation or groupware facilities.* These facilities include word processing/publishing, electronic mail, project planning tools, spreadsheets and financial planning tools, graphics packages, LAN-based calendar systems, FAX interfaces, electronic meetings, and image storage.

2. *Early delivery of strategically important applications.* These are applications that can put a competitor at a significant disadvantage.

3. *Savings from the delay or cancellation of mainframe purchases or upgrades.*

REFERENCES

1. Doherty, W. J., and R. P. Kelisky. 1979. Managing VM/CMS systems for user effectiveness. *IBM Systems Journal.* Volume 18, Number 1. 143–163.
2. Thadhani, A. J. 1981. Interactive user productivity. *IBM Systems Journal.* Volume 20, Number 4. 407–423.
3. ———. 1984. Factors affecting programmer productivity during application development. *IBM Systems Journal.* Volume 23, Number 1. 19–35.
4. Lambert, G. N. 1984. A comparative study of system response time on program developer productivity. *IBM Systems Journal.* Volume 23, Number 1. 36–43.

5. Butterline, M. A. Application Development Workgroup Final Recommendation. AT&T internal study available from AT&T Application Development Solutions, Orlando, Florida. March 10, 1989.
6. Moody, Fred. Mr. Software — How Bill Gates Programmed the Computer Industry. *New York Times Magazine*. August 25, 1991. 26.
7. Lewis, Peter H. Philippe Kahn of Borland, in His Own Words. *New York Times*. August 18, 1991.
8. O'Brien, Timothy L. Chairmen of the Bored Use Computers to Drive Meetings. *Newsday*. July 7, 1991. 62.
9. Roach, S. S. Productivity, Investment, and the Information Economy. *Economic Perspectives* (Morgan Stanley & Co.). March 14, 1984.
10. Roach, S. S. The New Technology Cycle. *Economic Perspectives* (Morgan Stanley & Co.). September 11, 1985.
11. Roach, S. S. America's Technology Dilemma: A Profile of the Information Economy. *Economic Perspectives* (Morgan Stanley & Co.). April 22, 1987.
12. Roach, S. S. Technology and the Service Sector: America's Hidden Competitive Advantage. *Economic Perspectives* (Morgan Stanley & Co.). September 25, 1987.
13. Roach, S. S. Technology and the Service Sector: America's Hidden Competitive Advantage. *Technology in Services: Policies for Growth, Trade, and Employment*. B. R. Guile and J. B. Quinn (eds.). National Academy Press, 118–138.
14. Roach, S. S. The Technology Trap. *Economic Perspectives* (Morgan Stanley & Co.). December 15, 1989. 6–18.
15. Roach, S. S., and R. S. Gray. The Productivity Puzzle: Perils and Hopes. *Economic Perspectives* (Morgan Stanley & Co.). April 10, 1986.
16. Bowen, W. The Puny Payoff from Office Computers. *Fortune*. May 26, 1986. 20–24.
17. Pennar, Karen. Special Report: The Productivity Paradox. *Business Week*. June 6, 1988. 100.
18. Port, Otis, et al. Special Report: How the New Math of Productivity Adds Up. *Business Week*. June 6, 1988. 103.
19. Panko, Raymond R. Is Office Productivity Stagnant? *MIS Quarterly*. June 1991. 190–203.
20. Jones, Capers. 1986. *Programming Productivity*. New York: McGraw-Hill.

3

The Costs of an Offloaded Development Environment

In the following chapters we will examine and select the hardware and software components for an offloaded development environment and make choices regarding installation, training, operations, administration, and maintenance. In this chapter we will examine the costs related to all these items and explore ways in which they can be minimized. In addition, there is a sample cost worksheet for a small offloaded development environment.

HARDWARE

Hardware and software are the two major costs associated with setting up an offloaded development environment. Unlike software, however, the overall price trend for hardware is downward. In this section we will examine the reasons for this downward trend and discuss ways to minimize costs.

Reasons for Downward Price Trends

The two major components that drive the prices of PC workstations and most servers are CPU microprocessors and memory chips. At the time of the writing of this book, CPU microprocessors (i.e., Intel 80X86 microprocessors) are under a lot of downward price pressure. This comes from a number of sources, including the following:

1. *RISC microprocessor manufacturers.* Reduced instruction set CPU microprocessors, which are used in non-PC workstations (e.g., Sun

workstations), are normally thought of as much more powerful than the Intel 80X86 line of microprocessors. However, with the 80486, Intel is starting to compete with the low end of the non-PC workstation market. This means the 80486 and RISC microprocessors will be competing directly against each other, which forces manufacturers of both types of microprocessors to lower prices.

2. *80X86 clones.* Some manufacturers are now making 80X86 workalike microprocessors at prices lower than Intel's. These lower prices are possible because workalike microprocessors are not manufactured under license but are the products of extensive reverse engineering programs. The best known of these workalikes is the AM386, produced by American Micro Devices. Intel, of course, is not pleased to see other companies enter their line of business. Especially since before the AM386 Intel had 100% of the 80386 market and enjoyed huge profit margins. However, Intel is not taking these clones lightly. In addition to taking steps in the courts to protect their product line, they are also allowing marketing considerations to drive microprocessor design, as evidenced by the SX series of microprocessors (i.e., 80386/SX and 80486/SX). With the 80386/SX, Intel applied a great deal of price pressure on 80286 microprocessor clone makers (despite the fact that these clone makers were licensed by Intel). The 80486/SX is now exerting price pressure on the unlicensed 80386 clone makers. There is, of course, no technical reason to make these SX microprocessors. The 80386/SX is merely a 32-bit 80386 microprocessor with a 16-bit interface instead of the normal 32-bit. The 80486/SX is a slowed-down 80486 (20 MHz versus 25 or 33 MHz) without a floating point unit. The decision to produce and market the SX series was solely an economic one. With the introduction of Intel's SX series the trend is clear. If American Micro Devices and other companies continue to reverse engineer and manufacture important CPU microprocessors, the prices of these microprocessors should continue to fall.

3. *Intel.* In order to better compete with RISC microprocessors and 80X86 clone microprocessor manufacturers, Intel has been lowering the price of their latest microprocessors. This, in turn, means that they also have to lower prices on their less powerful microprocessors in order to maintain a differential in price between microprocessors of various powers, knowing that nobody will buy 80386 microprocessors if the 80486s are only a few dollars more.

Memory chips (i.e., DRAM chips — Dynamic Random Access Memory chips), usually made in Japan, are the other major cost component of PC workstations and servers. In recent years, the prices of these chips have been falling and should continue to fall because of increasing competition from Korean and Singaporean manufacturers. However, as we have seen in the past, this has not always been the case.

In 1987, 256K DRAM chips — then the standard — could be purchased for about $4 apiece. Around this time, however, the United States government negotiated an antidumping trade pact with the Japanese government that covered DRAM chips. By 1988 there was an acute worldwide shortage of DRAM chips, with prices tripling. This, of course, hurt consumers of DRAM chips, as well as the makers of equipment that used DRAM chips, while giving huge profits to a few Japanese and American DRAM manufacturers. Fortunately, this shortage eventually corrected itself, and the prices for 256K DRAM chips fell to $1 apiece by 1990. Provided governments keep their hands off the chip industry, and competition is not stymied for other reasons, prices of memory chips should continue to fall.

How to Minimize Costs

Given that prices of the major components of PCs and servers continue to decline, it follows that PC workstation and server prices also will decrease. In order to minimize costs, however, the question of where to purchase your equipment becomes an important consideration.

Many different kinds of vendors sell servers, PCs, and PC-related equipment. These vendors range from discount houses that specialize in consumer and office equipment, to Value Added Resellers (VARs), to the manufacturers themselves. Some important attributes of each of these vendor types are listed below.

1. *Discount houses.* Discount houses charge very low prices, but they also offer very little service. The line of equipment they carry also may be limited to large selling items or generic items such as DRAM chips.

2. *Value added resellers.* VARs usually will carry a large selection of equipment from a number of different manufacturers. In addition to usually having equipment available for immediate delivery, they can usually offer assistance in its setup. Prices for equipment from VARs are usually higher than from other sources, but not always.

3. *Manufacturers.* Manufacturers usually prefer to deal only with large customers. For these customers they can provide equipment at very competitive prices, in addition to firsthand technical assistance. A problem with some manufacturers is that because of competitive pressures to keep inventories low, they might not be able to supply all needed equipment immediately.

Given the wide variety of discounts and services available and the amount of equipment needed to construct an offloaded development environment, in many situations it will pay to procure equipment from a variety of types of vendors. When comparing the cost of equipment from various vendors, keep in mind that list prices are not always a valid comparison criterion.

Another important consideration that can help to minimize costs is knowing where to skimp. Skimping on the right components can make an offloaded development environment affordable to organizations that are short on money. Skimping on the wrong components can be detrimental to the success of your project.

Where to Skimp

1. *PC Workstation.* In most situations it is not necessary to deploy the latest in PC workstation technology. For example, if you only plan to use character-based DOS tools like Micro Focus in the foreseeable future, then getting by with a 386/SX with a color monitor and a 100MB hard drive may be acceptable. However, if you plan to pursue the latest and greatest tools in the marketplace, a more powerful configuration may be required. The important thing to note is that when a new CPU microprocessor comes out it usually takes a couple of years for the software that can fully exploit the new microprocessor to be introduced. By then, of course, a new generation of microprocessors may be available, and your PC will have been subjected to a lot of wear and tear and may not have much life left in it. As a rule, get a PC workstation that you think can handle the tools you will be acquiring during the next two to three years.

2. *LAN.* When deciding on what LAN to get, there are not only technical considerations but cost considerations as well. Many LAN software packages run on multiple LAN hardware platforms. For example, Novell NetWare runs on IBM's Token Ring, NCR's WaveLAN, and AT&T's StarLAN. The cost for these LAN

hardware systems, of course, varies from product to product. A second consideration is the medium used to connect the LAN together. For example, IBM's Token Ring uses shielded twisted pair, whereas AT&T's StarLAN uses unshielded twisted pair (i.e., telephone wire). If your building is already wired with unshielded twisted pair, then installing a Token Ring using shielded twisted pair would be much more costly due to the expense of rewiring. Depending on the age of your building, environmental costs associated with cutting holes in asbestos-filled walls also may come into play.

3. *Computer Links.* When considering how to connect servers to other servers or servers to mainframes, consider the amount of traffic that is likely to go over the line. If speed is not essential and traffic will be low, consider dial-up communication links over direct links.
4. *2-Tier vs. 3-Tier Architecture.* If your operation is small (5 to 8 users) and is not expected to grow, then a 2-tier setup (i.e., PC workstations in place of 3270 terminals) may be viable.

Of course, skimping on the wrong components can result in an underpowered, problem-ridden environment. The following guidelines should be observed.

Where Not to Skimp

1. *Server.* Never, never, never skimp on server power (i.e., CPU microprocessor, DRAM chips, hard disk). Servers are always located at a critical choke point in the offloaded development environment. Having an underpowered server will slow down all users and make the transition to offloaded development more difficult. In addition, initial savings will be quickly consumed by expensive server upgrades. If you need an item to skimp on with the server, try the monitor. Fancy VGA graphics are almost never needed on a server. Character-based terminals will usually do nicely.
2. *2.5-Tier vs. 3-Tier Architecture.* As discussed in Chapter 7, there is no technical reason to choose a 2.5-tier environment (i.e., PC workstations connected directly to the mainframe and a LAN) over a 3-tier environment. There is also no financial reason. Both environments require LANs and servers, but the 3-tier consolidates communication links at a single server, while in the 2.5-tier each PC has its own link. This makes the 3-tier environment cheaper.

An important consideration when trying to minimize costs in some organizations is the year-to-year cost analysis. The major question is how many years is the PC workstation good for. This will vary depending on a number of factors.

1. *Maintenance.* Well-maintained PCs will last five years. PCs that are not cared for may only last three years. The important thing to bear in mind is that PCs are electromechanical devices that only have a certain life expectancy. Eventually they will break down and not be cost effective to fix.
2. *Power.* If the PC workstation had the latest technology at the time of procurement (e.g., a 486 in 1991), then the useful life of the workstation will be longer than had it been a low-end PC at the time of procurement. A fairly new development that also may extend the life of PCs is the introduction of upgradeable CPU slots — for example, a PC comes with a built-in 386 microprocessor, but it is equipped with a slot for a 486 upgrade card or microprocessor.
3. *Recycling.* After a PC has been used by a developer and he now needs an upgrade to a more powerful PC, the old PC can be given to someone who can use a less powerful PC, such as a manager or secretary. In some development environments, old PCs also can be used as print spoolers, such as in AT&T's StarGROUP/StarLAN system.

SOFTWARE

The second major cost associated with setting up an offloaded development environment is software. Unlike hardware, however, software's overall price trend is not downward. In fact, it some situations it is upward. In this section we will examine the reasons for this price trend and discuss ways to minimize the costs involved.

Reasons for Flat/Upward-Price Trends

Unlike the situation for PCs, where there are dozens of makers of fairly compatible products, there are only a few viable vendors of software tools for offloaded development environment PC workstations. In the area of COBOL tools, only Micro Focus and Realia have a significant presence in commercial DP shops, with Micro Focus having the largest share. (This situation may change, however, because of Realia's acquisition by Computer Associates.) In the area of COBOL code generators (i.e., lower CASE), there are only two major competitors, Intersolv's APS/PC and Computer Associates' TELON/PWS. In some areas, tool offerings are unique, such as Computer Associates' IDMS/PC. Thus, the reason for "sticky" prices on these products is probably a lack of competition.

How to Minimize Costs

When setting up an offloaded development environment, software is needed for both the server and the PC workstations. With server software (e.g., LAN software), prices are generally not high when you consider the number of users. For example, an unlimited server license for AT&T's StarGROUP LAN Manager package is less than $3,500. However, PC workstation software can be very expensive, especially when the number of users is limited to one. For example, Micro Focus COBOL Workbench lists for $3,000 and APS/PC Workbench lists for over $9,000 for some configurations. Thus, when determining where to concentrate cost-saving efforts, it's best to concentrate on the PC workstation side.

As with hardware, many different types of vendors sell PC software. And, as with hardware again, determining where to procure your software is a consideration that will directly affect your costs. Some important attributes of the various types of vendors are listed below.

1. *Discount houses.* Discount houses charge very low prices for software packages that sell in fairly large quantities. However, discount houses will normally not carry very expensive packages, or those that require a lot of tuning or training.
2. *Value added resellers.* VARs usually will carry a limited selection of complex software packages that they specialize in. In addition to usually having software available for immediate delivery, VARs can offer training and assistance with its installation. Prices for software from VARs are sometimes higher than from other sources, but not always.
3. *Software houses.* Software houses that produce complex/expensive packages (e.g., Micro Focus COBOL Workbench, APS/PC) will usually reserve availability for just themselves or certain

VARs. If you are looking for a large number of copies of a tool, the software house should be able to provide the best discount possible.

After identifying the appropriate vendors for the software tools you plan to purchase, questions regarding the terms of purchase come into play. Some of the terms that directly affect software costs include the following:

1. *Discounts.* This is a tricky area in that there are not a lot of set rules. Discounts can range anywhere from 0% to 80% of list. It depends on how hungry the vendor is, how much competition there is, and what the published discount schedule is like. It also can be influenced by what commitments the customer is willing to make (see items 2 and 3 below) and the list price of the products. Products with prices in the $2,000+ range per copy can be discounted significantly because there is "room to maneuver." Products in the several hundred dollar range usually can't be discounted as much. In order to get a good idea of how much of a discount to ask for, informal contacts among friends and colleagues who are also buying such tools can be useful. In cases where a vendor has a contract with the United States federal government, it is usually possible to get terms of the contract by reading the trade press or, if necessary, via the Freedom of Information Act.[1]

2. *Stockpiling.* One way to get discounts is to buy a large number of copies of a package up front and store them until they are needed. This should be avoided as new versions of software are always coming out, making previous versions obsolete. A good rule to follow is to buy only what you can make good use of in the short term (about two or three months).

3. *Cumulative contracts.* If a vendor is reluctant to give a significant discount without the purchase of a large number of packages, then try to get them to agree to a cumulative contract. That is a contract that gives bigger and bigger discounts for each additional copy of software that is purchased.

Another consideration that will directly affect software costs is whether to buy maintenance contracts for major software packages (these contracts include technical support, usually on the phone, and new releases of the product) or just purchase the new releases as needed. Usually users are better off when they just buy whatever upgrades they need. When a new release comes out, it should only be purchased if there is some new feature that is needed. As far as technical support goes, the author has never purchased a maintenance contract from a PC tool vendor and has never been refused technical support because of it.

PLANNING AND INSTALLATION

The costs of planning and installation are mostly attributable to the time spent by the people charged with the task of setting up and operating the offloaded development environment. The cost for this will either be expensive or *very* expensive, depending mostly on whether a prepackaged offloaded development environment is chosen or not. Prepackaged offloaded development environments, such as AT&T's Application Development Workgroup/COBOL, can save a lot of time during installation, because many of the time-consuming system integration tasks need not be performed.

Custom-designed offloaded development environments take more time to plan and install. This is due to the extra time needed to first learn about system integration subjects, such as linking servers to mainframes, and then to actually do the integration and setup.

Regardless of which option is chosen, *planning* for the offloaded development environment is the most time-consuming activity because of the number of steps it involves, including the following:

1. Selecting the candidates.
2. Selecting and configuring hardware and software packages.
3. Ordering communication links.
4. Ordering hardware.
5. Ordering software.
6. Making baseline measurements.

Of these activities, selecting and configuring the hardware and software is certainly the most time consuming. Depending on the environment being served, this can take anywhere from three to nine months. For more information on this see Chapter 8.

Installation of the offloaded development environment will also take time. Some of the steps involved here include the following:

1. Taking delivery of software.
2. Taking delivery of hardware.
3. Taking delivery of communication links.
4. Setting up the server.
5. Setting up user training.
6. Deploying PC workstations.

Of these activities, taking delivery of the various components will usually take the most time, usually 1 or 2 months. So overall, planning and installation will usually involve the full-time attention of a technical person for about 4 to 10 months. Those sites that desire a custom-designed environment should count on a longer start-up time than those that use a prepackaged environment.

In addition to time spent by resident technical people to plan and set up an offloaded development environment, there are other planning and installation costs. For those groups that select prepackaged environments, system start-up service packages are sometimes offered by the vendor or third-party consultants. These packages will usually consist of a visit to the customer's site by a technical person who will direct the local administrators in the setup and operation of the environment. User training may also be included. The cost of these services is approximately $500 to $2,500 per day per person. A low-cost, or no-cost, alternative is obtaining assistance from other administrators who are running the same or similar operations.

If your site has work rules that mandate the use of specific types of technicians to do hardware-related jobs (i.e., wiring, computer installation, etc.), these expenses also will need to be taken into account. Like other technical folks, these technicians can cost $500 to $1,000 per day.

TRAINING

The cost of training will obviously depend on the base of existing knowledge. For administrators, knowledge or training is needed in the following areas:

1. PC workstation operating system.
2. PC workstation tools.
3. LAN design.

4. Server operating system.
5. LAN and server administration and operation.
6. Project knowledge.

This training can take from three to five weeks. The cost, as with most technical training, can run around $300 per day, more if travel is involved.

For users, knowledge or training is needed in the following areas:

1. PC workstation operating system.
2. Offloaded development environment.
3. PC workstation tools.

Usually this training will last one or two weeks. If users are sent to an off-site course, the usual training charges apply. If more than five or six people are to be trained at one time, then having a trainer come to your site at $1,500 to $2,500 per day may be more economical. If on-site training is opted for, the set-up costs for a training room also have to be considered.

OPERATION, ADMINISTRATION, AND MAINTENANCE (OA&M)

The cost of OA&M is mostly made up of the cost of the local administrator. His or her duties will include the following:

1. Backing up the server and performing restores.
2. Controlling PC workstation hard drives.
3. Organizing and maintaining server hard drives.
4. Maintaining printers.
5. Controlling server access and security.
6. Monitoring activity levels.
7. Tuning the server.
8. Setting up and maintaining server libraries and shared directories.
9. Monitoring communication links.
10. Maintaining system-wide mailing lists.

11. Maintaining trouble logs.
12. Add new users or packages.

Given the above duties, it is obvious that a person with a significant technical background is required. Clerks and/or secretaries should not be put in charge of OA&M of offloaded development environments.

The next question to be addressed is the ratio of local administrators to users. A good ratio for offloaded development environments is 1 administrator per 50 users. A similar ratio has been advocated in regular office LAN environments by Wohl[2] and others. Part-time administrators can be used but only for very small environments (10 to 15 users) and only after the initial start-up period is completed (no matter what the size of the offloaded development environment, the initial start-up period requires a full-time administrator). Setups that have administrator ratios higher than 1 to 50 will usually find that the effectiveness of the environments will be greatly reduced, thus reducing the impact of the investment (see Chapter 4 for more information).

LEARNING CURVE

One last item that needs to be mentioned from a cost point of view is the learning curve of the users. Poor training, incomplete systems integration, and bad timing (i.e., introducing the offloaded development environment in the middle of a big project, rather than at the beginning) can all lead to long, drawn-out user learning curves. This is why there needs to be significant management pressure to use the environment, along with close monitoring of usage reports (e.g., mainframe chargeback reports, server usage statistics). Failure in any of these areas can lead to a significant rise in the cost of doing business without the expected savings. Table 3-1 is a sample of determining cost effectiveness.

SUMMARY

When considering the long-term trends in the pricing of hardware and software the key issue is competition. Currently, there is a lot of competition in the hardware arena and very little in software. In the short term though, where one purchases hardware and software (e.g., from a discount house, VAR, and/or manufacturers), can have a significant effect on the cost of constructing an offloaded development

Table 3-1. Sample cost worksheet.

Sample Cost Worksheet for 11 Users and 1 Administrator Using AT&T's Application Development Workgroup/COBOL System Integration Package

Item	Quantity	Price	Total
Hardware:			
386/SX (20MHz) PC workstation with 4MB RAM on motherboard	12	$1,500	$18,000
80MB hard drive			
VGA color monitor			
3.5" floppy drive			
keyboard			
video controller on motherboard			
disk drive controller on motherboard			
mouse controller on motherboard			
Mouse	12	$75	$900
486 (33Mhz) server with 16MB RAM on motherboard	1	$12,000	$12,000
600MB hard drive			
3.5" floppy drive			
keyboard			
320/525MB tape drive			
SCSI drive controller			
mouse controller on motherboard			
Video controller	1	$200	$200
VGA monochrome monitor	1	$100	$100
Synchronous communication board	2	$500	$1,000
Synchronous modems	4	$500	$2,000
10Mb StarLAN hub	2	$1,200	$2,400
10Mb StarLAN board	13 (1 for each computer)	$300	$3,900
Total for hardware			$40,500
Total for hardware per user (Total / 11 users)			$3,682

Table 3-1. Sample cost worksheet (continued).

Item	Quantity	Price	Total
Software:			
MS-DOS	12	$75	$900
386MAX	12	$75	$900
AT&T ADW/COBOL End User	12	$1,200	$14,400
SPF/PC	12	$150	$1,800
Micro Focus COBOL Workbench	12	$2,500	$30,000
XDB DB2 Workbench	12	$1,250	$15,000
PFS Professional Write	12	$150	$1,800
UNIX System V	1	$700	$700
3270 Emulator	1	$1,500	$1,500
RJE Emulator	1	$1,500	$1,500
AT&T PMX/StarMAIL	1	$1,250	$1,250
AT&T ADW/COBOL Server	1	$12,000	$12,000
AT&T StarGROUP LAN Manager	1	$3,500	$3,500
Total for software			$85,250
Total for software per user (Total / 11 users)			$7,750
Item	**Days**	**Price**	**Total**
Training:			
Administrator training:			
Introduction to UNIX	5	$300	$1,500
UNIX Administration	5	$300	$1,500
LAN Administration	5	$300	$1,500
Micro Focus COBOL Workbench	3	$300	$900
XDB DB2 Workbench	2	$300	$600
Total per administrator			$6,000
User training:			
Introduction to PCs/MS-DOS	1	$300	$300
Introduction to AT&T ADW/COBOL	1	$300	$300
Micro Focus COBOL Workbench	3	$300	$900
XDB DB2 Workbench	2	$300	$600
Total for 11 users			$23,100
Total per user			$2,100

Table 3-1. Sample cost worksheet (continued).

Item	Units	Price	Total
Installation:			
Hardware and wiring	24 hours	$100/hour	$2,400
ADW/COBOL Application Start-up Package (provided by vendor)	3 days	$500/day	$1,500
Planning and installation (performed by local administrator)	4 months	$4,000/mth	$16,000
Total			$19,900
Total per user (Total / 11 users)			$1,809
Total for hardware, software, training, and installation			$174,750
Total per user (Total / 11 users)			$15,886
Operation, Administration, and Maintenance:			
Administration (initial 4 months)	1 person	$4,000/mth	
Administration (after initial 4 months)	0.5 person	$2,000/mth	

environment. In addition, *where* one tries to be economical can have an effect on the usefulness of an offloaded development environment. Skimping to some extent is generally safe in the areas of PC workstations, LANs, and computer links but not wise with the server.

Along with hardware and software costs, there will be training and OA&M (operations, administration, and maintenance) costs. Training for users will usually last one week. Training for administrators can last several weeks, depending on the administrator's experience. For OA&M, 1 administrator is needed for every 50 users. For smaller shops, a part-time administrator can be used once the environment is established. When an offloaded development environment is just starting up, however, an administrator will be needed full time regardless of the size of the environment.

Finally, managers need to plan and schedule for the learning curve of the users. The users will need some time to become familiar with all the new tools that they will be using to do their work. Not allowing enough time to learn the new tools will result in the users reverting to their old mainframe-based tools and methods for building applications.

REFERENCES

1. Software Maintenance News. The True Cost of Software Tools (Part 2). *Software Maintenance News*. December 1986. 1–2.
2. Wohl, Amy D. Improving Productivity in the LAN-based Office. Downsizing Expo Conference Proceedings. September 10–12, 1991. D–8.

4

Planning Considerations

To use PC workstations effectively for mainframe development, a well-planned and carefully designed offloaded development environment must be created. At medium- and large-sized companies these development environments usually consist of PC workstations connected, via a LAN, to servers that are connected to mainframes or mainframe networks. The purpose of these environments is to provide mainframe developers with the advantages of the PC workstation without depriving them of the following benefits of the mainframe environment, thereby improving developer productivity.

1. Sharable files and databases.
2. Regular backups.
3. Password protection and security.
4. Source code control.
5. Multitasking.
6. Fast and cheap print service.

THE PITFALLS

While it's easy to see why a development environment that incorporates the best of the PC workstation and mainframe worlds is desirable, it's not so easy to design, install, and operate that environment. Possible pitfalls do exist, and they should be understood and addressed early in the planning in order to ensure success. Some of these pitfalls are described below.

1. *Radical change.* Moving to a PC-based development environment often means a radical change in the tools programmers use to do their work. Programmers will need to learn to use a new set of compilers, editors, and debuggers. They will have to become adept at using PCs and LANs as well. Developing these new skills will take some training and some time. And some motivation wouldn't hurt, either.
2. *Integration headaches.* Moving to a PC-based development environment means integrating PC hardware and software, LAN hardware and software, server hardware and software, and mainframe communications. In short, a number of very different systems have to be made to work well together. All this integration can lead to a lot of aggravation mainly because of the variety of problems that can arise. These problems include, but are not limited to, memory contention, interrupt and I/O address contention, software and hardware incompatibilities, improperly genned lines, and so on.
3. *Multiple vendor interfaces.* Moving to a PC-based development environment often means working with a large number of vendors in order to obtain the products and services needed to set up a useful environment (five or six different vendors is common).

AVOIDING THE PITFALLS

A comprehensive plan is essential to the successful design and implementation of an offloaded development environment. A good plan will not only assist in coordinating the large amount of preparation work that is required, but it will also help in gaining management support and in keeping user expectations realistic. An example of a step-by-step offloaded development environment rollout plan is detailed in Appendix A. Some of the more important aspects are examined in detail below.

It's All in the Approach

There are an infinite number of ways to approach the deployment of an offloaded development environment. These are the three most common.

"Let a hundred flowers bloom..."

When Mao Tse-tung said, "Let a hundred flowers bloom, let a hundred ideas compete," he sure wasn't talking about offloaded development environments. Unfortunately, some IS managers act as if he was by allowing their developers to buy and use whatever PC-based packages pique their interest, on the false belief that PCs automatically improve productivity.

This fallacy can be easily exposed by simply examining the incompatibilities that must be overcome between the relatively few tools on the mainframe (Languages: COBOL vs. COBOL II vs. PL/I vs. Assembler; DBMSs: IMS vs. IDMS vs. DB2 vs. a bunch of others). The movement of programmers from project to project, not to mention communication between systems, has been greatly complicated by this relatively small variety.

Now, for the PC world, multiply this situation by 10 (or maybe 100). The emergence of cheap computers has given rise to a large number of software companies, and these companies have deluged the market with many thousands of packages. Only now, more than 10 years after the introduction of the PC, is some market discipline (i.e., defacto standards beyond the basic operating system) starting to emerge (e.g., Microsoft Windows as a user interface, Micro Focus XM as a memory manager for COBOL and COBOL-related development packages). This same sort of discipline, imposed by management, is required to avoid turning their offloaded development environments into chaotic and expensive messes.

Flash Cutting

Flash cutting means converting a large number of developers (25 or more) from a mainframe development environment to an offloaded development environment simultaneously. Given the amount of effort it takes administrators to set up an offloaded development environment and the effort needed to get developers to use several new tools simultaneously, flash cutting can be viewed as the equivalent of devouring an entire turkey at one sitting rather than eating it over several days. Not only would the diner (i.e., administrator) be unable to digest the bird, she would have a tough time just trying to stay alive. While this may seem obvious to most technical people, it is unfortunately not obvious to all and is just the situation that some groups have put themselves into when offloading development to PC workstations.

While researching this book, the author visited the administrators of a number of offloaded sites. One site had around 150 users and was assembled in only six months. During the author's visit, much information was exchanged on technical aspects of offloaded development environments — the performance of various LAN servers, what was the best 3270 emulation package, the quality of technical support from various vendors, the timeliness of equipment deliveries. When asked how many of the 150 developers were making significant use of PC-based coding and testing tools the answer was "About 5." When the administrator was asked what he would be doing to increase this number, he shrugged his shoulders and said he was too busy keeping the offloaded development environment up and running to worry about things like that.

Unfortunately, this is not an isolated situation. It shows how some offloaded development environments can take on lives of their own without consideration of what they are contributing, or not contributing, to the productivity of their users.

The Gradual Approach

The gradual approach can be defined as the initial deployment of an offloaded development environment to a small number of developers (around 10). Once these developers become proficient in the use of the offloaded development environment, additional tools and users can be added as business needs dictate. This approach has several advantages and no real disadvantages. The main advantages are the following:

1. *Proper digestion.* The gradual approach allows the administrator the time to attend to the care and feeding of the offloaded development environment AND to "hold the hands" of the new users.
2. *Fewer loose wheels (standardization).* Fewer initial users means the administrator has more time for monitoring and controlling which tools are being used. This will help reduce integration and training costs later when more users are added to the environment.

The advantages of the gradual approach also help lower political and financial risks, in addition to providing a solid base (i.e., equipment and personnel) upon which to expand.

LANDING UPPER-MANAGEMENT SUPPORT

Probably the first thing that is needed before any effort to create an offloaded development environment is launched is the support of upper management. This support needs to come in several forms, including:

1. *Monetary.* The total cost for implementing an offloaded development environment can easily hit $15,000 to $20,000 per user. In many companies, the disbursement of this kind of money to vendors requires concurrence of upper management. Occasionally, upper management will ask questions about what the money they are spending is being used for. Thus, getting them involved from the beginning will keep these embarrassing moments to a minimum.
2. *Patience.* Set-up time — the time from conception to the operational system — will usually exceed six months. Time is also needed to allow for the users' learning curve, which will vary depending upon each group's particular situation. Upper management needs to understand this and plan for it in their schedules and budgets.
3. *Steadfastness.* In addition to high initial costs and long start-up time frames, there may be complaints that offloading is not saving any money or improving productivity. And, of course, this may be true in the beginning. However, upper management will need the determination to see the introduction of the offloaded development environment through to the point where the returns outweigh the costs.
4. *Harassing internal suppliers.* In many large companies development groups often have to go through a number of internal suppliers for things such as the installation of hardware, changes to building wiring, procurement of communication links to mainframes, and procurement of hardware and software. Sometimes these groups, for one reason or another, are slow or unresponsive. Aggressive upper management can help motivate these suppliers.

For these reasons, a well-informed and supportive management is essential to carrying a deployment effort forward to completion.

SELECTING THE SUPPORT TEAM

Before an offloaded development environment can be made operational, a local administrator needs to be selected. Local administrators are responsible for the care and feeding of the LAN, server, and communications, as well as providing on-site assistance to end users of the environment. The selection of the right administrator is usually critical to the success of an offloaded development environment.

The Right Administrator

Administrators come in two types. The most common type of administrators are folks who already have a significant knowledge of PC workstations, LANs, and servers but not a lot of mainframe experience. The others are folks whose background is mostly mainframe oriented. There are people who have good backgrounds in both areas, but they are rare and their procurement should not be expected. Thus, obtaining a well-rounded administrator will usually involve significant training.

When selecting an administrator, management should consider a wide range of characteristics, including technical background, diplomacy, approachability, enthusiasm, and cleverness.

1. *Technical background.* The design and set up of an offloaded development environment and the conversion of mainframe developers to the environment require significant knowledge of PCs, LANs, and servers, in addition to significant project and mainframe knowledge. Many sites with well-designed offloaded development environments and good operational records have very low levels of real offloading going on. Sometimes inadequate or ill-timed user training is the reason, but more often it's due to the local administrator being unwilling or unable to show users how to make good use of the workstation-based development tools. Thus, where possible, try to get personnel who are familiar with the kind of environment the users are presently working in. The administrator needs to keep focused on the final objective of offloading expensive development activities and not just the smooth operation of a PC/LAN system.

2. *Diplomacy.* Most administrators will be involved in the allocation of scarce resources, so diplomacy is an important part of their job. Local administrators also must interface with central support organizations to obtain timely services or favors. These organizations will include people who allocate and install mainframe communication resources, building wiring, hardware, and software. The ability to deal with a large number of vendors effectively is also important. Issues that must be dealt with here include order handling, price negotiation, and the procurement of product fixes and upgrades.

3. *Approachability.* Once trained in a particular tool, most developers would rather die than ask for help from some central authority, such as an administrator. Unfortunately, conversion to an offloaded development environment often means learning several tools at once, which is difficult. Thus, the local administrator should be someone that the users would not view as threatening or arrogant.

In fact, the individual should be outgoing, have a cheerful disposition, and not get visibly annoyed when users ask dumb questions or make stupid mistakes.

4. *Enthusiasm.* The local administrator must be a true believer in offloading development because he is the person from whom the users will be taking their lead. Indeed, in most situations, the administrator will be the only source of information that the users will have. Local and upper management also may be enthusiastic, but many developers will not view them as competent authorities, even if they started life as developers.

5. *Cleverness.* It should be remembered that when a local administrator is designing, assembling, testing, and debugging an offloaded development environment, she is doing a complicated systems integration job. She has to find the right combination of products, parameter settings, hardware settings, memory configurations, and so on that will provide the right set of functionality and operational reliability. Being able to fix very sticky technical problems is also a very large part of the job.

The Right Manager

Like the local administrators, local management of a group of users of an offloaded development environment should have certain characteristics in order to insure a successful implementation. In addition to hiring an administrator who fits the above criteria, local management also needs technical competence, commitment, and good people-handling skills.

1. *Technical competence.* In this case, technical competence means having some familiarity with the tools that will be used in the offloaded development environment and having some idea of their complexity, for example, how different they are from their counterparts on the mainframe. This is important because management needs to develop and implement a rollout plan that doesn't try to do too much, too quickly.

2. *Commitment.* Designing, setting up, and operating an offloaded development environment to the point where positive returns are being encountered takes time. Depending on the timeliness of assistance provided by supporting organizations and vendors, the start-up period could range from six months to one year. Therefore, a management that is committed to long-term improvements over short-term cost savings is required to sustain this kind of conversion.

3. *People handling.* The encouragement and reward of the people involved in the set up and use of an offloaded development environment should not be overlooked by management. Not only is it important for the administrator to feel he has the support necessary to complete his long-term objective of moving the users' work environment off the mainframe, but the users should be encouraged and rewarded for taking a risk to improve their long-term productivity. All this, of course, has to be accomplished while meeting short-term demands from the users' customers.

RECRUITING THE INITIAL USERS

Never underestimate the importance of the users selected for the initial deployment of the offloaded development environment. The main rule here is to recruit volunteers whenever possible. The chances for success will increase significantly with the use of volunteers over a group of conscripted developers. The reasons for this are that there will always be a number of annoying start-up problems when an offloaded development environment is first installed (e.g., incorrectly genned communication lines, incorrectly wired networks, defective equipment, lack of defined operational procedures). Volunteers will help the administrators shake out the new environment, rather than try to kill it when problems occur.

As mentioned above, it is also a good idea to keep the initial deployment team small, around 10 developers. Attempts to convert large groups, 25 or more, from a desert start will almost always result in failure. This is because the administrators will spend most of their time trying to keep the large number of computers up and running, instead of concentrating on how the users are actually using the offloaded development environment to do their work.

TRAINING

An important part of any good deployment plan is the procurement of effective and timely training for both administrators and users.

Administrator Training

The first group that will need training is the administrators. Their training will usually involve a much broader range of topics than the users will require, but this, of course, depends on the background of the administrator.

Administrator training will normally include the following areas:

1. *PC training.* If MS-DOS-based PC workstations are to be used, this training will probably not be necessary, as most administrators have PCs in their homes. If implementing OS/2 PC workstations, training will usually be needed. **Warning:** People planning on becoming administrators who do not have home systems of some sort (e.g., PC, Apple, UNIX) should be viewed with suspicion. Not having a home system shows a lack of interest in the subject.

2. *Project training.* If the proposed administrator does not have knowledge of the project or the environment in which it is being developed (e.g., COBOL-DB2), then training will be needed. Project training or knowledge is needed to understand resource and interface needs. Environment training is needed to assist with the evaluation and selection of developer tools.

3. *PC workstation tool training.* Administrators should have training in the main development tools that are being proposed for use in the offloaded development environment. PC workstation tool training provides the knowledge necessary to evaluate, select, and install the right combination of tools. This training is also important because, in many situations, the administrator will be the only local assistance for the users of the offloaded development environment.

4. *LAN design and operation training.* Training in LAN design — equipment requirements, wiring limitations, memory requirements (critical in MS-DOS) — is the last major piece of knowledge that the administrator needs. This training should obviously occur after the selection of the PC/LAN components, which will have occurred after the selection of the workstation tools. Training in the operations of the LAN server is also needed. This would include such things as installation and testing of LAN hardware/software, allocation of resources to users (e.g., private hard disk space vs. public hard disk space), the setting up of printing facilities, the setting up of e-mail facilities, server backups and restores, and communications from the server to other systems via 3270, RJE, modems, WANs, and so on.

A good source for the above types of training is usually the associated software and hardware vendors. Training or consulting companies are also a good source (in many cases providing training that is superior to the tool vendor).

An important consideration when setting up the above training is scheduling. Since there is a gap between the PC workstation tool training and the LAN design and operation training (this is because the LAN cannot be selected until the workstation development tools are chosen), the training schedule should take this into account. Other factors in scheduling include equipment delivery schedules (you don't want training too far in advance of the set up and use of the hardware/software) and the administrator's workload.

User Training

While user training is not as extensive as administrator training, its quality and timeliness is no less critical. User training will usually involve the following areas:

1. *PC training.* While extensive training is not needed here, PC training should include information on file and disk structure, basic PC commands, and security responsibilities such as the regular backup of critical files and the parking of hard disks before physically moving PCs.
2. *Offloaded development environment training.* Specifically, this includes training in the capabilities of the integrated support environment and how it works. Information on the differences between mainframe and PC workstation/LAN systems (e.g., EBCDIC vs. ASCII) should also be addressed.
3. *Workstation tool training.* This training not only involves the passing along of information on individual tools but how the tools work together (e.g., Micro Focus COBOL/2 Workbench and XDB-Workbench for DB2, which together form a COBOL-DB2 environment). Since these tools can be fairly complicated, a follow-up session, several weeks after conversion to the offloaded development environment, is usually a good idea.

The above training can usually be done in a single shot and should be done so whenever possible. This is because the individual pieces usually do not have significant value independent from each other.

When assembling a training environment, try to obtain a fully operational offloaded development environment. Also try to set up the training room with one PC workstation for every two users. This way, when the students get stuck, they have someone with whom to consult.

As with the administrator training, vendors or consulting/training companies should be able to provide the necessary courses. This training will usually last at least one week. Try to pick a time when the team is not under a lot of pressure to meet immediate deadlines. This way they will have the time to learn the new tools/environment fully and will not feel the need to revert to their old tools/environment because of time pressures.

SUMMARY

The purpose of an offloaded development environment is to provide mainframe developers with the advantages of the PC workstation without depriving them of the benefits of the mainframe environment including shareable files and databases; regular backups; password protection and security; source code control; multitasking; and fast/cheap print services.

Designing, installing, and operating a successful development environment is not easy. Possible pitfalls do exist, and they should be understood and addressed early in your planning. These pitfalls include, but are unfortunately not limited to, the radical change in work environment most developers will experience; the integration headaches encountered when trying to coerce a number of very different systems to work well together; and the need to interface with a large number of vendors in order to obtain the products and services needed to set up a useful environment. To avoid these pitfalls, a comprehensive, step-by-step, rollout plan is essential. Such a plan will not only assist in coordinating the large amount of preparation work that is required to successfully design and implement an offloaded development environment, but it also will help in gaining management support for the project and in keeping user expectations realistic. A sample rollout plan is outlined in Appendix A.

It is important to remember that the approach used to deploy an offloaded development environment can go a long way toward ensuring the environment's success. While there are a number of ways to approach initiation, a gradual, phased approach is best. This approach involves the introduction of the basic offloaded development environment to a small number of developers. As these initial users become proficient in the use of the environment, additional tools and users can be added.

Never underestimate the importance of selecting the appropriate support team and user group for your initial deployment effort. Once trained and experienced, these folks will become an invaluable source of knowledge that can be used to introduce offloaded development to the larger user community.

5

Selecting PC Workstation Software Tools

As mentioned in the earlier chapters, the main reason for setting up an offloaded development environment is to give application developers the ability to exploit the software tools that run in the PC workstation environment. This chapter will examine the selection criteria for these PC-based tools and discuss how some of the major tools meet these criteria. The categories of tools that will be examined include editors, language workbenches (2GLs and 3GLs), DBMS emulators, TP monitor emulators, and lower CASE tools (code generators+). Information on upper CASE tool selection criteria is also included. In addition, a section on supplemental tools (JCL emulators, data handling tools, regression testing tools) needed to round out an offloaded development environment can be found at the end of this chapter.

However, before we get into the detail of selection criteria, the activity of tool selection itself should be addressed. In the old days, when everything was developed on mainframes or large minicomputers, the question of which tools to procure was handled by a small number of people. With the introduction of offloaded development environments this has changed, primarily because PCs cannot be easily controlled by a central group. Because PCs are, after all, personal computers, large numbers of people are now software buyers and should be aware of the following guidelines when making software buying decisions.

1. *Keep the number of different packages per category to a minimum.* Getting everybody in a DP shop to use a single tool in a particular category is extremely useful. Not only is it usually

cheaper, because of larger volume discounts, it also helps to simplify training, installation, and the movement of technical personnel within the DP organization. Concentrating on fewer tools also will make it easier to increase the depth of an organization's tool know-how, while reducing the number of interface problems. This guideline also suggests that existing bases of tool usage should be carefully considered when selecting tools. Don't throw away these existing bases without a very good reason!!!

2. *Once a tool is selected, stick with it.* It is almost always more productive for a DP shop to select a tool and then concentrate on becoming expert users, rather than searching for the latest features in different tools. This is really the only sensible strategy for a number of reasons. These reasons include the fact that most vendors will respond to customer needs if the needs are technically possible and they are given a chance; the expense of retraining; the expense of retooling, which not only includes buying new software to replace existing software but also any conversion costs; and the consolidation of the software industry (mergers, buyouts, equity purchases). This last item is a great cause for concern when tool selections are driven by the desire to get away from a particular vendor because of previous bad experiences or the desire to go with a vendor because of previous good experiences. Mergers, buyouts, and equity purchases can easily turn such rationales upside down overnight.

The following section outlines the selection criteria for each category of PC-based software tool. A section on software tools in the marketplace follows.

SELECTION CRITERIA

A set of selection criteria for editors, language workbenches (i.e., 2GLs and 3GLs), DBMS emulators, TP monitor emulators, lower CASE tools (i.e., code generators+), and upper CASE tools is contained in Table 5-1. Detailed descriptions of the selection criteria can be found immediately after the table. Readers should, of course, tailor the selection criteria to meet their individual needs. As mentioned earlier, the selection criteria for the upper CASE tool is only a partial list. For a complete list, readers should consult a book on upper CASE tool selection and use.

Table 5-1. PC workstation software tool selection criteria.

Software Tool Categories

Editor — Editors
Lang — Language Workbenches
DBMS — DBMS Workbenches
TP — TP Monitor Workbenches
LCASE — Lower Case Workbenches
UCASE — Upper Case Workbenches*

* Only a partial list of selection criteria is listed in the table.

Requirements

E — Essential Requirements
I — Important Requirements
N — "Nice to Have" Options

Selection Criteria	**Editor**	**Lang**	**DBMS**	**TP**	**LCASE**	**UCASE**
1. Supports both EBCDIC and ASCII code format data files	E	E	E	E	E	
2. Runs in the chosen environment	E	E	E	E	E	E
3. Can handle large data files effectively	E	N	N	N		
4. Supports mainframe syntax and semantics	I	E	E	E	N/I/E	
5. Supports calls to associated DBMSs, TP monitors, and assembler routines		E			E	
6. Contains a batch compiler		E			E	
7. Contains a runtime facility		E				
8. Contains or uses a full screen debugging/unit testing tool		E	E	E	E	
9. Provides subsecond response time for trivial commands	E	E	E	E	E	E
10. Supports calls to other programs and copy members		E			E	
11. Uses language workbench tools where appropriate			I/E	I/E	I	
12. Debuggers/unit testing tools work at source code level			E	E	E	
13. Contains a screen painter				E	I	I
14. Generates code that is compatible with mainframe syntax and semantics			E	E	E	E
15. Generates code in the required language					E	I/E

Table 5-1. PC workstation software tool selection criteria (continued).

Selection Criteria	Editor	Lang	DBMS	TP	LCASE	UCASE
16. Generates high-quality, structured code					E	I
17. Generates online applications quickly					E	
18. Generates error-free code			E	E	E	E
19. Supports selected methodology						E
20. Can run computer-intensive functions in the background		I	I	I	I/E	I/E
21. Requires minimal training	E	I	I	I	I	I
22. Resembles and functions like its mainframe counterpart	I				N/I	
23. Provides consistent presentation within tool	I	I	I	I	I	I
24. Can precompile or compile at speeds comparable to the mainframe		I	I	I	I	
25. Supports mainframe-like error messages and codes	N	I	I	I	N/I	
26. Supports the same level of error forgiveness as the mainframe		I	I	I	N/I	
27. Provides DDNAME support similar to the mainframe		I				
28. Supports use of PC I/O facilities	N/I	N/I	N/I	N/I	N/I	N/I
29. Supports building of PC and client/server applications		I	I	I	I	
30. Vendor offers good telephone-based support	N	I	I	I	I	I
31. Vendor has reasonable upgrade policy	N	I	I	I	I	I
32. Includes good supporting documentation	N	I	I	I	I	I
33. Processes database calls quickly			I			
34. Contains support tools similar to the mainframe (e.g., DLT0, SPUFI)			I	I		
35. Allows users to do their own DBA functions			I		I	

Table 5-1. PC workstation software tool selection criteria (continued).

Selection Criteria	Editor	Lang	DBMS	TP	LCASE	UCASE
36. Is provided by a vendor with a good working relationship with other workbench vendors	N	I	I	I	I	I
37. Supports prototyping				N	I	
38. Contains report painters					I	
39. Supports the creation of simple and complex applications					I	I
40. Provides direct access to upper CASE and 3GL workbenches					I	
41. Does not force all applications into a particular structure					I	
42. Supports easy switching between target environments					I	I
43. Provides good on-site support					I	I
44. Offers a "train the trainer" program					I	I
45. Provides multiuser dictionaries/repositories					I	I
46. Supports immediate validation of inputs					I	I
47. Supports flexible data entry			I	I	I	I
48. Provides direct access to lower CASE and 3GL workbenches						I
49. Can be used without knowing a large number of commands	I					
50. Supports editing of different types of files	I	N				
51. Can be customized	N	N	N	N	N	N/I
52. Contains a help facility	N	N	N	N	N/I	N/I
53. Provides operating system access	N	N	N	N	N/I	N/I
54. Edit facility is syntax sensitive	N	N				
55. Can produce useful documentation		N	N	N	N	I
56. Supports mainframe-like arithmetic precision		N				
57. Uses mainframe jargon	N	N	N	N	N	N

Detailed Descriptions of Selection Criteria

The following list contains detailed descriptions of the selection criteria used in Table 5-1. Please note that the identification numbers for the criteria are the same in both the table and list.

1. *Supports both EBCDIC and ASCII code format data files.* Since the offloaded development environment will be used to build systems that process mainframe data (i.e., EBCDIC format data), tools that can handle both EBCDIC and ASCII formats are required.
2. *Runs in the chosen environment.* The selected tool should not require more resources to operate than are available in the offloaded development environment. For example, if the environment uses MS-DOS as the PC workstation's operating system and uses a LAN package that takes 150KB of low DOS memory, then the editor probably should not take any more than 400KB of low DOS memory. See Chapter 6 for information on selecting the operating environment.
3. *Can handle large files.* Since both data files will be utilized in the offloaded development environment, files as large as 2MB or 4MB may need to be processed. For an editor this may mean using some sort of paging system. When paging occurs, it should happen in a short period of time (less than one second). Initial load times for large files also should be considered.
4. *Supports mainframe syntax and semantics.* For language workbenches, DBMS, TP monitor, and sometimes lower CASE tools, conformance to mainframe syntax needs to be 100% and complete. The meaning of each command also needs to be exactly the same in both environments. In addition, support for all versions of a language that are likely to be used is required (e.g., IBM OS/VS COBOL and IBM VS COBOL II). Anything less than 100% compatibility can cause significant problems during the introduction of the offloaded development environment. For lower CASE tools the extent of this requirement will depend on the previous use of mainframe-based lower CASE.
5. *Supports calls to associated DBMSs, TP monitors, and Assembler routines.* Unless your company makes no use of DBMSs or TP monitors, this criterion is just as essential as language compatibility. Support for calls to Assembler routines is usually less essential but still important.
6. *Contains a batch compiler.* At the very least, all language workbenches and lower CASE tools should include a batch compiler.

7. *Contains a runtime facility.* In order to facilitate dynamic testing and the creation of PC-based applications, all language workbenches should include a runtime facility.

8. *Contains or uses a full screen debugging/unit testing tool.* All tools used to produce executable/procedural code should include access to a full screen debugger/unit testing tool that has at least the same functionality as COMPUWARE's XPEDITER COBOL debugger on the mainframe. The tool should have most of the following features:
   - Ability to set breakpoints.
   - Short set-up time.
   - Ability to change variables.
   - Ability to display multiple variables simultaneously.
   - Execution counts over multiple sessions (i.e., test coverage meter).
   - Ability to add or exclude code from execution at run time.
   - Ability to reposition execution position.
   - Ability to execute backwards.
   - Ability to record and play back a test session.
   - Ability to start and stop execution.
   - Ability to change the speed of execution.
   - Ability to generate the exact same results as batch compiler runs.
   - Ability to make use of color.

9. *Provides subsecond response time for trivial commands.* One of the main reasons for building an offloaded development environment is to exploit the subsecond response time of the PC workstation. Therefore, all trivial commands and movements between most screens within the workbench should be executed in subsecond time.

10. *Supports calls to other programs and copy members.* Since multimodular programming is practiced in most DP shops, the ability to call other programs is extremely useful. Support for calls to CA-PANVALET (++INCLUDE) or CA-LIBRARIAN (-INC) based copy members also may be necessary.

11. *Uses language workbench tools where appropriate.* DBMS, TP monitor, and lower CASE tools should be able to make use of the

language workbench's tools where appropriate. For example, the language workbench's debugger should be able to handle 3GL code with embedded DBMS statements.

12. *Debuggers/unit testing tools work at the source code level.* Components that work with source code should work at the source code level and not require users to work at the generated level.
13. *Contains a screen painter.* All TP monitor, lower and upper CASE tools should have a screen painter that generates the TP monitor code (e.g., CICS BMS, IMS MFS). The painters should be "active," that is, connected to the CASE or other dictionary.
14. *Generates code that is compatible with mainframe syntax and semantics.* Conformance of generated code to mainframe syntax needs to be 100% and complete.
15. *Generates code in the required language.* The variety of languages, DBMS, and TP monitor calls that a CASE tool can generate is limited. However, supported code should usually include COBOL, DB2, IMS(DB/DC), and CICS.
16. *Generates high-quality, structured code.* The quality of the code generated by a CASE tool should be high in case the tool is dropped and the code needs to be maintained manually.
17. *Generates online applications quickly.* Since most lower CASE tools are geared toward generating online applications, this type of work should be accomplished in a much shorter period of time than would be the case if only 3GL tools were used.
18. *Generates error-free code.* All tools that generate code should produce code that is free of syntax errors. In addition, CASE tools should produce code that is resistant to execution errors.
19. *Supports selected methodology.* The upper CASE workbench needs to support the data analysis and functional analysis methodology used within the DP shop (e.g., Martin, Jackson, Yourdon). Tools that handle the dictionary and diagramming functions may need to be extendable to handle local enhancements/modifications to a methodology.
20. *Can run computer-intensive functions in the background.* It is useful if computer-intensive activities that can run in batch mode on the mainframe, such as compiles or noninteractive dynamic tests, be able to run in a background mode on a PC. This frees up the foreground for human-intensive activities, such as coding

and editing. This feature may be a function of the offloaded development environment itself or of the individual tool.

21. *Requires minimal training.* Training for the various types of tools should not be more than the following:

Editor	—	1/2 day
Language Workbench	—	2 to 4 days
DBMS Emulator	—	1 to 2 days
TP Monitor Emulator	—	1 to 2 days
Lower CASE Tool	—	5 to 10 days
Upper CASE Tool	—	5 to 10 days

    Proficiency should be achievable with a few weeks of full-time use.

22. *Resembles and functions like its mainframe counterpart.* Having the offloaded development environment's editor and/or lower CASE tool look and work just like its counterpart on the mainframe can greatly speed up the introduction of users into the environment because little or no training is needed. For users with PC phobia, the availability of familiar tools in the brand new environment can be a make-or-break issue.

23. *Provides consistent presentation within the tool.* Having basic commands, such as exiting a process, moving forward and backward or from left to right, invoked by the same commands or function keys throughout the tool will make it much easier to learn and use. Following IBM's ISPF conventions (e.g., PF3 to exit, PF7 to move backward, PF8 to move forward) may be best of all.

24. *Can precompile or compile at speeds comparable to, or better than, the mainframe.* It is best if batch compiles can be performed at speeds at least comparable to those of the mainframe. Compile speeds that are appreciably slower than the mainframe will be frustrating for the user.

25. *Supports mainframe-like error messages and codes.* It is best if error messages or codes, such as an OC7 for a data exception on the mainframe, can be generated by the runtime environment of the workbench. Not having this capability will force more careful mainframe-based testing to be performed than otherwise would be needed.

26. *Supports the same level of error forgiveness as the mainframe.* It is extremely useful if the tool's compile, debugging, and runtime facilities generate an error for any condition for which the mainframe would generate an error. Having a stricter environment on the PC is also quite acceptable, but having a less strict environment will force more mainframe-based testing to be preformed than otherwise would be needed.

27. *Provides DDNAME support similar to mainframe.* It is best if the identification of input and output files within the source code is the same as on the mainframe (i.e., via DDNAMEs). The use of literal PC file names within the source code should not be required, although it is a handy option.

28. *Supports use of PC I/O facilities.* It is extremely helpful if the tools can accept input from a mouse for certain functions, such as screen or report painting. Functionality under a GUI (e.g., MS-Windows) may also be useful.

29. *Supports building of PC and client-server applications.* It is usually advantageous if the selected tools can support the creation of PC-based systems in addition to mainframe-based systems. Support for client-server system development and use of GUIs also should prove useful.

30. *Vendor offers good telephone-based technical support.* For most problems, a user or administrator should be able to get a helpful response in an hour or less. Twenty-four-hour support should be available in extreme emergencies.

31. *Vendor has reasonable upgrade policy.* The vendor should give free upgrades for the first year of use. After that, upgrades should be available for no more than 15% of the purchase price paid.

32. *Includes good supporting documentation.* Documentation should be complete. This means that all user features are documented and that all differences between the PC tools and their mainframe counterparts are fully explained. Tools that do not have documentation that identifies the differences between the PC tools and their mainframe counterparts should be viewed with suspicion.

33. *Processes database calls quickly.* It is important that database calls, within the debugger and runtime environments, be processed quickly enough to support unit and string testing. Power to support volume testing would be extremely useful.

34. *Contains support tools similar to the mainframe's.* It is advantageous for the DBMS workbench to have PC-based support tools similar to their mainframe counterparts, such as QMF and SPUFI for a DB2 workbench, DLT0 for an IMS workbench, and DML/O for an IDMS workbench.

35. *Allows users to do their own DBA functions.* It is important that setting up and modifying tables, databases, and security be allowed by the DBMS and lower CASE tools.

36. *Is provided by a vendor with a good working relationship with other workbench vendors.* Some tools are used in conjunction with tools/workbenches from other vendors. Having vendors who work with each other and have knowledge about the other's tools is extremely useful when trying to solve problems whose origin is not known.

37. *Supports prototyping.* Support for the building of online prototypes is usually quite useful for TP monitor and lower CASE tools.

38. *Contains report painter.* All lower CASE workbenches should have report painters that generate the required code (e.g., COBOL). The painters should be "active" — connected to the CASE dictionary.

39. *Supports the creation of simple and complex applications.* Both simple and complex application creations should be supported without much change in method.

40. *Provides direct access to upper CASE and 3GL workbenches.* When inside the lower CASE workbench, it is a great time saver to be able to access the upper CASE and 3GL workbenches without having to exit the lower CASE workbench first. This can be especially important when load times for the lower CASE workbench are significant.

41. *Does not force all applications into a particular structure.* If the lower CASE workbench forces all applications to use the same structure or design, it is important to consider the future impact and overall suitability of this approach.

42. *Supports easy switching between target environments.* CASE tools should be able to switch between generating code for one language, DBMS, or TP monitor to another with just a few keystrokes.

43. *Provides good on-site support.* When a group is first starting to use a CASE tool, on-site support, or "hand holding," is usually a

very good idea due to the complexity of most CASE tools. Sometimes several visits by hand holders may be required.

44. *Offers a "train the trainer" program.* Since CASE tools usually require a lot of training, it may be useful for large DP shops to have their own instructors trained in the teaching of the tool.

45. *Provides or uses multiuser dictionaries/repositories.* The dictionaries and/or repositories used by the CASE tools should handle interaction with multiple users simultaneously.

46. *Supports immediate validation of inputs.* Most inputs to a CASE tool should be immediately validated to the extent possible. This would include checks for consistency, integrity, and completeness.

47. *Supports flexible data entry.* The ability to load information as it becomes available is useful in organizations that are very resistant to changing local work procedures to accommodate a tool. Such flexibility would allow for functional analysis activities to be performed before data analysis activities and also would allow for easy modifications to previously entered inputs.

48. *Provides direct access to lower CASE and 3GL workbenches.* When inside the upper CASE workbench it is a great time saver to be able to access the lower CASE and 3GL workbenches without having to exit the upper CASE workbench. This can be especially important when load times for the upper CASE workbench are significant.

49. *Can be used without knowing a large number of commands.* Being able to do basic tool functions with just a few commands (five or six) will make the transition from mainframe to PC easier for users. However, because of the nature of most of these tools this criterion may only be achievable for the selected editor.

50. *Supports different file profiles.* It is very useful if the editing facility can make certain assumptions, such as what columns to display or what LRECL to use, based on the name extension of the file being processed (e.g., the ".CBL" in the COBOL program named DRIVER.CBL). When the editor does not have this information, it should be able to "learn" it when it first encounters a new file type.

51. *Can be customized.* It is often helpful if the tool can be expanded to include custom options as well as interfaces to other tools within the offloaded development environment. For upper CASE

tools, this criterion may be of more importance because of the need to accommodate customized methodologies.

52. *Contains a help facility.* A context-sensitive help facility (i.e., when you are in the editor's browse facility and ask for help it talks about the browse facility) can go a long way in shortening the learning curve for a new editor. It is also valuable to have a help facility that contains the same information as the accompanying paper documentation. When this is the case or when the help facility is extensive, a search facility within the help facility can be very handy. Remember, the more complex the tool, the more powerful the help facility should be.

53. *Provides operating system access.* When inside a tool, it is usually advantageous to be able to access the raw operating system without having to exit. This criterion becomes more important when the tool has long load times.

54. *Edit facility is syntax sensitive.* When editing source code, it is useful to have an editor that will perform syntax checking as the code is being entered. This is especially helpful for developers who are working in a language with which they are not yet familiar.

55. *Can produce useful documentation.* Programmers sometimes have a need to produce documentation for other parties or to meet the requirements of a local development methodology. The automatic generation of documentation (e.g., cross references, structure charts) can be extremely helpful.

56. *Supports mainframe-like arithmetic precision.* Having the ability to produce the same results as the mainframe with respect to the arithmetic precision of the execution environment is something that is quite useful, though not easily obtainable. For example:

    A = 2

    B = 3

    C = (A * B) / B

    Is C equal to 2 on both the mainframe and PC workstation?

57. *Uses mainframe jargon.* If the tool makes use of mainframe jargon, such as "data set name" or "member," the transition from mainframe to offloaded development can be made easier.

TOOLS IN THE MARKETPLACE

This section provides an overview of some of the major PC workstation software tools that are currently available. These include editors, language workbenches (COBOL, PL/I, and IBM Assembler), DBMS emulators (IMS, DB2, IDMS, and DATACOM), TP monitor emulators (CICS, IMS(DC), and IDMS(DC)), and lower CASE (APS/PC and CA-TELON/PWS).

Editors

While the editor for an offloaded development environment is probably one of the most inexpensive components, it is often one of the most important in terms of persuading users to switch to PC workstations. This is because the editor will usually be the tool in the environment to receive the heaviest use, at least when the environment is first set up.

PC-based editors come in two formats, as standalone packages and as part of language workbenches (see next section for more information on language workbenches). The editors that come with language workbenches, such as Micro Focus COBOL/2 Workbench and Realia COBOL, are usually quite good, but they are not emulations of mainframe editors. As mentioned earlier, one of the most important features of PC-based editors is mainframe emulation. A less powerful editor that emulates a mainframe editor should usually be chosen over a more powerful editor that does not emulate a mainframe editor. This is because offloaded development environment users spend more of their time using PC-based editors than any other tool, and having an editor that they are very familiar with eases the transition from mainframe to PC-based development.

Some of the more popular PC-based editors that emulate mainframe editors include the following:

1. *SPF/PC*. SPF/PC, by Command Technology Corporation, is an MS-DOS-based emulation of IBM's ISPF on the mainframe. It contains most of the features of ISPF (see Figures 5-1 and 5-2) and meets all the essential and important editor criteria listed above. The list price is approximately $245. Command Technology can be contacted at the following address:

   Command Technology Corporation
   1040 Marina Village Parkway
   Alameda, CA 94501
   Phone: (415) 521-5900
   FAX: (415) 521-0369

```
SPF/PC1  148K -------------- PRIMARY OPTION MENU ------------------- VER 02.10
OPTION ---
                                                            USERID   - IBMPC
   0  SPF/PC PARMS - Specify terminal and user parameters   TIME     - 15:24
   1  BROWSE       - Display source data or output listings TERMINAL - IBM
   2  EDIT         - Create or change source data           PF KEYS  - 48
   3  UTILITIES    - Perform SPF/PC utility functions
   4  FOREGROUND   - Invoke language processors in foreground
   5  SYSTEM INFO  - Display system information
   6  COMMAND      - Execute DOS commands
   C  CHANGES      - Display summary of changes for this release
   H  HELP         - Display information about SPF/PC
   U  USER         - Invoke user applications
   X  EXIT         - Terminate SPF/PC
 Press [F3]  to terminate SPF/PC

        +--------------------------------------------------------------+
        |    (C)COPYRIGHT COMMAND TECHNOLOGY CORPORATION 1983-89       |
        |                  ALL RIGHTS RESERVED                         |
        |            UNAUTHORIZED DUPLICATION PROHIBITED               |
        +--------------------------------------------------------------+
```

Figure 5-1. SPF/PC primary option menu.

```
EDIT1A h:\SYS1P001.CBL---------------------------------------- COLUMNS 0001 0072
COMMAND ---                                                     SCROLL ---   HALF
000279            SKIP1
000280        1000-RECEIVE-MAP.
000281            SKIP1
000282            MOVE '1000-RECEIVE-MAP' TO C-ERROR-PARAGRAPH.
000283            SKIP1
000284            EXEC CICS HANDLE CONDITION MAPFAIL(2000-CK-KEYS) END-EXEC.
000285
000286            SKIP1
000287            EXEC CICS RECEIVE MAP('SYS1M01')
000288                              MAPSET('SYS1S01')
000289                              END-EXEC.
000290            SKIP1
000291            IF EIBRCODE NOT = LOW-VALUES
000292                MOVE 'Y' TO WKC-WARNING-ERROR-SW
000293                GO TO 9900-CICS-ERROR.
000294            SKIP1
000295        2000-CK-KEYS.
000296            SKIP1
000297            MOVE '2000-CK-KEYS' TO C-ERROR-PARAGRAPH.
000298            SKIP1
000299            IF EIBAID EQUAL DFHPF1
000300                MOVE 'SYS1P002' TO TR-PROG-NAME
079 K AVAIL
```

Figure 5-2. SPF/PC edit option.

2. *SPF/2.* SPF/2, also by Command Technology Corporation, is an OS/2-based emulation of IBM's ISPF. In addition to the features found in SPF/PC, SPF/2 has a macro interface to REXX, IBM's SAA procedural language. The list price is approximately $295.
3. *Tritus SPF.* Tritus SPF, by Tritus, Inc., is an MS-DOS, MS-Windows, and OS/2-based emulation of IBM's ISPF and REXX. The introductory list price (prior to March 31, 1992) is $75. Tritus can be contacted at the following address:

   Tritus, Inc.
   Suite 360
   6034 West Courtyard Drive
   Austin, TX 78730-5014
   Phone: (512) 794-5800
   FAX: (512) 794-3833
4. *KEDIT.* KEDIT, by the Mansfield Software Group, is a PC-based emulation of IBM's XEDIT. It meets the essential and important selection criteria listed above and supports a macro interface to REXX under OS/2. The MS-DOS version lists for approximately $150 and a combined OS/2 and MS-DOS version has a list price of approximately $175. Mansfield Software Group can be contacted at the following address:

   Mansfield Software Group
   P.O. Box 532
   Storrs, CT 06268
   Phone: (203) 429-8402
   FAX: (203) 487-1185

Language Workbenches (3GLs and 2GLs)

The language workbench (i.e., compiler, debugger, syntax checker) is the heart of the offloaded development environment for programmers. All other tools (i.e., DBMSs emulators, TP monitor emulators, code generators) revolve around supporting the selected language workbench. This is useful because the workbench provides a set of standards, or target environment, for other vendors to shoot for when they build their tools.

In the United States, the three major languages (3GL and 2GL) used in mainframe DP shops are COBOL, PL/I, and IBM 370 Assembler. All of these languages are supported by PC-based workbenches and we will examine them in order of importance.

COBOL

PC-based COBOL workbenches/toolsets are supported by a number of vendors. The big three, Micro Focus, Liant, and Realia (now owned by Computer Associates), hold 90% of the market. Liant's product, RM-COBOL (i.e., Ryan McFarland), only supports portability between MS-DOS and UNIX. Support is not offered for IBM OS/VS COBOL or IBM VS COBOL II, so it is not suitable for offloading MVS development and will not be discussed here. Micro Focus and Realia both offer very useful workbenches for offloading mainframe COBOL development.

Micro Focus COBOL/2 Workbench

The Micro Focus COBOL/2 Workbench (Figure 5-3) is a product of Micro Focus Limited, a British company founded in 1976. Since the late 1970s Micro Focus has been offering various COBOL products, most notably their batch COBOL compiler. Micro Focus is the most established of the leading PC COBOL suppliers, with more than 50% of the market and a staff of over 400 employees. In addition to selling Micro Focus products under their own name, the vendor has OEM agreements with Microsoft and IBM to sell Micro Focus products under their names (when you buy a Microsoft or IBM PC COBOL compiler you are really getting a Micro Focus COBOL compiler). However, it should be noted that only Micro Focus sells the collection of tools known as the Micro Focus COBOL/2 Workbench.

Micro Focus COBOL/2 Workbench consists of the vendor's COBOL/2 (batch) Compiler and COBOL/2 Toolset. The workbench combines these with some extra tools to make a function-key-driven environment (i.e., as of release 2.5 of the Workbench). Users are guided through the workbench by a list of valid function key selections displayed at the bottom of the screen. When the standard function keys (F1 to F10) are not enough, single-character mnemonics and/or alternate menus, accessed via the <Ctrl> and <Alt> keys, are used.

The Workbench can operate in either EBCDIC or ASCII mode, allowing developers to build mainframe- or PC-based production systems. The Workbench also supports both the MS-DOS and OS/2 environments.

Developers start work by entering the Micro Focus full screen editor (Figure 5-4). The editor can be used without reference to the documentation. It does, however, function differently from ISPF (the function keys are different and there is no command line). The workbench is flexible enough to allow the use of a different editor, but certain functionality is lost when this is done.

```
                                                                      Banner 1200
                   +----------------------------------------+
                   |   Micro Focus COBOL/2 Workbench V2.5.18 |
                   |                                        |
                   |    Mainframe Development Environment   |
                   +----------------------------------------+

Incorporating: - Micro Focus COBOL/2, Toolset and Workbench

Highlights: - NEW - Data File Editor
            - NEW - On line Reference
            - NEW - Mouse support in the Editor, Animator and CSI
            - NEW - Floating point support
            - NEW - Intrinsic functions
            - IMPROVED - MFXFER new interface and improved transfer support
            - IMPROVED - configurable Editor
            - IMPROVED - Animate whole applications
            - Access to Mainframe Development tools
                  IMSVS86 and CICSVS86 (where available)

                        Issued Apr  8th 1991
                 Copyright (C) 1985,1991 Micro Focus Ltd.
Micro-Focus-Mainframe-Development-Environment-------------------------------------
F1=help F2=files F3=develop F4=execute F5=IMS F6=CICS     F8=config F9=Workbench
                                                                          Escape
```

Figure 5-3. Micro Focus COBOL/2 workbench (mainframe development environment) signon screen.

```
+SYS1P001.CBL----------------------------------------------------------------+
|              GO TO 6500-XCTL-TO-NEXT.                                      |
|          SKIP1                                                             |
|          IF EIBAID NOT = DFHENTER                                          |
|              MOVE -1      TO OPTIONL                                       |
|              MOVE 'Z810' TO WKC-ERR-CODE                                   |
|              GO TO 8000-RETRIEVE-ERR-CODE.                                 |
|          SKIP1                                                             |
|      3000-CHECK-COMMAND.                                                   |
|          SKIP1                                                             |
|          MOVE '3000-CHECK-COMMAND' TO C-ERROR-PARAGRAPH.                   |
|          SKIP1                                                             |
|          IF COMMANDL GREATER THAN ZERO                                     |
|              MOVE COMMANDI TO WK-COMMAND                                   |
|          ELSE                                                              |
|              GO TO 4000-CHECK-SELECTION.                                   |
|                                                                            |
|          IF WK-COMM4 = 'B001'                                              |
|             MOVE -1 TO OPTIONL                                             |
|             MOVE SPACES   TO COMMANDO                                      |
+----------------------------------------------------------------------------+
Edit-SYS1P001------520-lines----Line-311----Col-8-------Wrap-Ins-Caps-Num-Scroll
F1=help F2=COBOL F3=insert-line F4=delete-line F5=repeat-line F6=restore-line
F7=retype-char F8=restore-char F9=word-left F10=word-right       Alt Ctrl Escape
```

Figure 5-4. Micro Focus editor.

After a program is coded or edited, a single keystroke moves the program to the Micro Focus Checker. The Checker is essentially a full screen compiler. Users may watch their code as it is being syntax checked and compiled. The Checker can process various types of COBOL syntax, including IBM OS/VS COBOL and IBM VS COBOL II. When COBOL code is run through the Checker and a problem is found, a message is displayed and the user is asked if they want to continue checking (see Figure 5-5). If the answer is no, they are automatically put into the Micro Focus editor at the point where the error occurred. The error message from the Checker is also placed at the bottom of the editor's screen (see Figure 5-6). After the user fixes the problem, they reenter the Checker at the beginning of the program (not where the Checker had stopped previously). If a user wants to receive all her error messages before going back to the editor, this also can be done. The editor has a feature that allows for multiple-error messages to be displayed as they are needed.

After a program has been successfully processed through the Checker, another keystroke moves it to the Animator (Figure 5-7). The Micro Focus Animator is a full screen debugger/unit testing tool, much like COMPUWARE's XPEDITER. The main difference is that the Animator is faster and initializing a session is less complicated.

Animator has many useful features, including the following:

1. The ability to set breakpoints.
2. The ability to change and display multiple variables simultaneously. This is done with the variables displayed in little boxes which can be moved to the right side of the screen (see Figure 5-7).
3. Execution counts over multiple sessions. This feature turns the Animator into a nice test coverage meter. Information is displayed via numeric counts (see Figure 5-7), histograms, and/or by color coding the individual COBOL statements.
4. The ability to add or exclude code from execution at runtime.
5. The ability to reposition the point of execution (i.e., the next statement to be executed).
6. Dynamic structure charts. These show the execution flow of a program at a logical level.
7. The ability to start and stop execution and to change execution speed by hitting a single key is also included.

```
* Options:  ANIM ENSUITE(2) ERRQ EDITOR(mf) LIST NOFORM ANALYZE USE($cobdir\wbos
XDB - accepted - EBCDIC
* XDB Precompiler Pass 1
* XDB Precompiler Pass 2
W-Level messages:    0  E-Level messages:     0
* XDB End Precompile
--------------------------------------------------------------------------------
           MOVE WS-PROGRAM-ID  TO ML02-PROGRAM-ID.
           MOVE MESSAGE-LN02 TO CNTL-RPT-DATA.
           WRITE CNTL-RPT
                 AFTER ADVANCING 1 LINE.
           MOVE MESSAGE-LN03  TO CNTL-RPT-DATA.
           WRITE CNTL-RPT
                 AFTER ADVANCING 1 LINE.
           MOVE MESSAGE-LN06   TO CNTL-RPT-DATA.
           WRITE CNTL-RPT
                 AFTER ADVANCING 1 LINE.
           WRITE CNTL-RPT
                 AFTER ADVANCING 1 LINE.
           IF HAG-MSG-CODE EQUAL SPPACES
*  12-S********************************                                       **
**    Operand  is not declared
CONTINUE CHECKING PROGRAM ?   Yes/No/Zoom
--------------------------------------------------------------------------------
Checking SYS1P001, Ctrl+Break to Stop
```

Figure 5-5. Micro Focus Checker.

```
+SYS1P001.CBL---------------------------------------------------------------
              AFTER ADVANCING 1 LINE.
        IF HAG-MSG-CODE EQUAL SPPACES
           MOVE '   *** PROGRAM HAS COMPLETED SUCCESSFULLY ***
                   TO ML07-ABND-MSG
        ELSE
           MOVE '      *** PROGRAM ABENDED ***' TO ML07-ABND-MSG.
           MOVE MESSAGE-LN07  TO CNTL-RPT-DATA.
           WRITE CNTL-RPT
                 AFTER ADVANCING  1 LINE.
        IF MD09-AUX-MSG EQUAL SPACES
           NEXT SENTENCE
        ELSE
           MOVE MESSAGE-MD09 TO CNTL-RPT-DATA
           WRITE CNTL-RPT
                 AFTER ADVANCING 1 LINE.
        MOVE MESSAGE-LN05  TO CNTL-RPT-DATA.
        WRITE CNTL-RPT
              AFTER ADVANCING 1 LINE.
        MOVE MESSAGE-LN08  TO CNTL-RPT-DATA.
+---------------------------------------------------------------------------+
Edit-SYS1P001------1278-lines---Line-1200---Col-40------Wrap-Ins-Caps-Num-Scroll
F1=help F2=COBOL F3=insert-line F4=delete-line F5=repeat-line F6=restore-line
F7=retype-char F8=restore-char F9=word-left F10=word-right       Alt Ctrl Escape
 *  12 Operand  is not declared
```

Figure 5-6. Micro Focus editor (after finding error with Micro Focus Checker).

```
     SKIP1

     MOVE '2000-SEND-MAP' TO C-ERROR-PARAGRAPH.                      2
     SKIP1
     MOVE EIBTRMID TO MFTERMO.                                       2
     SKIP1
     EXEC CICS ASSIGN APPLID(MFREGIONO) END-EXEC.                    2
     SKIP1
     IF EIBRCODE NOT = LOW-VALUES                                    1
         GO TO 9900-CICS-ERROR.                                      -
     SKIP1
     EXEC CICS SEND MAP('SYS1M01')                                   1
                    MAPSET('SYS1S01')                     +EIBRCODE+
                    CURSOR                                |        |
                    ERASE                                 +--------+
                    FREEKB                             +SQLCODE----+
                    END-EXEC.                          |+0000000000|
     SKIP1                                             +-----------+
     IF EIBRCODE NOT = LOW-VALUES                     +WK-PGM-TRANS+1
         GO TO 9900-CICS-ERROR.                       |B000        |1
     SKIP1                                            +------------+
Animate-SYS1P001----------------------------Level=01-Speed=5-Ins-Caps-Num-Scroll
F1=help F2=view F3=align F4=exchange F5=where F6=look-up  F9/F10=word-</> Escape
Animate Step Wch Go Zoom nx-If Prfm Rst Brk Env Qury Find Locate Txt Do Alt Ctrl
```

Figure 5-7. Micro Focus Animator.

In addition to the editor, Checker, and Animator, Micro Focus COBOL/2 Workbench has a number of other useful facilities including the following:

1. *A batch compiler.* Of course, the Micro Focus COBOL/2 (batch) Compiler is included in the workbench. It uses the same compiler options and parameters as the Checker.
2. *A runtime environment.* A runtime environment is included in the workbench. When building a PC-based COBOL system, a runtime package from Micro Focus is required.
3. *COBOL Source Information (CSI).* This utility can trace a variable from its initial definition through every line where it is modified or tested. Flags identify the corresponding source lines, and users can suppress unflagged lines in order to make working on particular variables within very large programs easier. CSI also will identify unused variables, the location at which a given procedure is called, and what procedures it in turn calls.
4. *User tailorable menus.* The Micro Focus COBOL/2 Workbench gives its users access to the tools used to create the product, such as the menu handler. The standard menus can be altered and extra menus added to allow for direct access to third-party tools from the workbench.
5. *A Data File Editor.* The Data File Editor gives the user a facility similar to COMPUWARE's File-AID and DATA-XPERT. Data files, in ASCII or EBCDIC format, can be inspected and altered in an environment that displays individual records using a template from a COBOL copy book.
6. *A Session Recorder.* The Session Recorder is a keystroke capture and playback facility similar to CA-TRAPS and AT&T's ESCORT. It allows for the capture of keystrokes and screen images that can be used to drive and compare test sessions for regression testing purposes.
7. *XM.* XM is Micro Focus's extended memory manager. It provides access to memory above the 1 MB line in the MS-DOS version of the workbench. This memory manager is also used by vendors whose tools directly interface with the workbench (e.g., XDB-Workbench for DB2, Micro Focus IMS Option, Micro Focus CICS Option, CA-TELON/PWS).

Along with this large collection of tools comes a massive set of documentation, currently 12 volumes, some of which contain up to 400 pages. The documentation is complete except for a few areas (for example, the chapter on XM still does not document all of that utility's switches/parameters).

Against the above listed criteria for language workbenches, Micro Focus meets all of the "essential" items and most of the "important" ones. The main strengths of this workbench are the Animator debugger/unit testing tool and its flexibility and integration. One of its few weaknesses, however, is its somewhat long learning curve, which can be attributed to the richness of the environment.

In the future, Micro Focus is expected to introduce an object-oriented COBOL and to provide improved support for the building of GUI and client-server COBOL applications. They currently are participating in an American National Standards Institute (ANSI) effort to develop a set of standard OOP (Object Oriented Programming) extensions for COBOL.

The list price for all this is approximately $2,500 for a single-user copy without maintenance and approximately $3,000 for a single copy with maintenance. Micro Focus can be contacted at the following address:

Micro Focus Incorporated
2465 East Bayshore Road
Palo Alto, CA 94303
Phone: (415) 856-4161

Realia COBOL

Realia COBOL is a product of Realia, Inc., an American company founded in 1978 that has been offering various PC-based COBOL products since the early 1980s. In 1991, Realia was acquired by Pansophic, which in turn was acquired by Computer Associates. As of 1991, Realia held around 6% of the COBOL market and had a staff of less than 40 people. Now that Realia has access to much larger marketing and sales resources than it did when it was independent, its position in the market may change.

Realia's programming environment is not as fancy as Micro Focus's COBOL/2 Workbench. It does, however, supply the tools necessary to give users significantly increased productivity. Like Micro Focus, Realia COBOL can operate in either EBCDIC or ASCII mode, allowing developers to build mainframe- or PC-based production systems. It also supports both the MS-DOS and OS/2 environments.

Developers start work by entering Realia's full screen editor RED (see Figure 5-8). The editor is convenient and well designed and can be used without reference to the documentation. It does, however, function differently from ISPF (the function keys are different and there is no ever-present command line).

After a program is coded or edited, the user moves to the compiler. Realia's compiler can process various types of COBOL syntax, including IBM OS/VS COBOL and IBM VS COBOL II.

After a program has been successfully compiled, the user moves to RealDBUG, a full screen debugger/unit testing tool (Figure 5-9).

RealDBUG has the following many useful features:

1. *The ability to set breakpoints.* This includes the ability to display the execution of only certain ranges of code.
2. *The ability to display and change variables.* This is done with variables displayed in little boxes at the right side of the screen (see Figure 5-10).
3. *The ability to start and stop execution.*

In addition to the RED editor, the compiler, and RealDBUG, Realia COBOL has the following other useful facilities:

1. *A runtime environment.* A runtime environment is included in the workbench. When building a PC-based COBOL system, the runtime library may be linked to the COBOL application and distributed without payment of a royalty fee.
2. *RealFED.* RealFED is a data file editor that gives the user a facility similar to COMPUWARE's File-AID and DATA-XPERT. Data files, in ASCII or EBCDIC format, can be inspected and altered in an environment that displays individual records using a template from a COBOL copy book.
3. *DOS / 16M.* Realia makes use of Rational Systems' DOS extender named DOS/16M. DOS/16M allows users to obtain access to extended memory up to 16MB, and it is supported on 286, 386, and 486 PCs.

Along with this tool set comes a full-sized, 8-1/2 × 11-inch binder that contains detailed information on how to use the tools. As a language reference, Realia supplies the IBM VS COBOL II language reference manual.

```
                GO TO 6500-XCTL-TO-NEXT.
            SKIP1
            IF EIBAID NOT = DFHENTER
                MOVE -1      TO OPTIONL
                MOVE 'Z810' TO WKC-ERR-CODE
                GO TO 8000-RETRIEVE-ERR-CODE.
            SKIP1
        3000-CHECK-COMMAND.
            SKIP1
            MOVE '3000-CHECK-COMMAND' TO C-ERROR-PARAGRAPH.
            SKIP1
            IF COMMANDL GREATER THAN ZERO
                MOVE COMMANDI TO WK-COMMAND
            ELSE
                GO TO 4000-CHECK-SELECTION.

            IF WK-COMM4 = 'B001'
               MOVE -1 TO OPTIONL
               MOVE SPACES   TO COMMANDO
               GO TO 9000-SEND-MAP.

            IF (COMMAND-IS-NEXT-TRANS AND WK-COMM2-4 IS NUMERIC)
+-----+----+---+---+---+---+--------------------+-----------------------+------+
RED Version 4.004  sys1p001.cbl       C=07   M  I=00336 O=00310 H=00003 B1
```

Figure 5-8. Realia editor (RED).

```
+---------------------+--------+-------------------------------------------+
|Realia RealDBUG 4.000|PRIMES  |Enter next command                         |
+---------------------+--------+-------------------------------------------+
|   34|*  Compute the primes 10 times to increase timing accuracy.         |
|   35|*  Indicate all odd numbers are potential primes                    |
|   36|*  Indicate no primes have been found.                              |
|   37|*                                                                   |
|   38|     PERFORM CALC-MILLI-SECONDS                                     |
|   39|     MOVE MILLI-SECONDS TO BGN-MILLI-SECONDS.                       |
|   40|     PERFORM 10 TIMES                                               |
|   41|       MOVE ALL '1' TO PRIME-FLAGS-GROUP                            |
|   42|       MOVE ZERO TO TOTAL-PRIME-COUNT                               |
|   43|       SET PRIME-INDEX TO 1                                         |
|   44|       PERFORM COUNT-PRIMES                                         |
|   45|     END-PERFORM                                                    |
|   46|     DISPLAY 'COUNT:' TOTAL-PRIME-COUNT                             |
|   47|     PERFORM CALC-MILLI-SECONDS.                                    |
|   48|     SUBTRACT BGN-MILLI-SECONDS FROM MILLI-SECONDS                  |
|   49|         GIVING DISPLAY-MILLI-SECONDS.                              |
+--------------------------------------------------------------------------+
| Advance     Breakpoint   Examine      Find defn    Goto range   Jump back   |
| Look value  Next range   Program set  Quit Alt-F2  Range set    Step ranges |
| Trace       Unset range  View value   Where defn   eXecute set  0-9 Line num|
| CURSOR:                                                                  |
+--------------------------------------------------------------------------+
```

Figure 5-9. Realia RealDBUG.

```
+---------------------+--------+------------------------------------------+
|Realia RealDBUG 4.000|PRIMES  |Variable display mode, enter next command ...|
+---------------------+--------+------------------------------------------+
|   76|            GO TO COUNT-PRIMES.                                     |
|   77| CALC-MILLI-SECONDS.                                                |
|   78|     ACCEPT TIME-SYNC FROM TIME.                                    |
|   79|     PERFORM CALC-MILLI-SECONDS-LOOP.                               |
|   80|     MULTIPLY HH BY 60 GIVING MILLI-SECONDS.                        |
|   81|     ADD MM TO MILLI-SECONDS.                                       |
|   82|     MULTIPLY 60 BY MILLI-SECONDS.                                  |
|   83|     ADD SS TO MILLI-SECONDS.                                       |
|   84|     MULTIPLY 100 BY MILLI-SECONDS.                                 |
|   85|     ADD HUN TO MILLI-SECONDS.                                      |
|   86|     MULTIPLY 10 BY MILLI-SECONDS.                                  |
|   87| CALC-MILLI-SECONDS-LOOP.                              +---------+  |
|   88|     ACCEPT TIME-AREA FROM TIME.                       |HH       |  |
|   89|     IF TIME-AREA IS EQUAL TO TIME-SYNC                +--+------+  |
|   90|         GO TO CALC-MILLI-SECONDS-LOOP                 |15|31 35|  |
|   91|     END-IF.                                           +--+------+  |
+-------------------------------------------------------------------------+
| Change subscripts  Decrement subscripts  Hex modify   Increment subscripts |
| Offset entry       Quit or Alt-F2        Value modify                    |
|                                                                         |
| SCROLL: PgDn/Up F1 F2   REMOVE WINDOW: Return End Space Esc   HELP: Alt-A/Z |
+-------------------------------------------------------------------------+
```

Figure 5-10. Realia RealDBUG (view value).

Realia meets all of the "essential" and many of the "important" listed criteria for language workbenches. Its main strengths are the speed of the compiler, short learning curve, and ease of installation. Given the overall complexity of building an offloaded development environment, a short learning curve and an easy installation procedure for a major component, such as a COBOL workbench, can be very useful.

In the future, Realia is expected to introduce an object-oriented COBOL. They currently are participating in an American National Standards Institute (ANSI) effort to develop a set of standard OOP extensions for COBOL.

The list price for Realia COBOL is approximately $995 for a single user copy with maintenance. The vendor may be contacted at the following address:

Realia
10 South Riverside Plaza
Chicago, IL 60606
Phone: (312) 346-0642
FAX: (312) 346-4638

PL/I

There is only one well-known, PC-based PL/I compiler on the market — Liant Software Corporation's LPI-PL/I. It is available only in UNIX and MS-DOS formats, with the MS-DOS version only running on 386- or 486-based PCs. Liant, which also sells the RM-COBOL (i.e., Ryan McFarland) tool set, is mostly known as a maker of UNIX-based compilers and tools.

While LPI-PL/I does support certain ANSI PL/I standards, it does not support many of the nice IBM extensions that most mainframe PL/I programmers are used to, including the following:

1. Multiple specification pairs in PUT EDIT statements (only one pair is allowed per statement).
2. Array-to-array moves with the BY NAME option.
3. GET DATA and PUT DATA statements.
4. IGNORE option on READ statements.
5. Certain built-in functions, such as REAL, SUM, HIGH, LOW, ONCHAR, ONFIELD, and ONSOURCE.

6. Certain ON conditions, such as SIZE, STRINGRANGE, CHECK, TRANSMIT, RECORD, and AREA.

LPI-PL/I is perfectly fine for PL/I shops interested in creating MS-DOS or UNIX-based PL/I applications, but it is not suitable for offloading mainframe PL/I development.

IBM Assembler

With the migration of COBOL development to the PC workstation, there has been an increase in the need for support of PC-based mainframe assembler calls. This is because many DP shops have collections of reusable utility programs, written in IBM Assembler, that can be called from COBOL programs. To meet this need, both Micro Focus and Realia have come out with products to support IBM's Assembler H used on its 370 architecture mainframes. Micro Focus 370 Assembler came out in 1990, and Realia's Real370 in 1991.

Micro Focus 370 Assembler supports dynamic calls from COBOL programs executing under the Micro Focus COBOL/2 Workbench in both the MS-DOS and OS/2 environments. It supports the full instruction set including XA and floating point. It also has a macro processor that produces assembler code files consisting of the original assembler code plus expanded macros and code from copy statements. For those programmers interested in creating or modifying assembler programs on the PC, Micro Focus 370 Assembler has an Interactive Debugging Facility that allows programmers to monitor the execution of individual assembler instructions and inspect the contents of variables and registers. The list price for Micro Focus 370 Assembler is approximately $1,250.

Realia's MS-DOS and OS/2-based Real370 works like Micro Focus's assembler product and has similar facilities. However, in addition to working with Realia's product line, Real370 can be used in conjunction with Micro Focus COBOL. The list price for Real370 is approximately $995.

DP shops that use a large number of assembler routines in their COBOL programs may want to consider acquiring one of the above products. However, before doing so, buyers should consider the amount of work it would take to add another major workbench component to their offloaded development environment versus the amount of work it would take to create the PC-based COBOL routines needed to simulate the necessary IBM Assembler calls.

DBMS Workbenches

Since most mainframe DP shops create COBOL programs that interact with some kind of database, the DBMS workbench (i.e., pre-compiler, debugger, data handling tools) is the component of an offloaded development environment that enables most mainframe programmers to use language workbenches to their fullest capability.

In the United States, the two major DBMSs used in mainframe DP shops are IBM's DB2 and IMS(DB). Reflecting this popularity, there are multiple PC-based DBMS workbenches that support offloaded application development using these databases. In addition, there are workbenches supporting other major DBMSs, including Computer Associate's CA-IDMS(DB) and CA-DATACOM.

DB2

Currently there are many SQL interface packages that work with language workbenches, such as Micro Focus. The two best-known packages for offloading DB2 development to PC workstations are XDB-Workbench for DB2 and IBM's OS/2 Database Manager.

XDB-Workbench for DB2

The XDB-Workbench for DB2 is a product of XDB Systems, a Maryland-based company founded in 1983. Since 1986, XDB Systems has been offering various SQL-based products, including their own relational DBMS. One of their main products is the XDB-Workbench, to which they have made a commitment to achieve 100% mainframe DB2 compatibility.

XDB-Workbench includes the following capabilities of interest to the DB2 programmer:

1. Creates and alters databases, tables, and indices.
2. Inserts, updates, and deletes records in tables.
3. Interactively queries tables via SQL commands. This is much like SPUFI on the mainframe.
4. Generates reports from query results.
5. Creates menuing systems that can integrate all the functions of a PC-based application into a single system. This is useful for building small SQL-accessed relational databases.

6. Imports and exports data between mainframe DB2 tables and XDB tables.
7. Produces reports containing information on the structure of tables in a database.
8. Generates DCLGENs.
9. Imports DDL from the mainframe to create XDB tables.

The XDB-Workbench works closely with the Micro Focus and Realia workbenches. When a programmer wants to do COBOL-DB2 work, he loads the XDB SQL engine, followed by the COBOL language workbench. Once inside the COBOL workbench, he can compile COBOL code with embedded DB2 SQL statements by specifying an option pointing to XDB's SQL preprocessor. Afterward, he can test the COBOL-DB2 code at the SQL code level.

XDB-Workbench meets almost all of the requirements listed above. The following are the major advantages for mainframe DB2 developers using XDB-Workbench.

1. Short learning curve and minimal training requirements. Usually just a day is needed.
2. Good documentation (five volumes).
3. Vastly superior test environment when compared with the mainframe. Programmers have much better control over their test environment (i.e., much less need to interact with DBAs, individual control over security) and are insulated from other developers in their testing activities. This makes testing faster and of higher quality.
4. High degree of compatibility with mainframe DB2.

The areas to be concerned about include the following:

1. Nontrivial installation. Changes need to be made to the CONFIG.SYS and AUTOEXEC.BAT files, along with certain switch settings in the XDB-Workbench itself. BAT files also need to be created to load and flush the SQL engine before entering the language workbench and after exiting.
2. While XDB Systems strives for 100% compatibility with mainframe DB2, there are still some gaps. For example, XDB 2.4 does not support EXPLAIN, and ROLLBACKs and COMMITs do not

work when used in conjunction with a TP monitor emulator, such as Micro Focus CICS Option or Micro Focus IMS Option (i.e., the IMS(DC) portion of Micro Focus IMS Option). However, XDB Systems explains all the differences between its workbench and mainframe DB2 in Appendix D of the "XDB SQL Reference."

The XDB-Workbench can operate in either EBCDIC or ASCII mode, allowing developers to build mainframe- or PC-based production systems. The XDB-Workbench also supports both the MS-DOS and OS/2 environments. In addition to the workbench, XDB Systems also markets a number of other tools to build client-server applications and offload entire DB2 applications to smaller computers. The list price for XDB-Workbench is approximately $1,500. The vendor may be contacted at the following address:

XDB Systems, Inc.
14700 Sweitzer Lane
Laurel, MD 20707
Phone: (301) 317-6800

OS/2 Database Manager

IBM's OS/2 Database Manager, which operates under OS/2 Extended Edition, contains many facilities that are found in the mainframe DB2 environment. It is SAA compliant and well integrated into the OS/2 platform, but it is not suitable for offloading DB2 development. The reasons for this situation include the following:

1. No EBCDIC support. Having only ASCII support creates havoc when testing code that depends on a certain collating sequence (e.g., ORDER BY, UNION, GROUP BY, HAVING).
2. No support for NOT NULL WITH DEFAULT.
3. No support for SYNONYMs.
4. No support for DB2 index keywords: SUBPAGES, CLUSTER, PART, CLOSE, DSETPASS, and USING VCAT.
5. No support for DB2 table keywords: CREATE TABLE LIKE, AUDIT, IN, EDITPROC, VALIDPROC, and FIELDPROC.

Recently, a study conducted by Jonathan Sayles[1] concluded that Database Manager 1.3's DDL was only 37% compatible when compared against mainframe DB2 2.2's DDL. The same study also found that

Database Manager's DML was only 72% compatible when compared against mainframe DB2's DML. Thus, while Database Manager may be quite good for building OS/2-based relational database applications, it is not good for offloaded DB2 development or downsizing existing DB2 applications to PCs. This means that XDB-Workbench is the only viable tool for offloading mainframe DB2 development to PC workstations.

IMS(DB)

Despite the fact that IBM's IMS now has many competitors, including some from IBM itself, it is still the most widely used DBMS. Some reasons for this include the large community of trained and experienced IMS developers, a wide variety of supporting tools, and its reliability in handling large databases.

To support IMS developers there are two PC-based IMS workbenches in the marketplace, the Micro Focus IMS Option and Realia's RealIMS. Both packages provide facilities for the development of IMS(DB/DC) and CICS/DL/I applications, the latter when used in conjunction with a PC-based CICS workbench. Both are discussed below. The CICS facilities are discussed in the section on TP monitors.

Micro Focus IMS Option

The Micro Focus IMS Option was originally developed by the Stingray Software Company. The original name of the product was IMSVS86, and it was first released in 1987, with Stingray doing the product development and Micro Focus handling the sales and marketing. In 1991 Stingray was bought out by Micro Focus and the name of the product was changed to Micro Focus IMS Option. The Stingray development staff joined Micro Focus. Since its first release in 1987, the Micro Focus IMS Option has been constantly improved and is now in wide use at sites using the Micro Focus COBOL/2 Workbench.

The Micro Focus IMS Option includes the following capabilities of interest to the IMS programmer:

1. The ability to use the Micro Focus Animator. The IMS Option invokes an IMS control region before entering the Animator facility.
2. The ability to use the Micro Focus runtime facility. As with the Animator, an IMS control region is initiated before entry.
3. The ability to define screens sent to terminals from message processing programs (MPP) or formats sent to printers from

programs running in a region. This is accomplished using the MFSGEN facility.

4. The ability to paint screens and generate MFS code. This is accomplished using Micro Focus CO-MFS, which is purchased separately.
5. The ability to generate DBDs for each database accessed by a program. There is also a DBDMAP utility that can provide a hierarchical map of a single DBD.
6. The ability to initialize files for each genned DBD. This allocation of database files, along with the needed priming, is accomplished using the ZEROLOAD facility.
7. The ability to generate PSBs to specify the view of IMS resources that programs will be using. This is accomplished using the PSBGEN facility.
8. The ability to import and export data between mainframe IMS databases and PC-based IMS databases.

The Micro Focus IMS Option meets almost all of the selection criteria listed in the DBMS requirements section. The major advantages for mainframe IMS developers using Micro Focus IMS Option are the following:

1. Short learning curve and minimal training requirements. Usually just a day or two is needed.
2. Superior test environment when compared to the mainframe. Programmers have much better control over their test environment (i.e., much less need to interact with DBAs, no need to wait for lengthy or infrequently performed system regenerations) and are insulated from other developers in their testing activities. This makes testing faster and of higher quality.
3. High degree of compatibility with mainframe IMS.

The only area of concern is the few unsupported features. These include the following:

1. Checkpoint/restart does not include the backing out of database updates. Restart does not reposition any database or restore PCB contents.
2. System service calls are not processed.
3. Duplicate keys at the root level of an HDAM DBD are not supported.

4. Alternate response PCB definitions are not supported.
5. Bypassing of MFS system exits is not supported.

A more complete list can be found in Chapter 23 of the "IMSVS86 Operating Guide."

The Micro Focus IMS Option can operate in either EBCDIC or ASCII mode, allowing developers to build mainframe- or PC-based production systems. The IMS Option also supports both the MS-DOS and OS/2 environments. The list price for the Micro Focus IMS Option is approximately $1,000 when purchased with the Micro Focus COBOL/2 Workbench or approximately $1,250 when purchased separately. The CO-MFS package has a list price of approximately $300.

Realia's RealIMS

Realia's RealIMS was originally released in late 1989. RealIMS operates in conjunction with Realia COBOL and, if necessary, RealCICS to support the creation of IMS(DB/DC) or CICS/DL/I applications. Because RealIMS works in either EBCDIC or ASCII mode, developers can build mainframe- or PC-based production systems. It also supports both the MS-DOS and OS/2 environments.

The facilities provided by RealIMS give it functionality similar to the Micro Focus IMS Option. Some of the differences between the two packages include the following:

1. RealIMS supports BTS and DLT0 emulation.
2. RealIMS documentation is not as complete or as extensive as the documentation for the Micro Focus IMS Option. For example, there is no list of differences between RealIMS and mainframe IMS.
3. Because Realia's market share is much smaller than Micro Focus's and because RealIMS came out more than two years after the Micro Focus IMS Option (a.k.a. Stingray IMSVS86), there is not a lot of information on how the product performs in the field.

The list price for RealIMS, which contains both DB(DL/I) and DC facilities, is approximately $1,695. RealDL/I, which can be used in conjunction with RealCICS to build CICS/DL/I applications, has a list price of approximately $995.

Other DBMSs

In addition to support for DB2 and IMS, support exists for other mainframe DBMSs. These include Computer Associates' CA-IDMS and CA-DATACOM. However, unlike the multiple choices for DB2 and IMS, there is only one PC-based tool for each of these non-IBM DBMSs.

For CA-IDMS, it should come as no surprise that Computer Associates offers CA-IDMS/PC and CA-ADS/PC. With these tools, users may offload mainframe IDMS development to PC workstations or downsize existing applications to a PC/LAN environment. Some of the mainframe IDMS facilities emulated by the PC packages include IDD, ADSA, ADS/O, OLM, DML/O and IDMS(DC). There are also facilities to do database administration and SQL reporting.

For CA-DATACOM, support also comes from Computer Associates in the form of CA-DATACOM/PC and CA-IDEAL/PC. As with the PC-based IDMS tools, users may offload mainframe DATACOM development to PC workstations or downsize existing applications to a PC/LAN environment. CA-DATACOM/PC includes emulations of most of the mainframe facilities, including the data dictionary, data queries, and SQL access.

TP Monitor Workbenches

The TP monitor workbench (i.e., precompiler, debugger, screen painter), along with the DBMS workbench, are the two components of an offloaded development environment that enable most mainframe programmers to use the language workbenches to their fullest capability.

On IBM mainframes there are two major TP monitors, IBM's CICS and IMS(DC). Reflecting this popularity, there are multiple PC-based TP monitor workbenches that support offloaded application development using these monitors. In addition, IDMS(DC) is also supported by Computer Associates' PC-based IDMS tools. As the workbenches that support IMS(DB/DC) and IDMS(DB/DC) emulation were addressed in the section on DBMSs (i.e., Micro Focus IMS Option, RealIMS, CA-IDMS/PC), they will not be examined here. This leaves only CICS emulation, see below.

CICS

Currently there are three packages for offloading CICS development to PC workstations. They are Micro Focus CICS Option, Realia's RealCICS, and IBM's CICS OS/2.

Micro Focus CICS Option

The Micro Focus CICS Option was originally developed by Innovative Solutions, Inc. The original name of the product was CICSVS86 and it was first released in 1987, with Innovative doing the product development and Micro Focus handling the sales and marketing. In 1991 CICSVS86 was purchased by Micro Focus and the name of the product was changed to Micro Focus CICS Option. In addition to the purchase of the product, certain members of the Innovative staff joined Micro Focus.

The Micro Focus CICS Option includes the following capabilities of interest to the CICS programmer:

1. Availability of a CICS preprocessor that translates EXEC CICS statements into IBM OS/VS COBOL or IBM VS COBOL II code. All CICS commands are syntax checked, but certain commands do not generate runtime code. See below for more information.
2. Ability to use the Micro Focus Animator. Testing is performed at the EXEC CICS level, not at the generated level. When working with DB2 or IMS databases, the appropriate DB2 SQL and IMS DL/I facilities are made available.
3. Ability to use the Micro Focus runtime facility.
4. Ability to paint maps and generate BMS macros and COBOL copy books. Mapsets also can be constructed.
5. Ability to perform BMS macro imports for existing applications.
6. Ability to define CICS transactions via a Program Control Table (PCT). In addition, VSAM files can be defined to the system. IMS PSB and DBD generation facilities are available for building CICS/DL/I applications as well.

The Micro Focus CICS Option meets most of the selection criteria listed in the TP monitor requirements section. The major advantages for mainframe CICS developers using Micro Focus CICS Option are the following:

1. Short learning curve and minimal training requirements. Usually just a day is needed.
2. Superior test environment when compared with the mainframe. Programmers have much better control over their test environment (i.e., much less need to interact with support personnel, no

need to wait for lengthy or infrequently performed CICS table updates) and are insulated from other developers in their testing activities (i.e., there is no possibility of crashing a CICS region). The power of the Micro Focus Animator facility is also a major advantage. This makes testing faster and of higher quality.

3. High degree of compatibility with mainframe CICS.

The only area of concern is the unsupported features. Some of these include the following (as of version 2.2.H):

1. The SYNCPOINT command.
2. Certain command options, such as KEYLENGTH, SYSID, REQID, and USERID.
3. Most options of HANDLE and IGNORE CONDITION.
4. Most options of ASSIGN.

A complete list can be found in Appendix A of the "Micro Focus CICS Option Reference Guide and Tutorial."

The Micro Focus CICS Option can operate in either EBCDIC or ASCII mode, allowing developers to build mainframe- or PC-based production systems. The Micro Focus CICS Option also supports both the MS-DOS and OS/2 environments. The OS/2 version of Micro Focus CICS Option should not be confused with the Micro Focus CICS OS/2 Option. Micro Focus CICS OS/2 Option is an IBM product with some additional Micro Focus utilities. Micro Focus sells the product to sites interested in building CICS applications that run production on PS/2s or are interested in building CICS-based cooperative processing applications. See the section on IBM's CICS OS/2 for more information.

The list price for the Micro Focus CICS Option is approximately $1,000 when purchased with the Micro Focus COBOL/2 Workbench and approximately $1,250 when purchased separately.

Realia's RealCICS

Realia's RealCICS was originally developed by the Charandon Group of Canada and initially released in 1986. RealCICS operates in conjunction with Realia COBOL and, if necessary, RealDL/I (a subset of RealIMS) to support the creation of CICS/DL/I applications. Because RealCICS works in either EBCDIC or ASCII mode, developers can build mainframe- or PC-based production systems. It also supports both the MS-DOS and OS/2 environments.

The facilities provided by RealCICS give it functionality similar to the Micro Focus CICS Option. These are the major differences between the two packages (i.e., RealCICS 2.20 and Micro Focus CICS Option 2.2.H):

1. Degree of support for mainframe CICS commands. RealCICS supports more mainframe CICS commands than the Micro Focus CICS Option. For example, RealCICS offers complete support of the ASSIGN, CANCEL, DEQ, ENQ, and START commands and better partial support for the HANDLE and IGNORE CONDITION, SEND, RECEIVE, and WRITE commands than does the Micro Focus CICS Option. For more information see Chapters 2 and 10 of the "RealCICS Development System User Manual."
2. Extent and sophistication of the Micro Focus CICS Option tools versus the Realia tools. Micro Focus has the advantage here with its Animator product and other tools.

The list price for RealCICS is approximately $995. RealDL/I, which can be used in conjunction with RealCICS to build CICS/DL/I applications, also has a list price of approximately $995.

IBM's CICS OS/2

IBM's CICS OS/2 was originally developed at the IBM Lab in Hursley, England, and was initially released in 1990. It runs under OS/2 EE and is the first major IBM product available on a wide range of platforms (i.e., 3090s down to PS/2s). Since it is part of IBM's Systems Application Architecture (SAA), we should see a version of CICS for OS/400 in the near future. The two programming languages that can be used with the product are IBM's C/2 and Micro Focus's COBOL/2. For COBOL developers this means that testing and debugging can be performed using Micro Focus's Animator.

The main emphasis in the marketing of IBM CICS OS/2 has been to give developers a facility to build PS/2-based CICS systems and cooperative or client-server CICS systems. To accomplish this PS/2 CICS workstations can operate with or without a host attachment. They also can utilize a standard CICS API to allow workstations to communicate with other workstations. Only as an aside is it mentioned that IBM CICS OS/2 can be used for offloading the development of mainframe-based CICS applications.

Given the recent release of IBM CICS OS/2 and the lack of emphasis on using it to offload mainframe CICS development, there is not a lot of information on how the product performs in the field. Thus, any studies on the use of IBM CICS OS/2 in an offloaded development environment that are made public will be of great interest.

The list price for IBM CICS OS/2 is approximately $736 (onetime charge). The Micro Focus CICS OS/2 Option, which contains IBM's CICS OS/2 plus a BMS screen development facility and an integrated preprocessor to maximize integration with the Micro Focus COBOL/2 Workbench, has a list price of approximately $1,000 when purchased with Micro Focus COBOL/2 Workbench. Buyers should not confuse the OS/2 version of the Micro Focus CICS Option with the Micro Focus CICS OS/2 Option. They are different tool sets.

Lower CASE Workbenches

Once the users of an offloaded development environment become proficient in the use of language, DBMS, and TP monitor workbenches, they may choose to add a lower CASE workbench (i.e., code generator plus extra development tools). Lower CASE workbenches can provide users of language, DBMS, and TP monitor workbenches with additional reductions in initial application development time, greater coding consistency, and significantly reduced maintenance.

PC-based lower CASE workbenches are supported by a number of vendors. The two main products in the market today are Intersolv's APS/PC and Computer Associates' CA-TELON/PWS. Both of these tools have long histories and should be examined by all organizations interested in making further improvements to the development life cycles of their online applications.

Intersolv's APS/PC

Intersolv, formerly Sage Software, was one of the first companies to bring a major mainframe-based application development system down to the PC workstation. This happened when APS/PC was released in 1987 after having been offered on the mainframe for several years.

With APS/PC, programmers can develop online or batch applications that can be generated and tested on the PC workstation with the help of language, DBMS, and TP monitor workbenches, such as Micro Focus and XDB. Specifically, APS/PC can generate IBM OS/VS

COBOL, IBM VS COBOL II, IMS(DB), DB2, IDMS(DB), VSAM, IMS(DC), CICS, and ISPF Dialog code. (Note: ISPF Dialog code cannot be tested on the PC workstation because of a lack of a PC-based emulation facility.) APS/PC is available for both the MS-DOS and OS/2 environments and uses 8MB of RAM to operate.

The APS/PC package includes the following facilities of interest to most programmers:

1. *Screen painting facility.* APS/PC screen painting is performed by entering literals and data fields at the appropriate position on a screen. Information from the central Data Element Facility is used to populate fields on the screen with names, text, attributes, and field edits. The screen painter can generate DC code for IMS(DC), CICS, and ISPF Dialog.
2. *Prototyping facility.* Once screen painting and generation is complete, data can be entered into fields and displayed on any screen that uses the same data fields. Users may move from screen to screen, in any order, and make changes as needed.
3. *Online system generator.* After using the screen painting facility, developers enter an online generator named "Online Express." With Online Express a user fills in information on several screens to define the function and behavior of the program being built. The kind of information collected includes database accesses, PF key functions, and custom code points. Custom code, written either in COBOL or S-COBOL (i.e., APS/PC's COBOL-like 4GL), is required for mathematical calculations or unusual logic requirements. However, in most situations developers will be able to produce multifunction, multi-I/O programs with little or no custom code.
4. *Batch system generator.* Report creation is performed using a report painting facility. APS/PC report programs can produce up to 15 reports on one pass of data. Batch updates can be performed by coding programs in COBOL or the previously mentioned S-COBOL. It should be noted that the batch facility is included to supplement the development of online applications with small amounts of batch processing. APS/PC should not be used to build applications that are primarily batch oriented.
5. *Customization facility.* APS/PC has a complex but powerful facility that allows for automatic code insertion at an individual,

project, or organizational level. With the use of the Customization facility, an administrator could build security facilities or other functions into programs without the involvement or knowledge of programmers.

Here are some other areas of interest.

1. *Integration.* As for integration with other tools, APS/PC is quite powerful. APS/PC users can easily switch to the Micro Focus COBOL/2 Workbench, Micro Focus IMS Option, Micro Focus CICS Option, or XDB-Workbench. S-COBOL can be tested inside Micro Focus Animator, and XDB and IMS(DB) information can be imported. As for links to upper CASE tools, APS/PC has a bidirectional interface with Intersolv's Excelerator and KnowledgeWare's IEW/ADW. A shared repository is planned for APS/PC and Excelerator.
2. *Performance.* Given the power of APS/PC, it should come as no surprise that performance can be a little slow. APS/PC can take several minutes to load and the generating of screens and programs also can take significant amounts of time (3 to 10 minutes). Given this, APS/PC provides a multitasking facility that allows generating to be performed in the background, while the foreground is free for other tasks.
3. *Documentation.* The documentation for APS/PC is extensive (six volumes). It is PC oriented and the online help facilities are complete. A good index is provided.
4. *Training.* In the area of training, Intersolv offers several courses for APS/PC users. It also offers a "train the trainer" program. Training the typical user will take about seven days. Use of APS/PC should begin immediately after training is complete. Not using this complex product immediately after training will usually result in the users forgetting what they learned. Normally it will take about a month for new APS/PC users to become proficient. To help this introductory process, there should be an experienced user available to answer questions and point out the best way to do things (i.e., hand holding). It should be noted that APS/PC is only for users who are already experienced offloaded development environment users. The introduction of APS/PC should not occur at the same time users are being introduced to a set of language, DBMS, and TP monitor workbenches.

The list price for APS/PC is approximately $9,600 for a single user copy. The vendor may be contacted at the following address:

Intersolv
3200 Tower Oaks Boulevard
Rockville, MD 20852
Phone: (301) 230-3200

Computer Associates CA-TELON/PWS

TELON was the first code generator to be widely used on the mainframe. In 1989 Pansophic Systems came out with TELON/PWS for the PC workstation. In 1991 Computer Associates bought out Pansophic and renamed the product CA-TELON/PWS.

With CA-TELON/PWS, programmers can develop online or batch applications that can be generated and tested on the PC workstation with the help of language, DBMS, and TP monitor workbenches. Specifically, CA-TELON/PWS can generate IBM OS/VS COBOL, IBM PL/I, IMS(DB), DB2, VSAM, IMS(DC), and CICS code. (Note: Since there is no effective PL/I compiler for offloading mainframe development, the testing of PL/I programs cannot take place at the PC workstation level.) CA-TELON/PWS is available for both the MS-DOS and OS/2 environments and requires 512KB of RAM to operate.

The CA-TELON/PWS package includes the following facilities of interest to most programmers:

1. *Panel painting facility.* CA-TELON/PWS panel (i.e., screen) creation is performed by entering literals and data fields at the appropriate position on an ISPF-like screen. A dictionary of central information can be used to assign field edits. Consistency checks between fields are available.

2. *Prototyping facility.* CA-TELON/PWS provides for five levels of prototyping. The usual level of prototyping for most users will involve data mapping and screen execution without data access. Any changes needed can be made and displayed very quickly. CA-TELON/PWS offers users a more powerful set of prototyping tools than are found under APS/PC.

3. *Online system generator.* After using the panel facilities, developers enter an online screen definition facility. In this facility a user fills in information on several screens to define the function and behavior of the program being built. The kind of information

collected includes database accesses, PF key functions, and custom code points. Custom code is written in COBOL. Users should be aware that CA-TELON/PWS enforces a rather strict program flow on the developers. They will need to be aware of this flow and keep it in mind when designing programs. Also, as program complexity increases, the amount of custom coding will increase, thus reducing the effectiveness of CA-TELON/PWS. APS/PC is much more flexible than CA-TELON/PWS in the development of online programs.

4. *Batch system generation.* Report and update programs are created using the same tools as those used to build online programs. However, it should be noted that CA-TELON/PWS should not be used to build applications that are primarily batch oriented.

5. *Customization facility.* CA-TELON/PWS allows users to automatically add custom code at the beginning and/or end of all custom code points. In addition, an administrator can alter the code creating macros, which are written in Assembler. This, however, is a little dodgy because upward compatibility is not guaranteed. CA-TELON/PWS's method of customization is not as safe as APS/PC's method.

Some other areas of interest include the following:

1. *Integration.* CA-TELON/PWS does not directly interact with Micro Focus COBOL/2 Workbench or any of the other PC-based workbenches. To access these tools a user must exit CA-TELON/PWS. CA-TELON/PWS can, however, create, import, change, and export IMS(DB) and XDB information. As for links to upper CASE tools, CA-TELON/PWS can utilize a one-way interface with Excelerator, IEW/ADW, and Bachman.

2. *Performance.* CA-TELON/PWS has a very fast load time (~15 seconds) and fairly fast screen- and program-generating times (1 to 2 minutes). (Note: The CA-TELON/PWS generation step does not include the Micro Focus COBOL compile, as does the APS/PC tool.) Thus, CA-TELON/PWS is a faster product than APS/PC.

3. *Documentation.* Except for one volume, the documentation for CA-TELON/PWS is oriented toward the mainframe. Online documentation consists of a plain text copy of the written documentation without any search capability. However, a very useful help feature that CA-TELON/PWS provides is the ability to enter a "?" in any field to get a help screen on that particular field.

4. *Training.* In the area of training, Computer Associates offers several courses for CA-TELON/PWS users. It also offers a "train the trainer" program. Training the typical user will take around eight days. Use of CA-TELON/PWS should begin immediately after training is complete. Not using this complex product immediately after training will usually result in the users forgetting what they learned. Normally it will take about a month for new CA-TELON/PWS users to become proficient. To help this introductory process, there should be an experienced user available to answer questions and point out the best way to do things (hand holding again). It should be noted that CA-TELON/PWS is only for users who are already experienced offloaded development environment users. The introduction of CA-TELON/PWS should not occur at the same time that users are being introduced to a set of language, DBMS, or TP monitor workbenches.

The list price for CA-TELON/PWS is approximately $10,500 for a single user copy.

Upper CASE Workbenches

The purpose of this book is to facilitate the introduction of offloaded development to programmers in commercial DP shops. However, programmers are not the only group that can make effective use of such environments. Analysts also can derive significant productivity and quality gains from using upper CASE tools in an offloaded development environment. However, because of the complexity of the issues involved in selecting and using an upper CASE tool, no in-depth discussion of upper CASE workbenches is provided here. (This area could be the subject of a book all by itself.)

SUPPLEMENTAL OFFLOADED DEVELOPMENT ENVIRONMENT TOOLS

Supplemental tools are those packages that "round out" the offloaded development environment. They provide certain functionality that is not normally found in the above workbench tools. These include JCL emulators, mainframe sort utility emulators, data handlers, and keystroke capture/playback tools. Following is a list of packages available in each of these areas.

1. *JCL emulators.* JCL emulators provide the user with DDNAME emulation support on the PC workstation, thus eliminating the need to recode JCL into MS-DOS .BAT files or vice-versa. This can help significantly with the string testing of applications. Two JCL emulators in the marketplace are

    a. PROXMVS, available from:

        Proximity Software
        Suite 3C
        408 Headquarters Drive
        Millersville, MD 21108
        Phone: (301) 987-3400
        FAX: (301) 987-3446

    b. TransJCL, available from:

        Miller — Fairchild, Inc.
        10555 West 74th Street
        La Grange, IL 60525
        Phone: (708) 579-9560
        FAX: (708) 579-9587

2. *Mainframe sort utility emulators.* Being able to emulate a mainframe sort utility may be useful for some developers. Two sort emulators available today are

    a. SORTMVS, a SyncSort emulator from Micro Focus.

    b. PROXSORT, an IBM DFSORT emulator that is packaged with PROXMVS, from Proximity Software.

3. *Data handlers.* Data-handling tools provide the user with an easy way to view and alter mainframe data files on the PC workstation. Facilities and features of data handlers can include emulation of mainframe-based data-handling tools, translation between EBCDIC and ASCII formats, unpacking packed data fields, hex and character mode access, and the use of copy books as display templates. These tools are in competition with similar facilities embedded within some of the above workbenches. Two non-workbench-based-data handling tools are

    a. DATA EDITOR FACILITY, available from Micro Focus.

b. File-AID/PC, available from
   Compuware
   31440 Northwestern Highway
   P.O. Box 9080
   Farmington Hills, Michigan 48333-9080
   Phone: (800) 521-9353
   Phone (in Michigan): (313) 737-7300

4. *Keystroke capture/playback tools.* Tools that can capture and playback mainframe keystrokes are useful for constructing mechanized regression test systems. Two capture/playback tools that are available for PC workstations and/or servers are

   a. CA-TRAPS, available from Computer Associates.

   b. ESCORT Connectivity Software, available from AT&T/NCR.

Of course, there may be additional tools that offloaded development environment users need. These can include word processors, spreadsheets, graphics packages, and e-mail systems. The important thing to remember when choosing such packages is the "real" needs of the users and the adaptability of the package to the selected offloaded development environment.

SUMMARY

Since the main reason for setting up an offloaded development environment is to give applications developers the ability to exploit the software tools that run on PCs, the usefulness of the environment will largely depend on the PC workstation software tools selected. These tools can be categorized as follows: editors, language workbenches, DBMS emulators, TP monitor emulators, lower CASE tools, upper CASE tools, and supplemental tools.

A list of selection criteria for each category of PC workstation software tools has been provided in this chapter. Readers should tailor these lists to meet their individual needs and objectives.

REFERENCES

1. Sayles, Jonathan. DB2 Compatibility: XDB vs. Data Manager. *Proceedings of the 1991 XDB User Conference.* September 23, 1991. Session 6.

6

Determining the Workstation Operating Environment

Once the workstation software tools (editors, compilers, DBMS and TP emulators, CASE tools, and so on) have been selected, the workstation operating environment is chosen. This operating environment consists of the workstation operating system, memory management facility (if separate from the operating system), and workstation hardware. The sections that follow outline the options for each component of the workstation operating environment.

WORKSTATION OPERATING SYSTEM

The main choices for the workstation operating system are MS-DOS, MS-Windows, OS/2, and UNIX. A discussion of each system's usefulness and applicability to the offloaded development environment is provided.

1. *MS-DOS.* A few years ago, many vendors of workstation software tools believed that MS-DOS would soon be replaced by OS/2. Despite this belief, as of the writing of this book MS-DOS remains the most popular operating system for offloaded development environments. The attributes that make MS-DOS so popular among offloaded development environment implementors are the following:

    a. Simplicity. Its simple exec language, simple batch language, and easy installation procedures simply make choosing MS-DOS easy.

    b. Low price. MS-DOS is inexpensive to purchase and upgrade.

c. Support. MS-DOS is supported by a knowledgeable and well-funded vendor.

d. Portability. MS-DOS can run on any Intel 80X86 PC workstation with as little as 512KB of RAM.

e. Versatility. Tens of thousands of applications can run under MS-DOS, including tools from virtually all workstation software tool vendors.

f. Familiarity. Virtually anyone who can operate a PC is familiar, to some degree, with MS-DOS.

There are, however, two significant drawbacks to MS-DOS. The first, and most important, is memory management. Most users of MS-DOS PCs in large business environments are connected to LANs. The main concern when adding new packages to these LAN-using PCs is how much low DOS memory (i.e., usually the first 640KB) the package needs. Indeed, for many local administrators of LANs with MS-DOS-based clients, the world seems to revolve around the now infamous 640KB limit. To get around this often crippling limitation, some vendors offer memory management packages that allow system programs, such as device drivers, TSRs, certain MS-DOS resources (e.g., FILES, BUFFERS), and various LAN programs to be moved to high DOS memory, usually between the 640KB and 1024KB lines. These packages include Qualitas' 386MAX and Quarterdeck's QEMM, both of which are discussed in greater detail in the following section. In addition, certain workstation software tools come with memory managers that allow their tools to use memory all the way up to the 16MB line (e.g., Micro Focus XM). The use of both these types of memory management tools, however, does not guarantee that all the necessary workstation software tools will fit in the memory of an MS-DOS-based offloaded development environment. Even when they do it is usually not without considerable effort.

The second drawback with MS-DOS is its lack of a built-in multitasking capability. This does not mean that multitasking is not possible under MS-DOS (e.g., Micro Focus has a concurrent processing facility within its COBOL/2 Workbench); it just means that multitasking is not part of the operating system function. This can be a significant problem since most developers will, at some point, need to do computer-intensive activities such as compiles or batch tests.

2. *MS-Windows.* MS-Windows is the very popular GUI (graphical user interface) extension of MS-DOS. In addition to its popularity in the normal business environment, MS-Windows enjoys significant support in the area of offloaded development. Among the advantages of using MS-Windows as a workstation operating system are

   a. Simplicity. MS-Windows is an easy to install and easy to maintain mouse-driven operating system with consistent presentation from application to application.

   b. Low price. Like MS-DOS, MS-Windows is inexpensive to purchase and upgrade.

   c. Support. MS-Windows is supported by the same knowledgeable and well-funded vendor as MS-DOS.

   d. Low RAM requirement. Users can run MS-Windows and still have enough memory to run many applications in a small amount of RAM.

   e. Versatility. Thousands of applications can run under MS-Windows, including applications from many workstation software tool vendors.

   f. Significant user base. Many businesses have made MS-Windows their standard PC operating environment.

   g. Multitasking. Unlike MS-DOS, MS-Windows has a built-in multitasking capability.

   While all this sounds great, there are some drawbacks. Because MS-Windows runs on top of MS-DOS, there is still the problem of memory management. The same tricks that must be performed under MS-DOS usually must also be performed under MS-Windows. These include experimenting with memory management packages, such as 386MAX and QEMM, and using workstation software tool memory management programs like MicroFocus's XM. A second drawback is that while most vendors have announced that they are planning to convert their tools into standard MS-Windows applications (i.e., programs that can be called up in a window, transfer displayed information from one window to another, and so on), they are not there yet. Most tools still take over the whole screen when invoked (i.e., they do not operate in a window).

3. *OS/2.* OS/2 Version 1.X was the least popular of the top four PC workstation operating systems (MS-DOS, MS-Windows, OS/2, UNIX). It consisted of both an exec language-based environment and a GUI component that is much like MS-Windows. Despite OS/2's sales problems, many workstation software tool vendors introduced OS/2 versions of their tools. These OS/2 versions are usually identical to their MS-DOS counterparts.

   OS/2 Version 2.0, is promised to be "a better DOS than DOS, a better Windows than Windows and a better OS/2 than OS/2 (1.X)." Specifically, OS/2 2.0 is a 32-bit operating system, as opposed to MS-DOS, Windows, and OS/2 1.X, which are 16-bit systems. This allows users to make better use of 32-bit architecture workstations, such as the 386 and 486. Among the anticipated advantages of using OS/2 2.0 as a workstation operating environment are:

   a. Simplicity. Like MS-Windows, OS/2 is mouse driven and provides for consistent presentation from application to application.
   b. Support. OS/2 is supported by a well-funded vendor, IBM.
   c. Versatility. OS/2 2.0 is able to run DOS and Windows applications. In fact, OS/2 2.0 gives these applications more memory to run in than could be obtained in their native environments (i.e., OS/2 2.0 provides applications with approximately 610KB of RAM versus approximately 512KB for DOS, depending on the version, and 380KB for Windows). In addition, users have the ability to "boot" specific versions of DOS. OS/2 2.0 also is able to handle OS/2 1.X applications. All totaled, this means that OS/2 2.0 will be able to handle more applications than any other PC workstation operating system.
   d. Multitasking. With 32-bit processing, OS/2 2.0 delivers much better multitasking capability than the 16-bit-based systems. Also, through its use of preemptive multitasking, OS/2 2.0 gives priority to applications running in the foreground. This results in even better response time for those applications that users are currently interacting with. In addition, OS/2 2.0 provides for better protection between applications. This means that "misbehaving" applications will be able to be terminated without having to reboot the whole workstation.
   e. Easy memory management.

Among the disadvantages of using OS/2 2.0 as a workstation operating environment are

a. Large RAM requirement. Usually at least 8MB.

b. Large hard disk requirement. OS/2 2.0 by itself requires 20MB to 30MB.

c. Small base of existing users. Most businesses are still sitting on the fence waiting for OS/2 2.0.

Early versions of OS/2 2.0 have received positive reviews from the thousands of IBM customers who have been testing it. However, the important thing all offloaded development environment builders should remember is to personally test all software thoroughly, especially new operating systems, before making any large commitments. Over time it is expected that OS/2 2.0 will become a "solid" operating system.

4. *UNIX.* Of the four operating systems discussed in this chapter the only "real" operating system (multitasking and multi-user) is UNIX. However, as a workstation operating system for an offloaded development environment supporting IBM mainframe development, it suffers from some fatal flaws that often prevent its use. These include

   a. No mainframe DBMS emulation support. There are no IMS or DB2 emulators for UNIX.

   b. Little mainframe TP monitor emulation. For the most part, very few mainframe TP monitor emulators are available for UNIX. One exception is the CICS emulation package from UniSoft.

   c. Complexity. Programmers can work in the UNIX environment for many years and still be learning new things about it.

   The choice of PC workstation operating systems presented to today's builder of an offloaded development environment is not an easy one to make. MS-DOS, along with MS-Windows, can be chosen with their known problems (i.e., little or no built-in memory management, little or no multitasking capability). Or OS/2 can be selected with all its promise but rather shaky history. One thing is for certain and that is that whatever choice is made, there will be people who disagree with it. Hopefully by 1993 or 1994, there will be one clear choice in the area of PC workstation operating systems.

MEMORY MANAGEMENT SYSTEMS

As mentioned above, if MS-DOS or MS-Windows is chosen as the operating system, a memory management tool is usually required. Memory management tools come in two types. The first type is a tool to move system programs from low DOS memory (usually 0 to 640KB) to high DOS memory (usually 640KB to 1024KB), in order to give workstation software tools the low DOS memory they require to run. A discussion of the main tools in this area is provided below. The other type of memory management tools are those that come with certain workstation software tools and allow developers to use extended memory from the 1MB line all the way up to the 16MB line. A brief discussion on this type of memory manager is included at the end of this section.

Program-Moving Memory Managers

Program-moving memory management tools shift system programs (i.e., device drivers, TSRs, DOS resources such as FILES and BUFFERS, LAN programs) from low DOS memory to unused parts of high DOS memory. They can also extend the range of low DOS memory from 640KB up to 736KB by taking over unused memory earmarked for video graphics capabilities and assigning it to low DOS memory. The importance of maximizing low DOS memory is to provide workstation software tools, such as DBMS emulators and CASE tools, enough memory to execute while still giving other offloaded development environment components, such as the operating system and the LAN software, the low DOS memory they require.

The most popular of these program-moving memory managers are Qualitas' 386MAX and Quarterdeck's QEMM. Both of these tools can be purchased for less than $100 and provide the same functionality and similar results. Both tools give the user special memory analysis tools and maps, along with facilities to automatically change AUTOEXEC.BAT and CONFIG.SYS files. Usually, the difference in the amount of low DOS memory that can be saved between the two tools is no more than 1KB or 2KB. However, if an offloaded development environment configuration is particularly tight for low DOS memory, that 1KB or 2KB can, in some situations, be critical.

The important thing to note is that only one of these tools should be selected for a given offloaded development environment. Having some developers using 386MAX and other developers in the same group using QEMM will make life for the local administrator much more difficult because of the lack of a standard developer workstation configuration.

Another consideration in the area of program-moving memory managers is the impact of MS-DOS 5.0. This version of MS-DOS includes some program relocation features that allow certain MS-DOS components to be moved to high DOS memory. Thus, MS-DOS 5.0 on its own may yield enough low DOS memory to run all the selected workstation software tools and the supporting system software, such as the operating system and LAN programs. However, as with all custom memory management configurations, testing is an absolute necessity.

Workstation Software Supplied Memory Managers

Memory managers that come with workstation software tools, such as Micro Focus COBOL/2 Workbench and Realia COBOL, allow developers to use extended memory from the 1MB line all the way up to the 16MB line. This is essential when compiling and/or testing large mainframe programs that cannot fit in what remains of low DOS memory after everything else is loaded.

Once a language workbench is chosen, you are usually committed to its memory manager. For Micro Focus the memory manager is their own product XM. For Realia, the memory manager is Rational Systems' DOS/16M. When you select other workstation software tools that will be working closely with the language workbench, such as DBMS emulators, TP monitor emulators, or lower CASE code generators, they also must be able to work with the language workbench's memory manager. The inability to support a common memory manager will mean that certain workstation software tools will not be able to directly call other workstation software tools. This incompatibility may make an offloaded development environment difficult to use. Thus, communication and cooperation among the vendors of your selected workstation software tools is very important. The level of communication should be reflected in the documentation of the workstation software tools (i.e., the documentation should explicitly state how the DBMS, TP monitor, or lower CASE workbench invokes the language workbench's memory manager).

Overall, the effort needed to set up both these types of memory managers is not insignificant. It can take many days to determine the configuration that works for all the selected workstation software tools. Of course, these memory management problems may be avoided by selecting OS/2 as the workstation operating system.

WORKSTATION HARDWARE

Choosing workstation hardware is nowhere near as difficult as selecting a workstation operating system. Various hardware components include the following:

1. *CPUs.* As the only viable operating systems for an offloaded development environment are MS-DOS, MS-Windows, and OS/2, the only type of workstation hardware that can be used is the Intel 80X86 line. Given the requirements of a workstation's language, DBMS and TP monitor workbenches, the minimum Intel CPU is the 80386/SX. This is especially true if MS-Windows is used. 80286-based PCs can support some workbench software tools but not as well as 80386-based PCs. As of 1990, there should be no reason to buy new 80286 PCs for any part of an offloaded development environment. For OS/2 2.0 workstations, or those workstations using lower CASE code generators or many upper CASE tools, the minimum useful CPU is usually an 80386/DX 25 or 33MHz. Table 6-1 matches Intel CPUs to major offloaded development environment software components.

   Another important consideration in choosing the workstation CPU is the brand. If your budget permits, try to use well-known brand name PCs (e.g., IBM, COMPAQ, AST, AT&T). They may cost more than less-well-known brands, but they make up for it in improved support — not only from the CPU vendor but from the other hardware and software vendors. If you have a problem loading a program or adding a hardware accessory to a COMPAQ PC, you are much more likely to get quick and useful assistance from the vendor than if you were using a "Fred's PC."

2. *Monitors.* There are not a lot of choices here. Color VGA monitors have become the standard and are more than sufficient for most workstation software tools. One exception to this is certain upper CASE tools that require extra large monitors to display complex graphics or diagrams.

3. *Hard disks.* The best advice here is "not too big, not too small." The right size will mostly depend on the number and the type of workstation tools selected. Language workbenches, along with one or two associated DBMS and TP monitor emulators, will usually fit nicely on a 100MB hard disk. Most lower and upper CASE tools will usually require a 200MB hard disk. If OS/2 is

the selected operating system (OS/2 2.0 takes roughly 20MB to 30MB), add a little extra to your hard disk requirement. Do not get extremely large hard disks (i.e., 300MB+). They usually encourage waste on the user's part and are difficult to maintain.

Table 6-1. Intel CPUs.

Workstation Operating System/Software Tool	Minimum Useful Intel-based CPU
MS-Windows	80386/SX 16 or 20MHz
Micro Focus COBOL/2 Workbench (MS-DOS)	
Micro Focus IMS Option (MS-DOS)	
Micro Focus CICS Option (MS-DOS)	
Realia COBOL (MS-DOS)	
RealIMS (MS-DOS)	
RealCICS (MS-DOS)	
XDB DB2 Workbench (MS-DOS)	
EXCELERATOR (MS-DOS)	
OS/2	80386/DX 25 or 33MHz
Micro Focus COBOL/2 Workbench (OS/2)	
Micro Focus IMS Option (OS/2)	
Micro Focus CICS Option (OS/2)	
Realia COBOL (OS/2)	
RealIMS (OS/2)	
RealCICS (OS/2)	
XDB DB2 Workbench (OS/2)	
APS/PC (MS-DOS, OS/2)	
TELON/PC (MS-DOS, OS/2)	
Bachman/Analyst (OS/2)	
EXCELERATOR (OS/2)	

4. *Floppy drives.* The high-density 3.5" floppy drive is now the standard. If the users have a significant number of old 5.25" floppy diskettes, an additional floppy drive of that type may be useful.

5. *RAM.* The minimum amount of RAM for most PC workstations is 4MB. That is enough for a language workbench and one associated DBMS or TP monitor emulator. A language workbench with two or more DBMS or TP monitor emulators or a code generator will usually need 8MB. Many upper CASE tools and OS/2-based workstations will need at least 16MB. For specific information consult with the technical support folks of your workstation software tool vendor. Do not rely on the "minimum requirements" list in the tool's documentation.
6. *Additional accessories.* Try to resist the temptation to add a lot of fancy options to your PC workstations, such as tape drives, FAX boards, or CD-ROM systems. Only get what is really needed! Remember, not only do these kinds of things drive up the cost of your offloaded development environment, they slow down your PC workstations.

SUMMARY

The workstation operating environment consists of the workstation operating system, its memory management facility, if separate from the operating system, and the workstation hardware. The "real" choices for the workstation operating system are MS-DOS, MS-Windows, and OS/2. Among MS-DOS's virtues are its simplicity, low price, vendor support, portability, versatility, and significant existing user base. Its major drawbacks, however, are its poor memory management and lack of a built-in multitasking facility. For MS-DOS to be a viable workstation operating system for an offloaded development environment, a supplemental memory management tool is almost always required. MS-Windows espouses many of the same virtues as MS-DOS and, in addition, provides a built-in multitasking facility and requires only a moderate amount of RAM. But because MS-Windows runs on top of MS-DOS, there can still be memory management problems. OS/2 2.0, with its easy memory management, powerful multitasking, and ability to support existing MS-DOS and Windows applications, appears to be the best choice, but more field testing will be needed to verify this. Hopefully, a definitive workstation operating system will emerge in the near future.

Because the choice of a workstation operating system dictates to a large degree the options for workstation hardware, decisions in this area are not too difficult to make. Since MS-DOS, MS-Windows, and

OS/2 are currently the only viable workstation operating systems, the only type of workstation hardware that can be used is the Intel 80X86 line. CPU, RAM, and hard disk requirements will vary depending on the software tools selected. Remember not to rely on the "minimum requirements" list in the documentation of the software tools. It is best to get the "real" story from the technical support folks of your software tool vendor.

7

Connecting It All Together

After selecting PC workstation software tools (compilers, debuggers, DBMS, and TP monitor emulators) and determining the workstation operating environment (operating system, memory management tools, and workstation hardware), the issue of connecting the workstations to each other and to the target mainframe production environment must be addressed. In addressing the issue of connectivity, an architecture, either 2-tier, 2.5-tier, or 3-tier, must be selected. Once the architecture has been selected, the local area network (LAN), server, and communication packages are chosen. Additionally, the decision on whether or not to use an offloaded development environment system integration package must be made. This chapter discusses each of these areas in depth, providing, to some extent, actual product descriptions.

OFFLOADED DEVELOPMENT ENVIRONMENT ARCHITECTURE

The important thing to remember when selecting an architecture for an offloaded development environment is that the objective is to give the users an environment that provides the functionality they expect (i.e., at least the functionality they were getting on the mainframe) in a cost effective way. The criteria for selecting an offloaded development environment architecture is presented here. A description of each architecture, including its strong and weak points, follows. Included in the list of architectures, for comparative purposes, are both the traditional single-tier and the channel-attached, single-tier development environments.

Selection Criteria for an Offloaded Development Environment Architecture

Here is a list of selection criteria for an offloaded development environment architecture, ranked by order of importance. Readers should, of course, tailor this list to suit their individual needs.

1. Essential Offloaded Development Environment Architecture Requirements
   a. Subsecond response time for most commands. In a number of studies (see Chapter 2) the availability of subsecond response time for trivial commands has been found to have a very favorable impact on user productivity.
   b. Reduced demand for expensive mainframe resources. Since many programmers within a mainframe-only development environment can easily incur charges of $1,000 per month, the reduction of these expenses is essential to keeping most commercial DP shops cost effective.
   c. Access to powerful PC-based development tools. Since most new development tools on the market today run on PC workstations, access to this environment is essential.
   d. Low operating costs. Since one of the main objectives of using an offloaded development environment is saving money by reducing mainframe usage, it is essential that operating costs associated with the offloaded development environment do not consume most of the savings.
   e. File sharing. Unless the users primarily work on one-man projects, the easy sharing of files (i.e., source code, test data files, designs, and specifications) is essential.
   f. Fast access to files. This requirement reflects the need for the offloaded development environment to be easy to use. Environments that have cumbersome procedures for accessing files or other resources will not be successful.
2. Important Offloaded Development Environment Architecture Requirements
   a. Short learning curve. Since some of the workstation software tools (e.g., language workbenches, CASE tools) will have long or fairly long learning curves, it is important that the basic supporting work environment be easy to learn and understand.

b. Access to multiple platforms. More and more DP shops are being asked to build client-server applications or to give existing applications GUI front ends (e.g., MS-Windows). Access to the platforms that support this kind of development (i.e., MS-DOS, OS/2, UNIX) is an important first step.

c. Access to multitasking facilities. Since most developers spend a considerable amount of time performing computer-intensive activities (compiles, certain dynamic tests, file transfers, e-mail), it is important to be able to run these tasks in the background while freeing up the foreground for human-intensive tasks, such as editing.

d. Easy to assemble and maintain. Since assembling an offloaded development environment usually means performing a systems integration job, it is important that the components be easy to install and maintain.

e. Makes use of existing facilities. Since most DP shops will already have existing wiring and communication facilities, it may be important that these facilities be reused in order to keep costs to a minimum.

f. Easy to customize. Given the variety of development tools in the marketplace, it is important to a DP shop's effectiveness to be able to add new and/or different tools as they are needed and to be able to customize the offloaded development environment to suit the user's changing needs.

g. File access security. As mentioned above, easy access to files is essential to a successful offloaded development environment. But in most DP shops it's not the only concern. Having files secured against unauthorized access is also important. This may be in the form of protected directories/libraries of files or individually protected files.

h. Formalized backup. As part of the need for file security a scheme for providing easy archiving and restoration of files on a daily basis is usually very important.

i. Source code control (library). As in the mainframe development environment, the effective control of source code is important in order to keep more than one developer from making changes to a particular file at any one time.

   j. Access to server-based tools. In order to keep costs to a minimum, it is often important to utilize server-based versions of software tools, rather than purchase multiple copies of the PC version of the same tool.

   k. Quick and cheap printing facilities. The ability to print files quickly and cheaply is usually of significant value to most application developers.

3. Nice to Have Offloaded Development Environment Architecture Options

   a. Access to e-mail. The usefulness of e-mail, from an office automation point of view, is generally acknowledged. See Chapter 2 for more information.

   b. Help facility. The offloaded development environment should have a context-sensitive help facility (i.e., when you are in the environment's file transfer facility and ask for help, you are presented with information about the file transfer facility). It is also good to have a help facility that contains the same information as the accompanying paper documentation. When this is the case, or when the help facility is extensive, the ability to do a mechanized search within the help facility can be very handy.

   c. Operating system access. It's useful to be able to access the raw operating system without having to leave the environment.

Offloaded Development Environment Architecture Options

We will now examine the various offloaded development environment architectures and compare each against the criteria above. Included in this list, for comparative purposes, is the traditional single-tier mainframe-based development environment and the channel-attached, single-tier mainframe-based development environment.

Traditional Single-Tier Mainframe Development Environment

The traditional single-tier mainframe development environment is made up of 3270 (dumb) terminals that access the mainframe via a mainframe network (Figure 7-1).

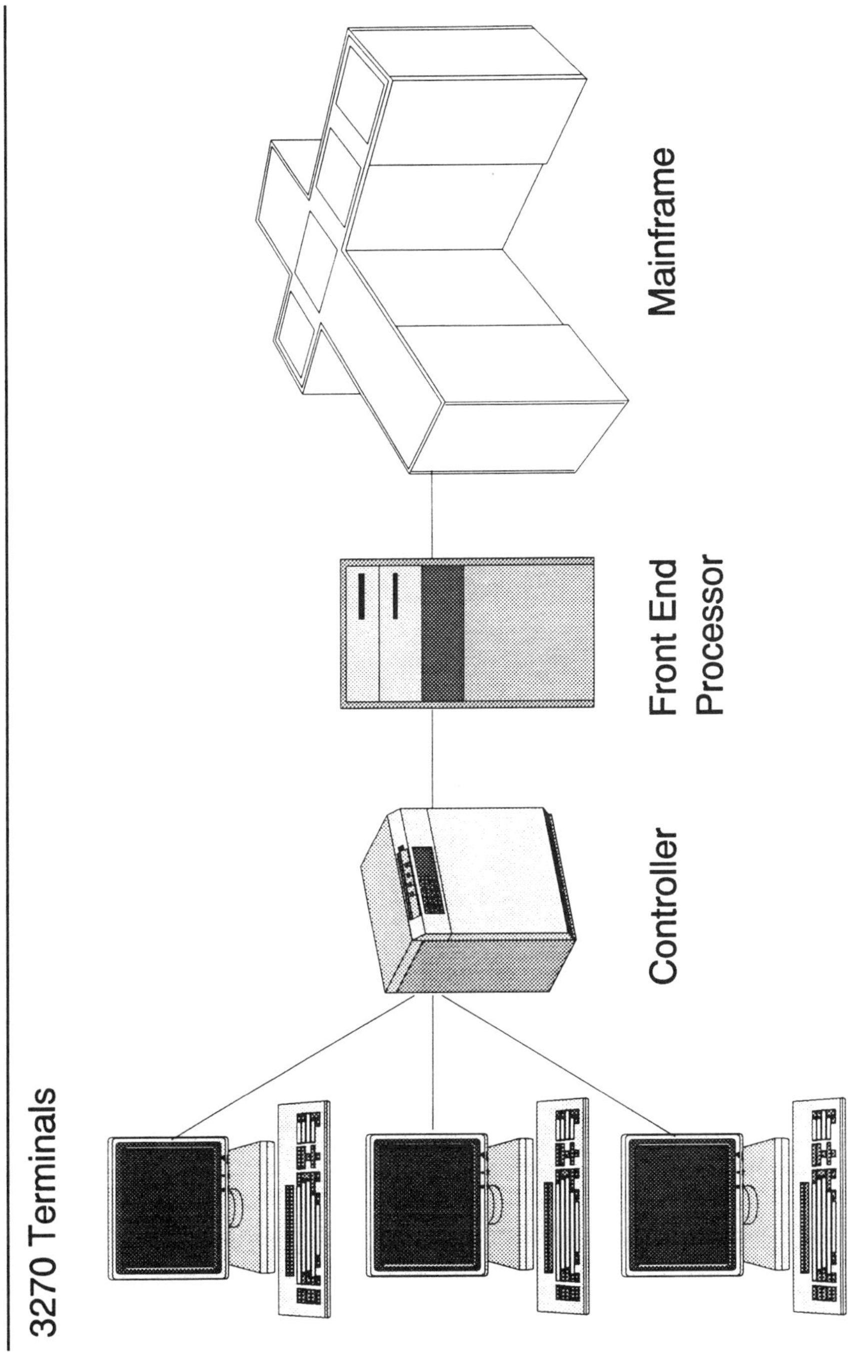

Figure 7-1. Traditional single-tier mainframe development environment.

Some of the advantages of the traditional single-tier environment include the following:

1. *Low operating costs.* All, or most, operating costs are built into the mainframe usage charges.
2. *File sharing.* Since all files are on a single computer, file sharing is usually easy.
3. *Fast access to files.* Since all files are on a single computer, file access is usually fast.
4. *No learning curve.* There is no learning curve because there is nothing new to learn.
5. *Access to multitasking facilities.* One thing mainframes are very good at is multitasking.
6. *File access security.* In addition to having easy access to files, files can easily be secured against unauthorized access.
7. *Formalized backup.* As part of the need for file security, daily backups are performed on most mainframes. These backups are generally stored off-site.
8. *Source code control (library).* If source code control is important to a mainframe's users, a package such as CA-PANVALET or CA-LIBRARIAN is usually installed.

The disadvantages of the traditional single-tier environment include the following:

1. *Multisecond response time for most commands.* Multisecond response time for trivial commands will usually decrease developer productivity by 30% or 40%. See Chapter 2 for more information.
2. *No access to powerful PC-based development tools.* Since most new development tools on the market today run on PC workstations, the lack of access to this environment is a serious detriment to the long-term competitiveness of most commercial DP shops.
3. *No access to multiple platforms.* More and more DP shops are being asked to build client-server applications or give existing applications GUI front ends (e.g., MS-Windows). The lack of access to the platforms that support this kind of development is detrimental to the long-term competitiveness of most commercial DP shops.

4. *Difficult to customize.* In most large organizations it usually takes six months to a year, sometimes longer, to get special or new system software added or upgraded on the mainframe.

5. *No quick and cheap printing facilities.* In many DP shops it can take up to several hours to get a print out. This can hinder the effectiveness of the application developers.

Channel-Attached, Single-Tier Mainframe Development Environment

The channel-attached, single-tier mainframe development environment is made up of 3270 terminals that directly access the mainframe (i.e., directly attached to a mainframe channel). Sometimes special channel-attached equipment is involved (Figure 7-2).

Some of the advantages of the channel-attached, single-tier environment include the following:

1. *Subsecond response time for most commands.* In a number of studies (see Chapter 2) the availability of subsecond response time for trivial commands has been found to have a very favorable impact on user productivity.

2. *Low operating costs.* All, or most, operating costs are built into the mainframe usage charges.

3. *File sharing.* Since all files are on a single computer, file sharing is usually easy.

4. *Fast access to files.* Since all files are on a single computer, file access is usually fast.

5. *No learning curve.* There is no learning curve because there is nothing new to learn.

6. *Access to multitasking facilities.* One thing mainframes are very good at is multitasking.

7. *File access security.* In addition to having easy access to files, files can easily be secured against unauthorized access.

8. *Formalized backup.* As part of the need for file security, daily backups are performed on most mainframes. These backups are generally stored off-site.

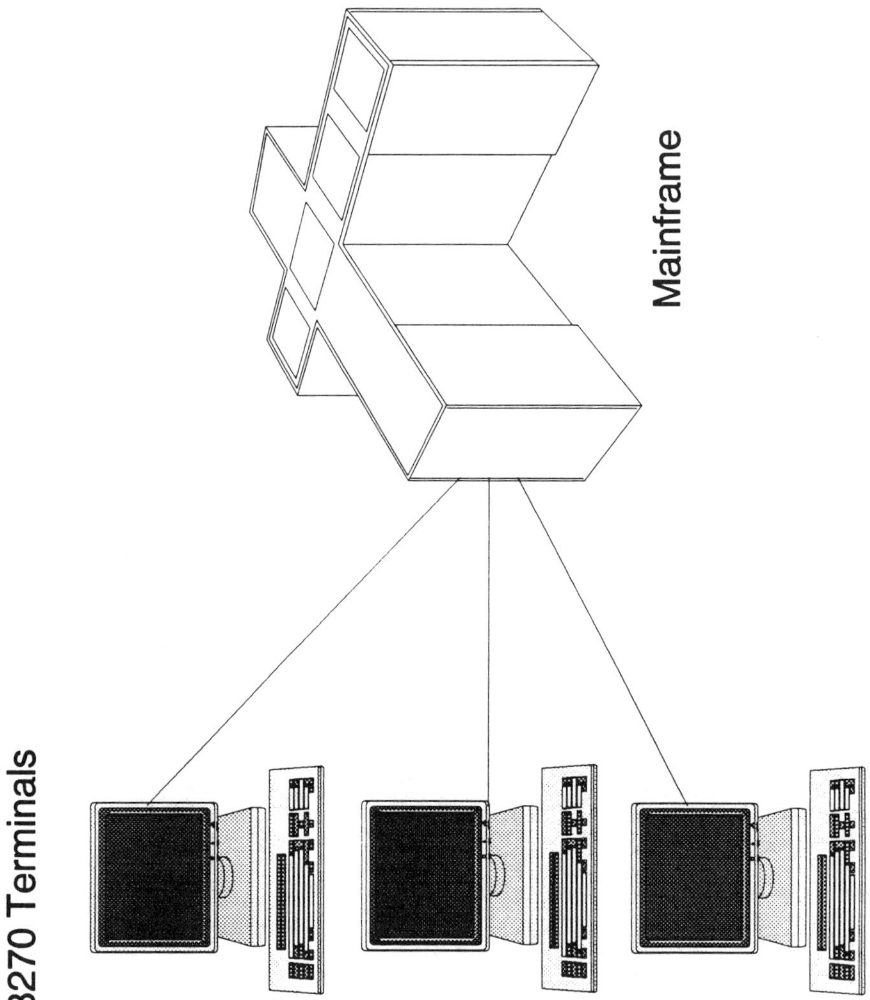

Figure 7-2. Channel-attached, single-tier mainframe development environment.

9. *Source code control (library).* If source code control is important to a mainframe's users, a package such as CA-PANVALET or CA-LIBRARIAN is usually installed.

The disadvantages of the channel-attached, single-tier environment include the following:

1. *High mainframe utilization rates.* Because more commands can be executed, the rate at which mainframe resources are used is usually 30% to 40% higher than in the traditional one-tier environment. This, in turn, may increase the need for more mainframes. However, per-project mainframe costs should not be higher. See Chapter 2 for more information.
2. *No access to powerful PC-based development tools.* Since most new development tools on the market today run on PC workstations, the lack of access to this environment is a serious detriment to the long-term competitiveness of most commercial DP shops.
3. *No access to multiple platforms.* More and more DP shops are being asked to build client-server applications or give existing applications GUI front ends (e.g., MS-Windows). The lack of access to the platforms that support this kind of development is detrimental to the long-term competitiveness of most commercial DP shops.
4. *Difficult to customize.* In most large organizations it usually takes six months to a year, sometimes longer, to get special or new system software added or upgraded on the mainframe.
5. *No quick and cheap printing facilities.* In many DP shops it can take up to several hours to get a print out. This can hinder the effectiveness of the application developers.

Two-Tier Development Environment

The two-tier development environment is just like the traditional single-tier environment except that PCs with emulation boards (e.g., IRMA, Attachmate) are used in place of 3270 terminals. In the two-tier environment no LANs are used to connect the PCs together (Figure 7-3).

Some of the advantages of the two-tier environment include the following:

1. *Subsecond response time for most commands.* In a number of studies (see Chapter 2) the availability of subsecond response

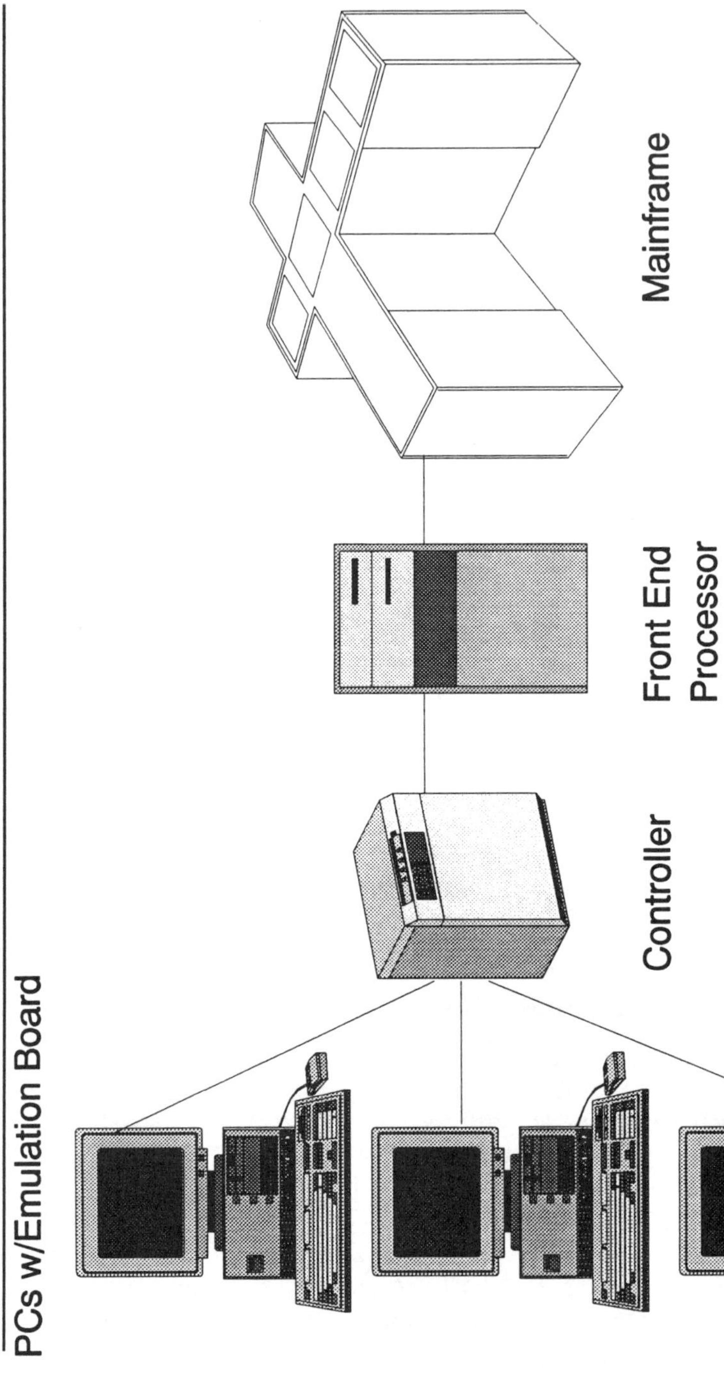

Figure 7-3. Two-tier development environment.

time for trivial commands has been found to have a very favorable impact on user productivity.

2. *Reduced demand for expensive mainframe resources.* Reductions in mainframe charges of 50% over the traditional single-tier environment are possible.

3. *Access to powerful PC-based development tools.* The two-tier environment can take advantage of many, but not all, of the powerful PC workstation software tools. Some tools (e.g., APS/PC) require a LAN to be effective.

4. *Short learning curve.* Because the environment is fairly simple (i.e., users are just substituting a PC with an IRMA board for a 3270 terminal), there is not much of a learning curve.

5. *Access to multiple platforms.* More and more DP shops are being asked to build client-server applications or give existing applications GUI front ends (e.g., MS-Windows). With the two-tier architecture, users get access to MS-DOS and/or OS/2.

6. *Access to multitasking facilities.* Since most developers spend a considerable amount of time performing computer-intensive activities (compiles, certain dynamic tests, file transfers, e-mail), it is important to be able to run these tasks in the background while freeing up the foreground for human-intensive tasks, such as editing. In some situations, developers in the two-tier environment may have some multitasking capability (e.g., Micro Focus Concurrent Processing Facility, OS/2, MS-Windows).

7. *Easy to assemble and maintain.* Since assembling an offloaded development environment usually means performing a systems integration job, it is important that the components be easy to assemble and maintain. Two-tier environments are generally easier to assemble and maintain than 2.5- or 3-tier environments because there are fewer components.

8. *Makes use of existing facilities.* Since most DP shops will already have existing wiring and communication facilities, it may be important that these facilities be reused in order to keep costs to a minimum. Two-tier environments make use of existing wiring and mainframe communication facilities.

9. *Operating system access.* It's useful to be able to access the raw operating system without having to leave the environment. Two-tier environments give users MS-DOS and/or OS/2 access, in addition to their usual mainframe access.

The disadvantages of the two-tier environment include the following:

1. *High operating costs.* Since each user is now responsible for the operation of a powerful PC, the cost of computer operations increases.

2. *Difficult file sharing.* Unless the users primarily work on one-person projects, it is essential that file sharing (i.e., source code, test data files, designs, and specifications) not only be available but also be easy to use. Under the two-tier environment, the only means of sharing files is at the mainframe or via floppy diskettes (i.e., "sneaker net").

3. *Slow access to files.* Since one main goal of implementing an offloaded development environment is increased programmer productivity, it is imperative to the success of the environment that file access not only be easy but also be quick. Offloaded development environments without access to shared directories of files and/or access to quick file transfer facilities are usually less effective than 2.5- or 3-tier environments.

4. *Difficult to customize.* Since there is little means of control over PC workstations in the two-tier environment, the addition of new software packages or upgrades to existing packages is usually done on an individual basis. As a result, system administration can become a nightmare due to the lack of an enforceable standard workstation configuration.

5. *Little file access security.* Standalone PC workstations tend to be easy targets for people looking for sensitive files because many of them are not password protected.

6. *No formalized backup.* Users of standalone PCs are usually told to back up their files on a regular basis. Unfortunately, this is usually a cumbersome activity that few users perform. The exception to this is those folks who have had hard disk problems in the past.

7. *No source code control (library).* In the mainframe development environment, the control of files (i.e., source code) is important in order to keep more than one user from making changes to a particular file at any one time. Unless two-tier environment developers make use of the mainframe's source code control facilities, which can be cumbersome for PC-based users, there is usually no source code control at all.

8. *No access to server-based tools.* In order to keep costs to a minimum, it is often important to utilize server-based versions of software tools, rather than purchase multiple copies of the PC version of the same tool. Two-tier environment users do not have this option.

9. *No quick and cheap printing facilities.* Because two-tier environment users cannot access LAN-based printers, they usually need to have dedicated printers in their cubicles. While this provides for quick turnaround of print requests, it is a costly solution (i.e., one printer for one or a few users).

2.5-Tier Development Environment

The 2.5-tier development environment is just like the two-tier environment except that the PC workstations are linked together via a LAN and have access to a server. The 2.5-tier environment differs from the three-tier environment in that emulation boards (e.g., IRMA, Attachmate) are still used in the 2.5-tier environment to access the mainframe (see Figure 7-4).

Some of the advantages of the 2.5-tier environment include the following:

1. *Subsecond response time for most commands.* In a number of studies (see Chapter 2) the availability of subsecond response time for trivial commands has been found to have a very favorable impact on user productivity.

2. *Reduced demand for expensive mainframe resources.* Reductions in mainframe charges of 75% over the traditional single-tier environment are possible.

3. *Access to powerful PC-based development tools.* The 2.5-tier environment can take advantage of powerful PC workstation software tools.

4. *Access to multiple platforms.* More and more DP shops are being asked to build client-server applications or give existing applications GUI front ends (e.g., MS-Windows). With the 2.5-tier architecture, users get access to MS-DOS, OS/2, and/or UNIX.

5. *Access to multitasking facilities.* Since most developers spend a considerable amount of time performing computer-intensive

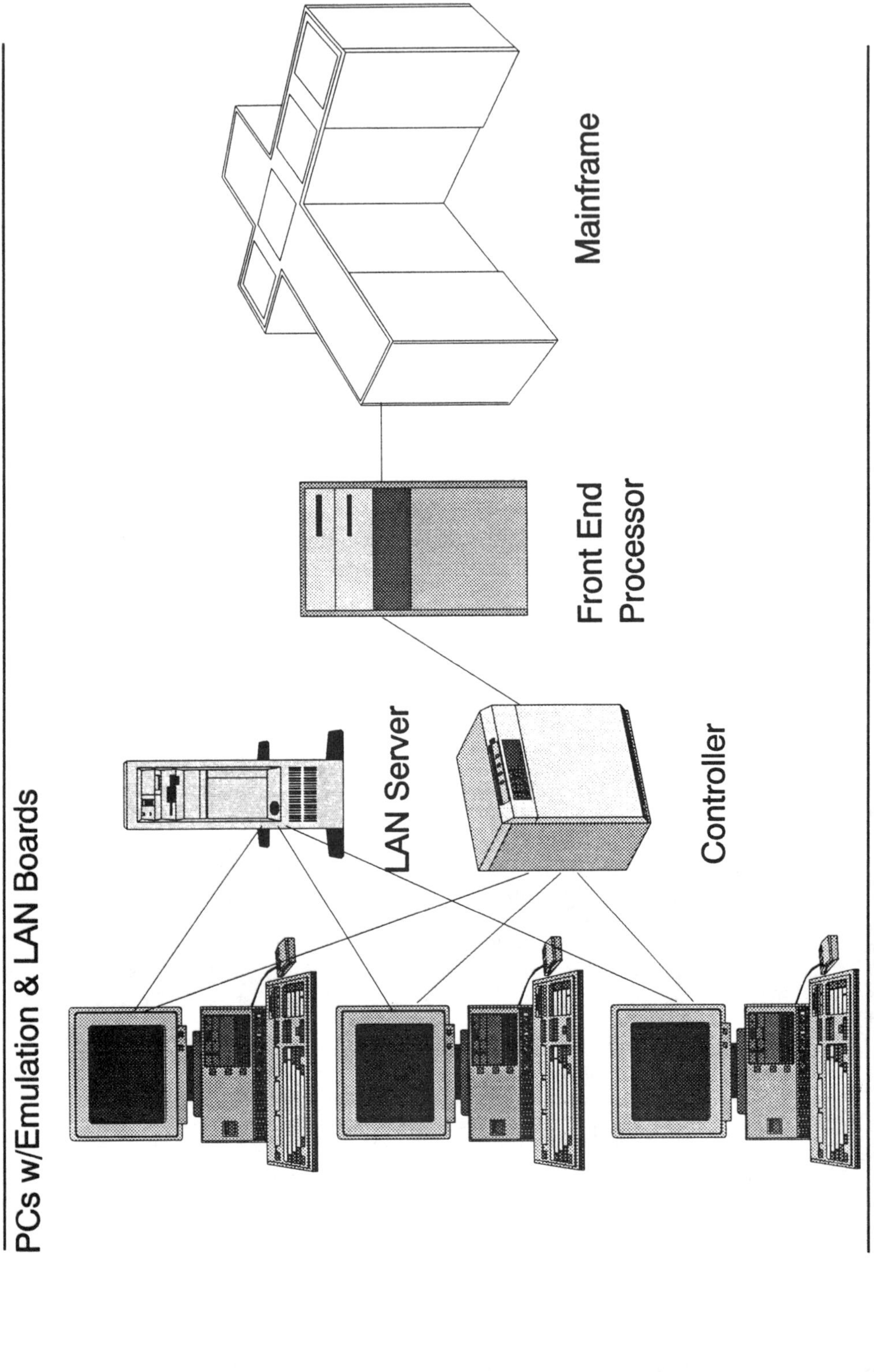

Figure 7-4 2.5-tier development environment

activities (compiles, certain dynamic tests, file transfers, e-mail), it is important to be able to run these tasks in the background while freeing up the foreground for human-intensive tasks, such as editing. The 2.5-tier environment gives users the option of moving certain background processing to the LAN server.

6. *Operating system access.* It's useful to be able to access the raw operating system without having to leave the environment. The 2.5-tier environments give users MS-DOS, OS/2, and/or UNIX access, in addition to their usual mainframe access.

The disadvantages of the 2.5-tier environment include the following:

1. *Long learning curve.* Considering that some of the workstation software tools (e.g., language workbenches, CASE tools) will have long or fairly long learning curves, it is important for the basic supporting work environment to be simple to learn and understand. Environments with more than two tiers generally require some training. This is especially the case when the extra tier has significant functionality.
2. *Inefficient use of multitasking facilities.* The major problem found in most 2.5-tier environments is that these environments do not make good use of the server's capabilities. For example, if a server is only used to share printers and deliver e-mail, but not handle file transfers or library management, it is probably being underutilized.
3. *May not be simple to assemble and maintain.* Offloaded development environments with more than two tiers require a certain amount of systems integration and therefore may not be easy to assemble and maintain.
4. *Requires extra facilities.* Since 2.5-tier environments require that a LAN be added in addition to the existing mainframe network, a substantial amount of extra wiring will be required. This contrasts with the 3-tier environment that can usually reuse the existing links (i.e., 2.5-tier environments have at least two communication links, a 3270 link and a LAN link, emanating from each PC workstation, whereas in 3-tier environments the PC workstations only have one communication link, a LAN link).

Three-Tier Development Environment

The three-tier development environment is different from the environments previously discussed in that the PC workstations are not directly linked to the mainframe network. The only links the PC workstations have are LAN links to a server. The server, in turn, is linked to all the facilities the offloaded development environment users need, such as 3270 mainframe access, RJE mainframe access, e-mail, and other servers (Figure 7-5).

Some of the advantages of the three-tier environment include:

1. *Subsecond response time for most commands.* In a number of studies (see Chapter 2) the availability of subsecond response time for trivial commands has been found to have a very favorable impact on user productivity.
2. *Reduced demand for expensive mainframe resources.* Reductions in mainframe charges of 85% over the traditional single-tier environment are possible.
3. *Access to powerful PC-based development tools.* The three-tier environment can take advantage of powerful PC workstation software tools.
4. *Access to multiple platforms.* More and more DP shops are being asked to build client-server applications or give existing applications GUI front ends (e.g., MS-Windows). With three-tier development, users get access to MS-DOS, OS/2, and/or UNIX.
5. *Access to multitasking facilities.* Since most developers spend a considerable amount of time performing computer-intensive activities (compiles, certain dynamic tests, file transfers, e-mail), it is important to be able to run these tasks in the background while freeing up the foreground for human-intensive tasks, such as editing. The three-tier environment usually gives users the option of moving certain background processing to the LAN server. A characteristic of servers in a three-tier environment is that they are used for more than just printer access and file sharing.
6. *Operating system access.* It's useful to be able to access the raw operating system without having to leave the environment. Three-tier environments give users MS-DOS, OS/2, and/or UNIX access, in addition to their usual mainframe access.
7. *Makes use of existing facilities.* Since existing DP shops will already have existing wiring and communication facilities, it may be important that these facilities be reused in order to keep costs to a minimum. Three-tier environments can usually make use of existing wiring and mainframe communication facilities.

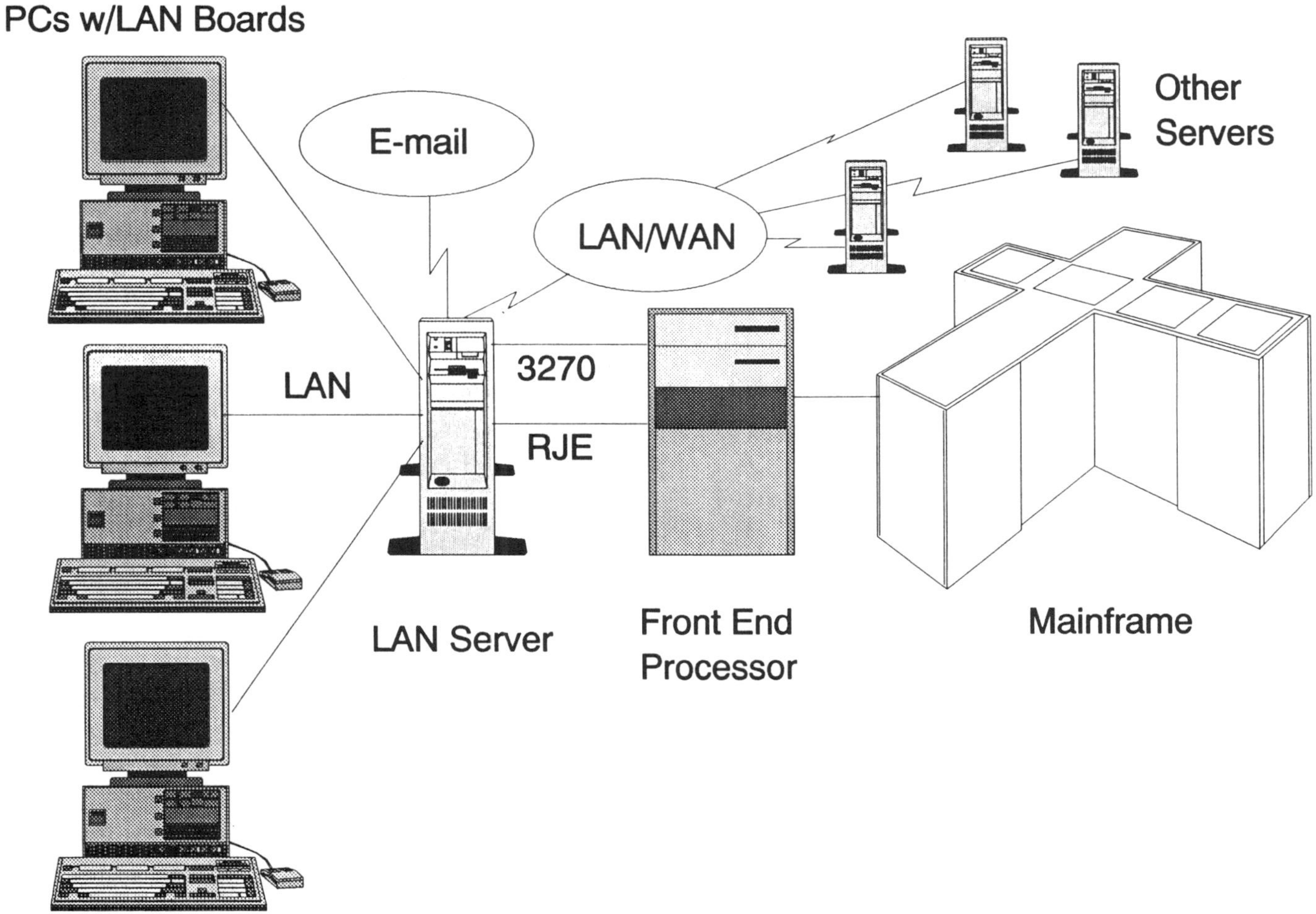

Figure 7-5. Three-tier development environment.

The disadvantages of the three-tier environment include the following:

1. *Long learning curve.* Considering that some of the workstation software tools (e.g., language workbenches, CASE tools) will have long or fairly long learning curves, it is important for the basic supporting work environment to be simple to learn and understand. Environments with more than two tiers generally require some training. This is especially the case when the extra tier has significant functionality.

2. *May not be simple to assemble and maintain.* Offloaded development environments with more than two tiers require a certain amount of systems integration and therefore may not be easy to assemble and maintain.

Conclusion

For almost all DP shops there are only two viable architectures from which to choose, two-tier or three-tier. The two-tier environment should be selected by the following:

1. *Small DP shops.* That is, shops with less than 10 developers that do not expect to grow. This is because there is a question of economies of scale. The costs of a LAN, server, and support may be too high to justify the use of more complex architectures.

2. *DP shops that handle mostly one-person projects.* Since shops that handle mostly one-person projects have little need for significant communication among developers (i.e., file sharing, source code control, e-mail), a two-tier environment may be more appropriate than a three-tier environment.

Three-tier environments should be selected by all other DP shops. Three-tier environments are almost always more powerful and cost effective than 2.5-tier environments because they make more efficient use of the LAN, server, and PC workstations for the following reasons:

1. The 2.5-tier environments typically offer only print serving and e-mail at the server level.

2. Servers in three-tier environments usually emulate 3270 controller functions, eliminating the need for 3270 controllers and PC-based emulation boards (e.g., IRMA, Attachmate).

3. Three-tier environments usually process file transfers as background processes on servers as opposed to 2.5-tier environments that process transfers as foreground processes on PC workstations. Using servers for file transfers is much more efficient because the server can make use of the RJE facilities, which are intended for file transfers, whereas PC workstations are usually restricted to 3270 communications, which are intended for interactive traffic.
4. Three-tier environments are likely to have server-based source code libraries, while 2.5-tier environments usually will not.

LOCAL AREA NETWORK (LAN)/SERVER HARDWARE AND SOFTWARE SELECTION

In this section we will examine LAN hardware and software, together with server hardware and software. This is done because the use of certain LAN hardware and software packages in many cases implies the use of certain combinations of server hardware and software (e.g., AT&T StarGROUP LAN Manager requires a server running under UNIX).

However, two important things should be kept in mind when putting together the supporting network for an offloaded development environment. The first is that the mixing and matching of components to some degree is usually possible. The other is that, in some situations, whole environments can be purchased from one vendor. Deciding between the two scenarios is usually a matter of choosing between lower prices and better support. Procuring hardware components at commodity prices is often an attractive option, but receiving comprehensive offloaded development environment support can be equally important. What is finally selected will depend on the technical, financial, political, and cultural needs and resources of the procuring organization.

Unlike some other parts of this book, this section will not devote a lot of space to examining products in depth. This is because there are too many products — especially hardware — on the market and they are constantly changing. Also, the latest information can usually be obtained from a variety of technical journals and magazines. Instead, the emphasis of this section will be on selection criteria for LAN/server hardware and software and their relative importance in the construction of an effective offloaded development environment. A brief discussion of the major products available can be found at the end of the section.

Selection Criteria for Offloaded Development Environment LAN/Server Hardware and Software

A list of selection criteria for offloaded development environment LAN/server hardware and software follows. It is ranked by order of importance and, as previously suggested, readers should reorder this list to suit their individual needs. It also should be noted that some selection criteria may conflict with other selection criteria. Users will need to balance these differences to suit their individual situations.

1. Essential Offloaded Development Environment LAN/Server Hardware and Software Requirements

   a. Supports selected architecture. For most organizations this means that the LAN/server hardware and software should support the three-tier architecture as previously described.

   b. Supports selected PC operating systems and software tools. The selected LAN software should support MS-DOS and/or OS/2. Compatibility with selected software tools (compiler, debugger, code generator, upper CASE tool) is also essential (e.g., both the selected LAN software and software tools fit in the available memory of the PC workstation).

   c. Physical environment conforms to LAN distance limitations. The selected LAN hardware must be able to handle the physical environment (e.g., the physical position of the users cannot exceed the distance limitations of the LAN hardware).

   d. Be easy to use and expand. The LAN operating system commands that the users invoke to link to resources must be easy to use. The LAN/server hardware and software should be easily expanded to accommodate minor changes, such as the addition of a few users (i.e., the server should not have to be reconfigured and/or rebooted for small changes).

   e. Offers adequate vendor support. As the LAN environment will be the user's link to the world, any down time is a major problem. Competent 24-hour telephone support for the important LAN/server hardware and software components should be available.

   f. Can coexist with servers and workstations running different versions of the LAN operating system. If your organization will have multiple LANs, they will usually need to be linked together eventually. When this happens, it is very unlikely that all the LANs will be running the same version of the LAN operating system or that all the LANs will be able to upgrade simultaneously. Therefore it is very important that new versions of the LAN operating system be downward compatible with earlier versions.

g. LAN/server operating system is multitasking. Non-multitasking MS-DOS-based servers are almost never acceptable in an offloaded development environment. Multitasking LAN operating systems are needed because only they can supply services to a large number of nodes/users and handle multiple gigabytes of data.

h. Supports e-mail access. E-mail is an essential office automation feature of offloaded development environments. E-mail services should be able to handle binary files. Access to e-mail services, such as ATTMail, AT&T Easylink, or MCIMail may also be desirable.

i. Requires small amounts of RAM on MS-DOS PC workstations. If MS-DOS workstations will be used, the LAN operating system should not require large amounts (75K or more) of precious low DOS memory. Excessive demands for such memory may prevent the use of some software tools.

j. Server can use an uninterruptable power supply (UPS). Because servers are usually the repository for important files, the server should have a UPS in case of a power outage. This will allow the server to be brought down gracefully in the event of an outage, without any files being damaged.

2. Important Offloaded Development Environment LAN/Server Hardware and Software Requirements

    a. Moderate cost. For those on tight budgets, the ability to use commodity-priced LAN hardware and an inexpensive LAN operating system (less than $4,000) may be important.

    b. Adequate administrative tools for LAN operating system. All multitasking LAN operating systems should have administrative tools, such as error/status logs, network error reports, and dynamic activity monitors that can track open files, logged on users, and CPU load factors.

c. High-speed backup of PC workstations. Since backing up important PC workstation files is an essential function of the LAN, being able to perform this task at high speeds is important.

d. Supports multiple drive on servers. The server should be able to support multiple drives depending on the space requirements of the users. Server hard disk support in the ratio of 100 MB per user should be possible, although a more common figure is 20MB to 40MB per user.

e. Environment allows easy connectability to other systems. Most successful LANs eventually need to be connected to other LANs. Therefore, adherence to standards and open systems (i.e., low use of proprietary software, hardware, wiring/cabling, and signaling schemes) is important.

f. Provides an acceptable division of services at the server level. The ability to have a single server offer file, print, and communication services is usually important to the economic viability of the offloaded development environment. However, the ability to distribute these services across multiple servers may also be important in certain situations.

g. Large RAM addressability for server. In order to expand the server to meet all possible user needs, an offloaded development environment server should be able to address a large amount of RAM (at least 64MB).

h. Provides adequate printer support. An offloaded development environment LAN should be able to support multiple printers (at least one per five users). These printers should be located close to the users' desks.

i. Uses existing hardware knowledge base. If a DP shop has spare computers that can function as servers, or has a large amount of knowledge about a particular line or type of computer, a lot of time and training can be saved if the selection of the LAN environment coincides with this previous experience.

j. Provides adequate security. It is best if access to server-based files and directories is controlled by passwords, group membership, and time of access. Access to resources, such as printers, should also be controllable. See Chapter 9 for more information.

k. Programmable server. Some LAN operating systems work on top of a server operating system (e.g., AT&T StarGROUP LAN Manager works on top of UNIX System V), while other LAN operating systems "take over" the whole server (e.g., Novell NetWare). Adding additional programs to servers running regular operating systems is usually easier and safer than adding programs to servers that have been completely taken over by a LAN operating system (e.g., if a UNIX package fails, it is generally less likely to crash the LAN than if a Novell Loadable Module (NLM) that is directly accessing NetWare fails).

l. Open server hardware versus proprietary server hardware. Using open (i.e., nonproprietary) hardware is important in keeping costs down and vendors responsive to customer needs. For example, you can buy a 486 computer from a wide variety of sources and get a wide range of features and prices. However, you can only buy a VAX from Digital and with less variety of features and prices.

m. Open LAN operating system versus proprietary LAN operating system. Using proprietary LAN operating systems adds to the cost of an offloaded development environment, because they are only available from a single source and that source controls their pricing. Usually buyers want the ability to choose from multiple vendors when it comes time to expand or upgrade their environment. Using a UNIX or OS/2-based LAN operating system, such as LAN Manager, gives the user much more flexibility when expanding or upgrading than a LAN operating system like NetWare.

n. Environment components are widely used. Just as selecting a brand name PC, such as IBM, COMPAQ, AST, or AT&T, makes it easier to get support from software tool vendors (see Chapter 6), selecting widely used LAN/server hardware and software improves the quality of vendor support you will receive. In addition to support, the use of popular LAN/server components will usually give buyers access to a wider variety of tool options.

3. Nice to Have Offloaded Development Environment LAN/Server Hardware and Software Requirements

   a. High-speed network. Access to high-speed LANs (10Mb/second or 16Mb/second) is nice to have but not essential for most offloaded development environments. If a proposed site is already wired for "slow" LAN service (1Mb/second to 4Mb/second), there is usually no need to replace it. This is because offloaded development environments almost never need access to large amounts of data. They mostly deal in source code and test data files. However, if a site is not wired at all for LAN service, installing a 10Mb/second or 16Mb/second LAN is the usual course, because they only cost a little more than the slow LANs.

b. LAN operating system supports use of multiprocessor servers. Offloaded development environments are usually not very CPU intensive at the server level. Therefore, having a LAN operating system that can function on multiprocessor servers is, at best, a nice to have option.

c. Server supports use of UPS with unattended shut-down capability. Some uninterruptable power supplies (UPS) have the ability to automatically bring down a server without human intervention. This is important for some types of applications but usually not for offloaded development environments. This is because offloaded development environments require a local administrator to monitor the environment and assist the users. When there is a power problem, it is very easy for the administrator to bring down the server manually.

d. LAN operating system can share PC-based printers. If space is tight, printers may be located in the work areas of individual users, rather than in a common area. Therefore it is useful if the LAN operating system can support network access to printers attached to PC workstations of individual users.

e. Supports large number of users. Having a LAN environment that can support large numbers of users (100+ users per server) is usually not needed for most offloaded development environments. This is because it is usually not a good idea to have more than 50 users per server or local administrator.

f. High-speed server CPU. Just as it is unnecessary for an offloaded development environment server to have multiple processors, it is not very important for the server to be of exceptional power (i.e., special RISC chip). For most offloaded development environments, a moderately priced 386- or 486-based server will do nicely.

g. Moderate RAM requirement for server. The ability to use the selected LAN operating system effectively, without having to load the server with large amounts of RAM (more than 16MB), may be of some importance.

Offloaded Development Environment LAN/Server Hardware and Software Options

The LAN operating systems discussed in this section generally meet all the essential requirements and most of the important requirements presented above. The following list does not include all the possible LAN operating systems, but it does cover all the different types of LANs (e.g., proprietary hardware support versus open hardware support, UNIX-based versus OS/2-based versus proprietary-based operating system, LAN Manager versus non-LAN Manager). As stated before, your requirements may differ from the above.

LAN Operating Systems and Supporting LAN Hardware (Except Server)

1. *Novell NetWare.* Novell NetWare is by far the most popular LAN operating system. Support and knowledge of NetWare are available from many sources. NetWare operates as its own proprietary operating system on the server, which means that it does not run under OS/2 or UNIX. (Note: Recently Novell issued Portable NetWare to allow other vendors to implement NetWare in other environments, such as UNIX and OS/2.) Because NetWare takes over the whole server, it operates at very high speeds when compared with other LAN operating systems. NetWare supports various types of LAN hardware, including Token Ring and 3Com Etherlink.
2. *AT&T StarGROUP LAN Manager.* AT&T's StarGROUP LAN Manager supports Microsoft's LAN Manager specification. It operates under UNIX on the server and provides OS/2 and MS-DOS client support. Because it uses UNIX on the server, it offers a good environment for running other supporting offloaded development environment utilities. However, because it runs under a sophisticated operating system (i.e., UNIX), it is slower than proprietary systems such as NetWare. StarGROUP supports various types of LAN hardware including Token Ring, 3Com Etherlink, and StarLAN.
3. *3+Open LAN Manager.* 3Com's 3+Open LAN Manager supports Microsoft's LAN Manager specification. It operates under OS/2

on the server and provides OS/2 and MS-DOS client support. Because it runs under a relatively sophisticated operating system (i.e., OS/2), it is slower than proprietary systems such as NetWare. 3+Open supports various types of LAN hardware including Token Ring and 3Com Etherlink.

4. *Banyan VINES.* Banyan's VINES is a fairly popular proprietary LAN operating system that operates under UNIX on the server and provides MS-DOS client support. Because it uses UNIX on the server, it also offers a good environment for running other supporting offloaded development environment utilities. However, because it runs under a sophisticated operating system (i.e., UNIX), it is slower than other proprietary systems, such as NetWare. VINES supports various types of LAN hardware including Token Ring and StarLAN.

5. *Digital's VMS Services for PCs.* Digital's VMS Services for PCs is a proprietary LAN operating system that runs on VAX hardware and provides MS-DOS and OS/2 client support. Because it runs under VMS on the server, it offers a good environment for running other supporting offloaded development environment utilities. However, as with UNIX-based LAN operating systems, Digital's product is slow when compared with a proprietary system such as NetWare. VMS Services for PCs provides DP shops that have significant experience with IBM and DEC an easy way to access the benefits of offloaded development.

Server Hardware

When it comes to selecting a particular server, almost any 80386-based server (33MHz or better) or 80486-based server will do, provided it is on the list of approved servers for the selected LAN operating system. If the vendor of the LAN operating system also sells servers it may be wise to get both from the one vendor. This usually reduces the chance of compatibility problems and eliminates a lot of potential finger pointing by vendor support groups when problems arise.

There are more features of importance when selecting an offloaded development environment server.

1. *Large amounts of addressable RAM.* The minimum should be 32MB. The optimum would be at least 64MB.

2. *Large amounts of addressable hard disk space.* Several gigabytes is very desirable.

3. *High-speed I/O bus.* A 32-bit bus is essential (i.e., no 386/SX-based servers).

SELECTION OF MAINFRAME COMMUNICATION METHODS AND FACILITIES

When constructing an offloaded development environment, the question of how to best link the offloaded development environment and the mainframe needs to be addressed. The link is important because reliable file transfer between the offloaded development environment and the target mainframe is essential. Also, offloaded development environment users need online access to the mainframe in order to perform final integration and systems testing of their applications.

However, a problem arises because there are not many good ways to tie a mainframe to an offloaded development environment server or PC workstation. In fact, there are not many not-so-good ways to tie the two together. This is because the world of mainframe connectivity is a lot different from the world of server and PC workstation connectivity. Thousands of terminals, printers, and other devices are linked to a mainframe via networks of front end processors (FEPs) and controllers. All this is very foreign to servers and PC workstations.

The two methods used to give offloaded development environments mainframe access (i.e., online and/or file transfer access), are 3270 (i.e., 3278 for monochrome display terminals or 3279 for color display terminals) and RJE (Remote Job Entry). Because these methods were built for 3270 (dumb) terminals and RJE devices, they cannot be used to communicate with servers or PC workstations without modifications. Therefore, to make all this work the server and PC workstations will need to appear to the mainframe as 3270 terminals, RJE printers, RJE punches, RJE readers, and/or RJE consoles. This is done with emulation hardware and software packages that will be described below. It should be noted that another method of communication, LU 6.2, may be useful to users interested in building cooperative processing applications that need peer to peer communications. This area, however, is beyond the scope of this book.

There are two places where 3270 and RJE emulation can be performed, the PC workstation level and the server level. In the following paragraphs we will examine the topologies used at both levels and their respective strengths and weaknesses.

PC-Based Emulation

We will now examine the options available for PC-based 3270 emulation and discuss the reasons for selecting or not selecting it. PC-based RJE emulation will not be addressed as it is not a viable option for an offloaded development environment. (It would be too expensive for a group of offloaded development environment users to each have their own RJE link.)

PC workstations can emulate 3270 terminals and devices in several ways. The most popular methods include the following:

1. *3270 emulation hardware and software.* In Figure 7-6, a PC workstation with an emulation board and software connects to a local controller (e.g., IBM 3274/6, AT&T 6500). The controller is then connected to a local or remote FEP (front end processor) which is connected to a mainframe. Standard communication protocols (e.g., SNA/SDLC, BSC) are used between the PC workstation and the controller. The only change made in the communication facilities is that the controller usually needs to be informed that the 3270 device at the end of the line is a PC workstation with an emulation board and not a standard 3270 terminal.
2. *Protocol converters.* In Figure 7-7, a PC workstation is connected via its serial port to a protocol converter box. The protocol converter changes the PC workstation's asynchronous signals into SDLC or BSC signals that the mainframe can understand. The converter, in turn, is connected to a local or remote FEP (front end processor) which is connected to a mainframe. Some protocol converter boxes can handle multiple PC workstations, while some single-line converters reside on installable PC boards.
3. *3274/6 emulation hardware and software.* In Figure 7-8, a PC workstation with an emulation board and software connects to a local or remote FEP which is connected to a mainframe. The difference between this option and the first two is that the PC workstation emulates a controller rather than a 3270 terminal. Since most controllers and controller emulators can support 32 mainframe links, this option is usually more than is needed by most offloaded development environment users.

Whether or not to use PC-based 3270 emulation depends primarily on what kind of architecture has been selected. In situations where an offloaded development environment is using a 2- or 2.5-tier architecture, the best PC workstation 3270 emulation configuration for

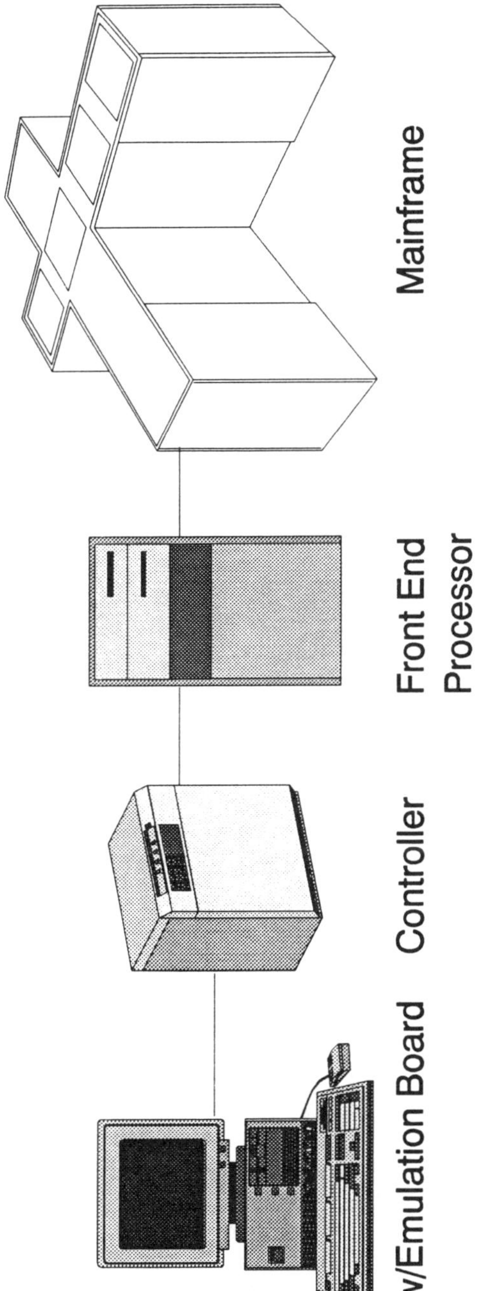

Figure 7-6. 3270 emulation.

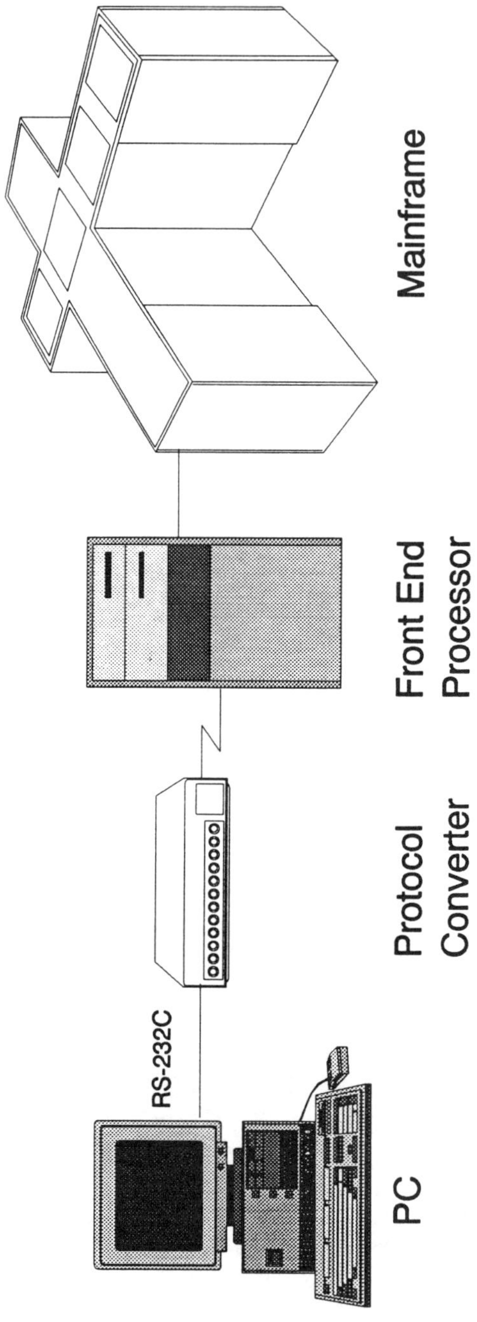

Figure 7-7. 3270 emulation with protocol converter.

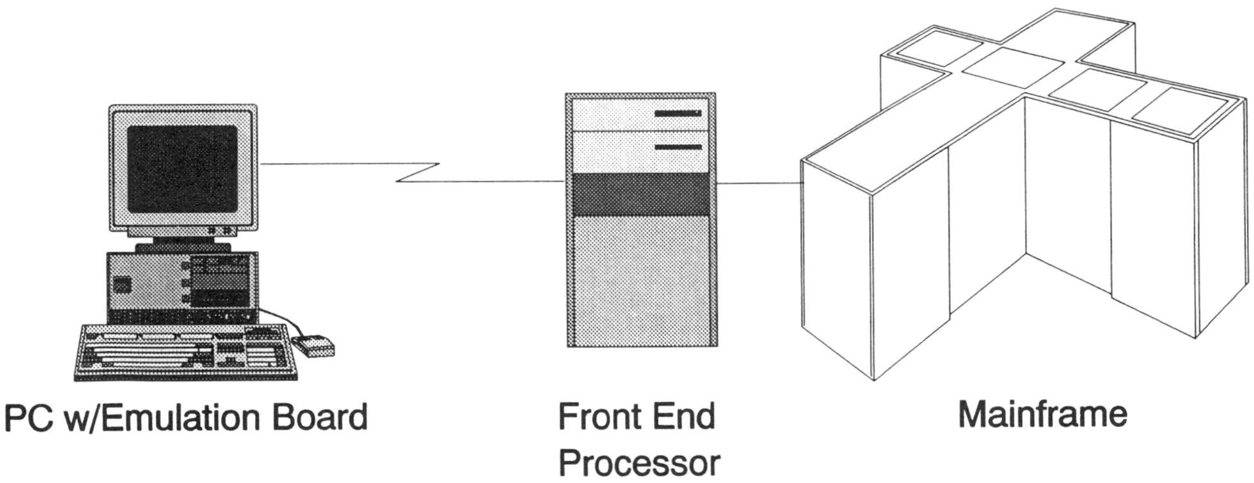

Figure 7-8. 3274/6 controller emulation.

almost all situations is that pictured in Figure 7-6 and described in item 1 above. This option provides for terminal emulation that is usually as fast as a real 3270 terminal and is very easy to set up. In medium- to large-scale environments, however, it is usually not as economical as the server-based 3270 emulation used in 3-tier architectures. This is because server-based emulation normally requires only one emulation board and software package, whereas PC-based 3270 emulation requires emulation hardware and software for each user.

File transfer using PC-based 3270 emulation packages is not recommended unless there are very few offloaded development environment users or the file transfers are performed very infrequently. This is because most 3270-based file transfer solutions are slow, cumbersome to use, and degrade response time for other 3270 users doing interactive work. Thus, most offloaded development environments should avoid using PC-based 3270 emulation and use server-based 3270 emulation instead.

Server-Based Emulation

In this section we will examine the options available for server-based 3270 and RJE emulation. A discussion of the reasons for selecting or not selecting certain options follows.

Servers usually emulate 3270 terminals and devices by emulating the controllers (e.g., IBM 3274/6, AT&T 6500) that the terminals and devices talk to. This emulation is normally accomplished using LAN gateway packages (i.e., controller emulation hardware and software that knows about the LAN). For the most part, the 3270 emulation packages are used primarily for online access to the mainframe, but some packages include file transfer facilities.

Servers can also communicate with mainframes via RJE. In this situation the server, with the help of RJE emulation hardware and software, emulates RJE devices such as printers, punches, readers, and consoles. RJE emulation packages are used for high-speed, low-impact file transfers between the server and mainframe. The two main configurations for server-based 3270 and RJE communications are the following:

1. *Centralized server-based emulation processing.* In Figure 7-9, a server with an emulation board and software connects to a local or remote FEP which is connected to a mainframe. PC workstations access the server's emulation facilities via the LAN. The

number of active links between the server and FEP may be as small as one (i.e., the 3270 and RJE emulation software share an emulation board — not recommended) or as many as three or four (i.e., one RJE link and several 3270 links). Having multiple 3270 links may be useful in situations where large numbers of users will need simultaneous access (e.g., to do mainframe-based stress testing) or when the practical capacity of a single emulation link is exceeded (i.e., nearly all controller emulation packages claim to be able to handle 32 simultaneous sessions, but the useful limit may be much lower). Figure 7-9 shows a server with one RJE and one 3270 link.

2 *Decentralized server-based emulation processing.* In Figure 7-10, multiple servers with emulation boards and software connect to a local or remote FEP which is connected to a mainframe. PC workstations access the servers' emulation facilities via the LAN. As with the centralized server emulation architecture, the number of active links between the servers and FEP may be as small as one or as many as three or four (see the above configuration description for more information on this aspect). Having multiple servers sometimes improves the processing speed of the emulation facilities; this is especially important for real time processing. It can also help simplify the operation of the offloaded development environment, as local administrators will not have to worry about various server-based processes interfering with each other. Figure 7-10 shows two servers supporting an offloaded development environment. One server handles 3270 online mainframe access, while the other handles file serving (i.e., file sharing and file transfers) and printing.

The use of server-based 3270 emulation should be the standard for all but the smallest offloaded development environments. The main reason for this is low cost when compared with 3270 terminals or PC workstations using 3270 emulation packages. One or two server-based communications boards and an emulation program are a lot cheaper than a controller and a load of terminals or a controller and a load of emulation boards and software packages for PC workstations. This holds true even if dedicated 3270 server(s) are used. However, there are drawbacks to server-based 3270 emulation. Server-based packages are usually much more difficult to set up than PC-based packages. This sometimes becomes evident when local administrators ask communication technicians to attach their servers to mainframe FEPs. Another drawback is the speed of some server-based 3270 emulation

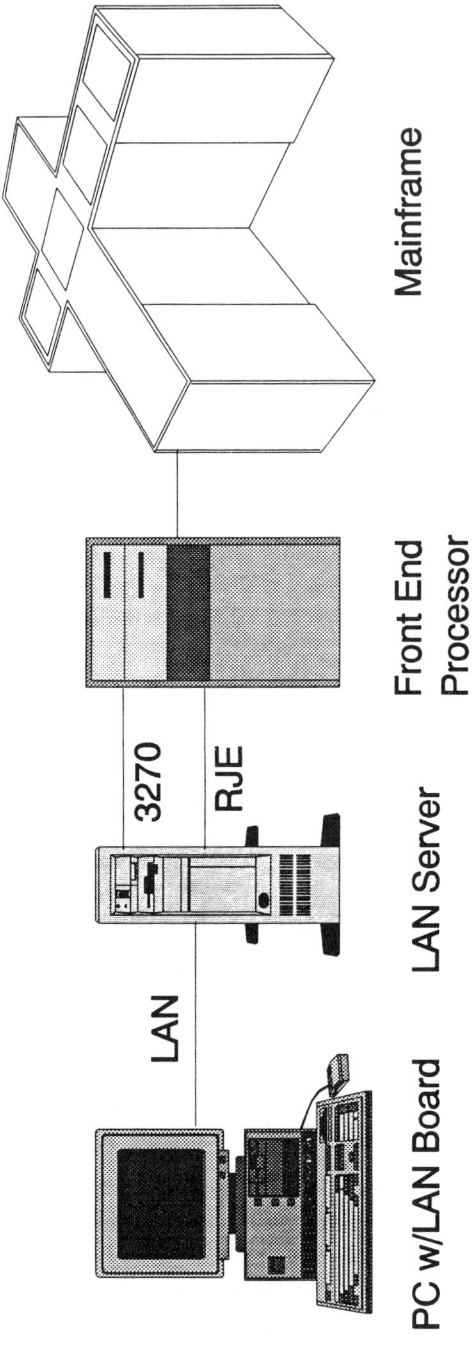

Figure 7-9. Centralized server-based emulation.

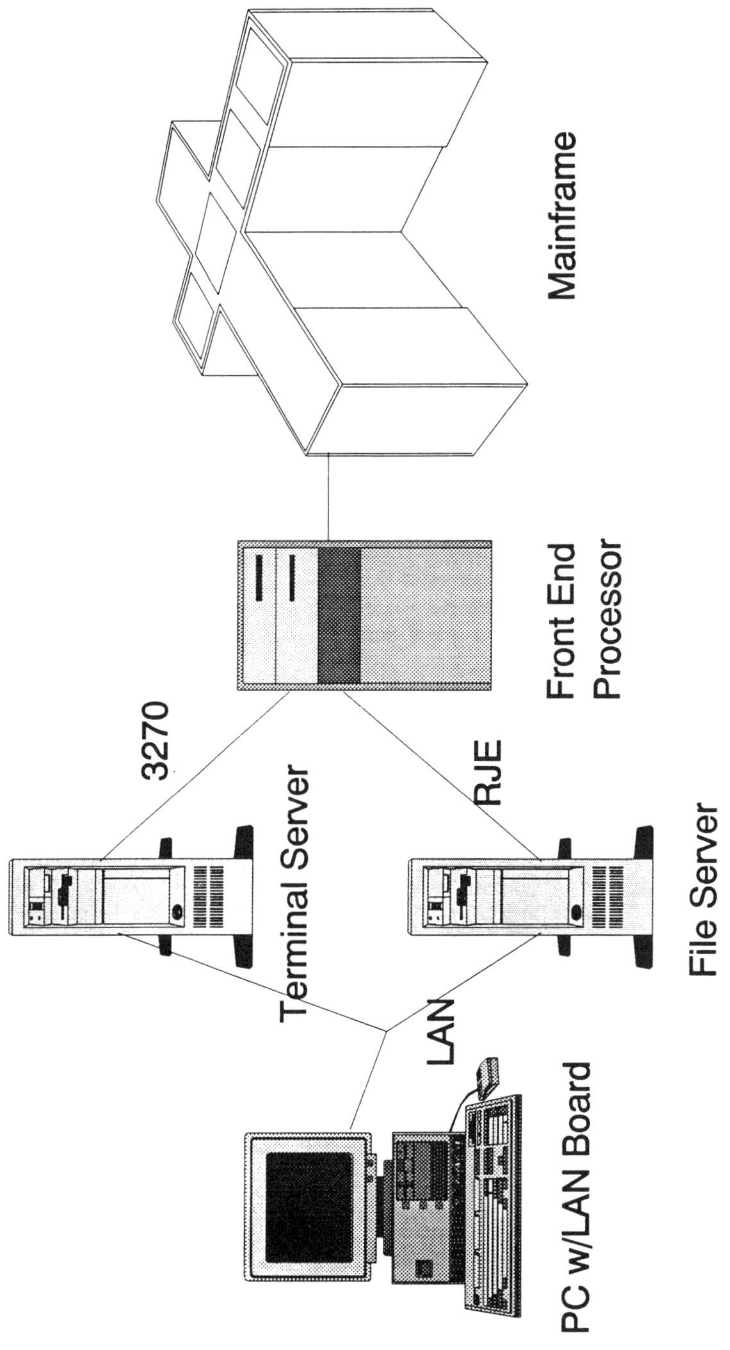

Figure 7-10. Decentralized server-based emulation.

packages, especially those used in a centralized server architecture. These packages can be slow when compared to PC-based packages or regular 3270 terminals. However, the management of some offloaded development environments may view slow 3270 online access as an advantage in that it gives the users more of a reason to use the PC-based development tools.

As for server-based RJE file transfer, there are a number of advantages that make this facility a desirable part of almost all offloaded development environments. The first is speed. RJE was built to move source code and data files around quickly. The second is that RJE is built for file transfer and 3270 is not. The users who still remain on standard 3270 terminals doing interactive work will be very grateful when they realize that the large number of file transfers normally associated with an offloaded development environment are not being carried out over 3270 communication links that they share. However, as with server-based 3270 emulation, there are drawbacks to server-based RJE emulation. The main drawback is complicated setup. Not only does the installer have to deal with the difficulties of linking a mainframe to a UNIX or OS/2 server, he or she usually will have to arrange for the server to emulate an RJE punch or an RJE reader, in addition to an RJE printer and console. In many mainframe DP shops, it has been at least 10 years since the last request for such services. Thus, setting up an RJE emulation facility may become a search for a "lost art."

3270 Emulation Selection Criteria

Whether the selected platform for 3270 emulation is the server or PC workstation, the criteria for selecting the right package is primarily the same. Here is a rank ordered list of selection criteria for 3270 emulation packages (i.e., hardware and software). As with the lists of other selection criteria, the importance of any particular item will depend on individual need.

1. Essential 3270 Emulation Requirements
    a. Supports the selected architecture. For most organizations, this means using server-based 3270 emulation to support the three-tier architecture as described previously.
    b. Supports the selected platform. It is required that the 3270 emulation package supports the exact operating system, hardware, LAN hardware/software, and mainframe communication

protocol (i.e., SDLC/SNA or BSC) being used. Compatibility with selected software tools (compiler, debugger, code generator, upper CASE tool) is also essential.

c. Be easy to use and expand. The 3270 emulation software commands that the users invoke to access the mainframe should be easy to use. Server-based 3270 emulation software should also be easily expanded to accommodate minor changes, such as the addition of a few users (i.e., the server does not have to be reconfigured and/or rebooted for small changes).

d. Provides adequate vendor support. As the 3270 emulation package will be the offloaded development environment users online — and possibly file transfer — link to the mainframe, any down time is a major problem. Competent telephone support for the package should be available.

e. Requires small amounts of RAM on MS-DOS PC workstations. If the 3270 emulation will be PC-based and MS-DOS will be used, the package should not require large amounts (75K or more) of precious low DOS memory. Excessive demands for such memory may prevent the use of some software tools.

f. Supports an adequate number of users. If server-based 3270 emulation is being used, the package should be able to support at least one session for all users simultaneously. This can only be checked with field testing.

g. Provides print screen support. Users should be able to print screen images by hitting the <Prt Sc> key or some other keystroke combination.

h. Provides complete keyboard mapping. All mainframe keystrokes should be supported, including high-value function keys, PA keys, field mark, and so on. Keyboards should also be able to be remapped, if needed.

i. Supports transfer of different types of files (if 3270 is used for file transfer). The emulation packages should be able to transfer source code, flat data files, packed data files, fixed-length files, and variable-length files. Translation facilities (EBCDIC to ASCII/ASCII to EBCDIC) can be turned on or off depending on the type of file being transferred.

2. Important 3270 Emulation Requirements

   a. Provides an acceptable division of services at the server level. If the 3270 emulation package is operating at the server level, the ability to have a single server offer file, print, and communication (e.g., emulation) services may be important to the economic viability of the offloaded development environment. However, the ability to distribute these services across multiple servers may also be important in certain situations.

   b. Provides adequate security. If a 3270 emulation session is terminated by turning off the PC workstation, rather than by properly logging off, the session should automatically be terminated so that no other user can "pick up" that session.

   c. Provides high-speed communication. The speed of the emulation package should be almost as good as a standard 3270 terminal connected to the mainframe via conventional means.

   d. Supports background processing. If the 3270 emulation package is to be used for file transfer, background processing should be supported.

   e. Provides high-quality documentation. All documentation for emulation packages should be complete. This is because the users will be using one piece of hardware to emulate another.

   f. Offers competent support. Competent support is sometimes extremely helpful when using emulation packages.

   g. Requires only a moderate amount of RAM on the server. The ability to use the selected emulation package effectively, without having to load the server with large amounts of RAM, may be of some importance.

   h. Is easy to use. It is best if all emulation packages are easy for the end user to use. Easy installation is also advantageous in that it can shorten the amount of time needed to set up an offloaded development environment.

3. Nice to Have 3270 Emulation Requirements

   a. Is moderately priced. For server-based 3270 emulation, the cost of the package (i.e., software and communication board, but no modems) should be under $4,000. For PC-based 3270 emulation, the cost should be under $1,000.

b. Makes use of an existing knowledge base. If a DP shop currently uses a 3270 emulation package, a lot of time and money can be saved if this same package is selected for the offloaded development environment.

c. Supports multiple concurrent sessions. It is useful if each user can pull up multiple 3270 sessions concurrently (at least three). Whether or not this is the case will depend not only on the emulation package but on how the communication link has been set up. For server-based 3270 emulation, this requirement does not imply that every user needs multiple sessions simultaneously (e.g., genning for 30 sessions for 10 users is ridiculous, but 15 sessions for 10 users may be desirable).

d. Supports the simultaneous display of multiple concurrent sessions. The ability to see multiple concurrent sessions at the same time can be very valuable for some users.

e. Supports the building of client-server applications. The ability to build client-server applications with special interface tools may be useful for certain groups.

f. Supports color emulation. The ability to emulate 3279 color terminals is a nice feature that most users appreciate.

RJE Emulation Selection Criteria

Normally the platform for RJE emulation is the server. This is because RJE resources are usually too expensive to be allocated at an individual PC workstation level (i.e., it is unrealistic to give 100 offloaded development environment users 100 RJE remotes).

Here is a rank ordered list of selection criteria for RJE emulation packages (i.e., hardware and software). As with the other lists of selection criteria, the importance of any particular item will depend on individual need.

1. Essential RJE Emulation Requirements

    a. Supports the selected architecture. For most organizations this means using server-based RJE emulation to support the three-tier architecture as described previously.

    b. Supports the selected platform. It is required that the RJE emulation package supports the exact operating system, hardware, LAN hardware/software, and mainframe communication protocol (i.e., SDLC/SNA or BSC) being used. Compatibility with selected software tools (compiler, debugger, code generator, upper CASE tool) is also essential.

c. Is easy to use and expand. The RJE emulation software commands that the users invoke to access the mainframe should be easy to use. The emulation software should be easily expanded to accommodate minor changes, such as the addition of new RJE remote IDs (i.e., the server does not have to be reconfigured and/or rebooted for small changes).

d. Provides adequate vendor support. As the RJE emulation package will be the users' file transfer link to the mainframe, any down time is a major problem. Competent telephone support for the package should be available.

e. Supports transfer of different types of files. The emulation package should be able to transfer source code, flat data files, packed data files, fixed-length files, and variable-length files. Translation facilities (EBCDIC to ASCII/ASCII to EBCDIC) can be turned on or off depending on the type of file being transferred.

2. Important RJE Emulation Requirements

   a. Provides an acceptable division of services at the server level. If the RJE emulation package is operating at the server level, the ability to have a single server offer file, print, and communication (e.g., RJE emulation) services may be important to the economic viability of the offloaded development environment. However, the ability to distribute these services across multiple servers may also be important in certain situations.

   b. Provides high-speed communication. The speed of the RJE emulation package should be able to support the file transfer needs of the users. It is best if the minimum transfer speed is 9600 baud.

   c. Supports background processing. The RJE emulation package should operate unattended and in the background.

   d. Provides high-quality documentation. All documentation for emulation packages should be complete. This is because the users will be using one piece of hardware to emulate another.

e. Offers competent support. Competent support is sometimes extremely helpful when setting up and using emulation packages.

f. Requires only a moderate amount of RAM on the server. The ability to use the selected emulation package effectively without having to load the server with large amounts of RAM may be of some importance.

g. Is easy to use. It is best if all emulation packages are easy for the end user to use. Easy installation is also advantageous in that it can shorten the amount of time needed to set up an offloaded development environment.

h. Supports the removal of JES messages or header records. If files are downloaded via RJE printer emulation, it is very useful if the JES messages are removed automatically. For files transferred via RJE punch emulation, header and/or trailer records should be removed.

i. Supports transfers of files with large LRECLs. It is best if files with LRECLs of up to 32KB can be transferred.

j. Supports dial-up and direct link access. It is extremely helpful if automatic dial-up and sign-on are supported.

3. Nice to Have RJE Emulation Requirements

a. Is moderately priced. For server-based RJE emulation, the cost of the package (i.e., software and communication board, but no modems) should be under $4,000.

b. Makes use of an existing knowledge base. If a DP shop currently uses a particular RJE emulation package, a lot of time and money can be saved if the same package is selected for the offloaded development environment.

c. Supports multiple concurrent sessions. It is helpful if the RJE emulation package can handle simultaneous RJE printer, punch, and reader sessions, if necessary.

3270 and RJE Emulation Vendors

There are two types of vendors that offer 3270 and RJE emulation packages. The first group consists of most large-scale computer vendors, including the following:

1. IBM
2. DEC
3. AT&T/NCR

The second group consists of vendors that specialize in emulation and communication packages:

1. Digital Communications Associates (DCA)
2. Attachmate
3. Rabbit Software
4. Systems Strategies (now part of NYNEX)
5. Cleo Communications

The type of vendor to select will depend on whether the buyer is interested in complete or partial solutions from a major vendor, with the vendor handling part or all of the systems integration, or if the buyer is interested in assembling the offloaded development environment on his or her own.

OTHER COMMUNICATION LINKS

In addition to connecting an offloaded development environment to a target mainframe, it is usually beneficial to connect an offloaded development environment to other systems via an additional set of communication links. These links may be permanent or temporary, outgoing or incoming, elaborate or simple. The purpose of these links is to give local users outgoing access to other systems and outside users incoming access to your system. Some of the reasons for establishing other communication links include the following:

1. *Electronic mail.* The ability to link servers and/or PC workstations to other systems, such as other servers or commercial e-mail services (e.g., ATTMail) for the purpose of transferring e-mail has a direct effect on the value of an offloaded development environment's e-mail component. This is because the value of an e-mail system is mostly a question of economies of scale. The more people who have access to an e-mail system, the more it is used and, thus, the more valuable it becomes. An e-mail system with a very limited universe of users is not very valuable.
2. *User dial-out and dial-in via the public network.* The public phone network is the biggest WAN of all. With access to the public network, users can access their server or PC workstation from

home or while on the road. They can also access a large variety of public systems (business information systems) and private systems (other company systems). Access to the public network, especially incoming access, has extensive security implications. See Chapter 9 for more information.

3. *Access to other offloaded development environment servers.* In DP shops with two or more offloaded development environments, access to other servers is usually valuable. The reasons for this include the transfer of e-mail (as mentioned in item 1); the sharing of libraries of code, specifications, designs, and test inputs; access to data files or databases; and the temporary transfer of personnel from one group using an offloaded development environment to another group using a different offloaded development environment.

4. *Access to online technical support.* Since operating and administering an offloaded development environment is often a complex task, at least for the administrators, access to external technical support resources is very helpful. This can include outgoing access to vendor bulletin boards; and incoming access to system software by technical support personnel; and incoming or outgoing access to other offloaded development environment systems depending on whether the administrator is the giver or receiver of assistance.

5. *Central collection of user and system metrics.* In large DP shops there is usually a group that collects certain metrics (e.g., server usage levels, LAN usage levels, code library metrics). Providing these metric-collection groups with incoming access gives them the opportunity to build mechanized systems to collect this kind of information.

6. *Access to groupware.* In DP shops that have multiple offloaded development environments, there may be certain groupware packages that all servers may not have but may need access to. These packages are usually used infrequently and, consequently, their installation on multiple servers may not be cost effective.

7. *Access to devices on other networks.* Being able to access devices, such as special printers, plotters, FAX boards, and so on, on other networks may be useful. Access to these devices may be via LAN, WAN, or direct access to other servers.

Once it is decided what kinds of external communication will be needed, the communication method(s) must then be selected. The reasons for selecting one or more methods will depend on the availability of certain services and facilities, performance needs, security, and costs. The main methods are the following:

1. *WANs.* WANs, or Wide Area Networks, allow users to access hundreds or thousands of computers and other devices (printers, modem pools) over a large physical area. WANs are usually slower than LANs but are less expensive.

2. *LANs.* Linking offloaded development environments together on a single LAN makes the sharing of facilities very easy for end users. The links are usually of very high speed and very high cost. It can also complicate the administration of the offloaded development environments because of the added security and network implications that must be addressed.

3. *POTS lines with modems.* Plain Old Telephone Service (POTS) lines, used in conjunction with modems, are a cheap but slow method of access to external systems and facilities. They are usually effective in situations where access is infrequent and speed is not an issue.

Of course, multiple methods may be selected depending on the combination of user and administrator needs. In addition, each method carries certain implications that must be planned for, such as network administration and security. However, the benefits of some of these communication links, especially when they are centralized at the server, can more than make up for their costs.

INTEGRATED OFFLOADED DEVELOPMENT ENVIRONMENT PACKAGES

An integrated offloaded development environment package is a collection of software and hardware that ties together the various software tools, communication facilities, operating systems, and hardware platforms into a single environment (i.e., from the user's point of view). Such packages are basically the equivalent of NewWave or Cooperation, but they are specifically designed for mainframe application developers. To date there is only one integrated offloaded development environment package on the market, AT&T's Application Development Workgroup/COBOL, or ADW/COBOL for short. (Note: ADW/COBOL should not be confused with KnowledgeWare's Application Development Workbench (ADW).) A description follows.

AT&T Application Development Workgroup/COBOL

Introduced in 1989, ADW/COBOL enjoys wide use within AT&T's internal mainframe application development community. It is also used at a significant number of other companies and institutions within the United States. The product brings together PC workstations (MS-DOS and OS/2 2.0 based), UNIX servers, and mainframes into a single development environment for COBOL programmers and CASE users. (Note: MIS, project leaders, and analysts can also tie into the environment and share some of the benefits.) There are a number of significant advantages to using an integrated offloaded development environment package, such as ADW/COBOL. The following list documents those advantages and should be considered an evaluation criteria for this type of package.

1. *Saves set-up time and trouble.* Building an effective offloaded development environment on one's own can be a dirty and time-consuming job that can easily take six months or longer. Buying an integrated offloaded development environment package can save much of that time (usually more than 50%) and a lot of the confusion.
2. *Makes local administration easier.* Local administration chores like emptying out certain directories, tracking down lost files, and monitoring the status of communication links are handled by integrated offloaded development environment packages.
3. *Provides missing functionality.* Integrated offloaded development environment packages should handle the functions that the individual software tools, such as Micro Focus and SPF/PC cannot handle (e.g., movement of whole PDSs from mainframe to PC workstation, automatic loading of mainframe files into server libraries).
4. *Provides more efficient / better integrated functionality.* The processing of time-consuming tasks in the background (e.g., file transfers, e-mail) and the seamless linking of mainframe, server, and PC workstation into one environment (e.g., single-key access to the various platforms) are very important features of an integrated offloaded development environment.
5. *Supplies a simple, menu-driven user interface.* Having a simple, and more importantly a consistent, interface presented to the users provides two main benefits. The first is that a simple interface shields the user from having to know a lot about the raw

operating systems on the server and PC workstations. The second is that offloaded development environment users can easily be moved to different groups so long as the new group is also using the same integrated package.

6. *Provides a standard configuration.* The variety of PC and server-based software and hardware products on the market is almost beyond comprehension. Buying an integrated offloaded development environment package limits the software and hardware choices significantly. It also allows for central control of software tool configurations.
7. *Provides access to a knowledgeable support team.* The vendors of integrated offloaded development environment packages will have a significant knowledge of how to bring together a large variety of tools and packages into a single development environment. This can be extremely useful if a buyer needs to set up a development environment in a short period of time.

Depending on your point of view, there are some disadvantages to using an integrated offloaded development environment such as ADW/COBOL. These disadvantages include the following:

1. *A standard configuration requirement.* Using a specific integrated offloaded development environment package limits the buyer to a comparatively small set of software and hardware choices. To groups that want the freedom to bring in new packages (i.e., software or hardware) on a whim, having an integrated offloaded development environment can be constraining.
2. *Unresolved installation and administrative issues.* Having an integrated offloaded development environment eliminates some set-up headaches but not all. Buyers will still have to coordinate the delivery of a large number of products, arrange to have communication lines installed, and arrange for user and administrator training.
3. *Cost.* Vendors of integrated offloaded development environment packages need to provide a lot of support to customers. This comes at a price.

The list price for ADW/COBOL is $25,000 for the server portion and $12,000 for each client package. (Note: Each client package handles eight users; single-user client packages are available.) The vendor can be contacted at the following address:

AT&T Application Development Solutions
200 South Orange Avenue
Orlando, FL 32801
Phone: 1-800-545-4ADW

SUMMARY

The most important thing to remember when selecting an architecture of an offloaded development environment is that the objective is to provide the users with at least the same functionality they were getting on the mainframe (and at best, much more) in a cost effective way. This chapter examines the benefits and drawbacks for each type of architecture (i.e., 2-tier versus 2.5-tier versus 3-tier). Included in this analysis, for comparative purposes, are the traditional single-tier architecture and channel-attached, single-tier architecture. For almost all DP shops there are only two viable architectures, 2-tier and 3-tier. The 2-tier environment should be selected by small DP shops with less than 10 developers that do not expect to grow, or by DP shops that handle mostly one-person projects requiring no significant communication among developers. The 3-tier environment should be selected by all other DP shops. The reason for this is that 3-tier environments are almost always more powerful and cost effective than the other possible environments. This is because they make more efficient use of the LAN, server, and PC workstations.

Once the architecture has been chosen, the LAN/server hardware and software as well as the mainframe communication methods and facilities must be selected. A list of selection criteria for LAN/server hardware and software has been provided in this chapter. Readers should tailor this list to meet their individual needs and objectives.

The two methods used to give offloaded development environment users access to the mainframe for either online activities or file transfers are 3270 and RJE emulation. 3270 emulation can be performed on either the PC workstation or the server. RJE emulation, however, should only be performed on the server as it is far too expensive at the PC workstation level. Where emulation is performed will largely depend on the architecture selected. A list of selection criteria for both 3270 emulation and RJE emulation has been provided in this chapter. As always, readers should tailor these lists to meet their individual needs and objectives.

Two important things should be kept in mind when putting together the supporting network for an offloaded development environment. The first is that the mixing and matching of components, to some degree, is usually possible. The second is that, in some situations, whole environments can be purchased from one vendor. Deciding between the two scenarios is usually a matter of choosing between lower prices and better support. Procuring hardware components at commodity prices is often an attractive option. But receiving comprehensive support from the vendor of an integrated offloaded development package can be more important.

8

Setting Up and Operating an Offloaded Development Environment

In Chapters 5, 6, and 7 we examined the components that make up offloaded development environments. In this chapter we will examine the following issues connected with setting up and operating such an environment.

- The testing of components
- The ordering of components
- The laying out of hardware
- Installation
- Rollout plans
- The four stages of user involvement
- The defining of local procedures
- User support

TESTING COMPONENTS

Before ordering a full set of offloaded development environment components, it is important to test a representative sample of the selected products on a small and inexpensive scale. There are many reasons for this, and we will be examining them in detail in this section. However, most of these reasons fall into three main categories: lying sales representatives, hardware/software incompatibilities, and application incompatibilities.

1. *Lying sales representatives.* The job of most sales representatives is to find a way to sell the largest possible quantity of equipment to their customers. Unfortunately, this practice is not always synonymous with selling the customer what they really need. This is why sales representatives, on occasion, may forget to mention certain important facts (e.g., the sales representative's package works with Micro Focus COBOL but not the Micro Focus IMS Option). In some extreme cases sales representatives even lie. But more often than not, it is the sales representative's inexperience with her products that leads to ill-informed customers. This inexperience is usually characteristic of vendors that are undergoing rapid expansion (watch out for companies whose "old-timer" sales representatives are those who have been with the company for just a year). Thus, for your own protection, verify all important claims before making any large purchasing commitments.

2. *Hardware and software incompatibilities.* Given the large number of software packages that must work together as part of an offloaded development environment, it is easy to see why 100% compatibility is not easy to attain, at least not without some work by the customer and the vendor. In the case of software packages that are relatively new, the level of support offered for other supporting products may be lacking. For example, a number of development packages support the Micro Focus COBOL Workbench but not the XDB-Workbench for DB2 or the Micro Focus IMS Option.

   But software is not the only area where incompatibilities can hinder the success of an offloaded development environment. In the area of software/hardware compatibility a similar situation exists. Ten years after the introduction of the PC there are still dozens of PC makers. Most of these makers offer several different models of PCs, and within the production life of each model there may be several different versions (i.e., different ROM BIOS, even different CPUs). The average software vendor usually does not have a sample of each type of PC workstation. Therefore, unpredictable results can arise when a package is tried out on a particular PC for the first time.

   Finally, hardware-to-hardware incompatibilities also can be a problem. Users may buy their PCs from one vendor, their memory boards from another, and their LAN boards from a third. If we throw in video controllers, mouse controllers, and other types of

I/O controllers, the chances for a conflict (e.g., interrupt addresses, memory addresses) are significant. One obvious solution to this problem may be the procurement of all hardware from one vendor. However, this is not always possible and may be very expensive when it is.

3. *Application incompatibilities.* Even though potential users may be the subject of extensive surveys and interviews, not all facts related to application compatibility may surface. For example, an application may need to make significant use of the referential integrity facilities of DB2 but may not find the same facilities on the DB2 PC workbench. This is why critical existing application components need to be tested on a PC workstation before committing significant resources.

What Problems to Look For When Testing the Environment

At a minimum, testing out the new development environment involves the procurement of a single PC workstation of the exact model and type that is proposed for deployment, along with all proposed software packages. To ensure that all possible problems are identified, a LAN and server of the exact model and type that is proposed also would need to be set up. Whichever test environment is selected, PC and software or PC, LAN, server, and software, the tester needs to obtain a representative sample of test inputs. These inputs include critical system components and examples of all interfaces, including calls to DBMSs and TP monitors, as well as interlanguage calls.

Once a test environment is set up and representative samples of test inputs are obtained, a test plan is drawn up (see the next section for an example). At a minimum, the plan should address the issues listed below. Other issues that are deemed important to your particular situation should be added as needed.

1. *"RAM Cram."* Most MS-DOS PC workstation users, whether running spreadsheets, word processors, or compilers, have seen plenty of error messages complaining about a shortage of memory (i.e., low DOS memory: 0 to 640KB). When the user is a client on a LAN, these messages become more common. Thus, "RAM cram" becomes a major problem and is particularly prevalent in offloaded development environments that have many components competing for chunks of low DOS memory.

When assembling and testing an offloaded development environment, note that it will take a significant amount of time to set all system parameters correctly and to determine what can be loaded into expanded memory and what must stay in low memory. Table 8-1 lists some of the candidates for movement to expanded memory and their approximate sizes.

Table 8-1. Items that may be able to be moved to high DOS memory.

Item	Size
LAN Client Software	~ 100K+
BUFFERS (config.sys)	~ 15K
Mouse Driver	~ 10K
FILES (config.sys)	~ 3K
LASTDRIVE (config.sys)	~ 2K
ANSI.SYS (config.sys)	~ 2K

Other variables that need to be taken into account are the version of MS-DOS and type of video used (e.g., CGA, EGA, VGA; monochrome vs. color). Until MS-DOS 5.0 was introduced, every successive version had taken more and more low DOS memory. Choosing the right version of MS-DOS will alleviate the offloaded development environment's RAM cram situation. The video selected for the PC workstation also will have an impact since different types of video use different areas of the high DOS memory.

Needless to say, this area can be extremely hairy and trying to figure it out alone can be extremely difficult. This is why it is often worthwhile to look to the following other sources for information.

- Vendor manuals
- Vendor support personnel
- Other folks using the same equipment
- User groups
- Vendor/third party magazines and journals
- Vendor/third party BBS

2. *Tool highwater marks.* Tool "highwater marks" refer to the maximum amount of memory used by a particular tool. Some tools or workbenches are in fact collections of tools, each with its own memory requirements. Thus, when testing one of these workbenches, each individual component/tool must be examined.

3. *Memory manager compatibility.* Some tool sets, like Micro Focus COBOL Workbench, have their own memory managers. These packages allow their associated tools to run in extended memory. An important thing to check when using one of these tools is that your particular PC workstation is supported. Most major PC brands and models are supported, but because of differences in the method used to access machine resources, certain machines may not work. If there are questions about or problems with memory manager compatibility, consult with the vendor before continuing your test. Usually the fix will involve an unusual setting of memory manager parameters. The worst-case scenario may involve shipping a sample PC to the vendor.

4. *Hardware interrupts.* All PCs have interrupts that the user may specify for their own use. These interrupts are intended for additional controllers (mouse, I/O, video) or communication boards (LANs). However, sometimes the default interrupt settings on different boards will be the same. When this happens, time will be needed to determine a unique interrupt setting for each board. The approach used is basically trial and error, testing the various possible combinations until you find a combination of settings that work. The most important thing here is to come up with a configuration that is simple and standard for all users. Local administrators do not want to get into the situation where interrupt settings differ from one PC to another. This would make the standardization of software and hardware installation impossible and would force the testing of each individual PC.

5. *Memory addresses.* As with hardware interrupts, memory addresses may need to be specified and tested for various components (LAN communication boards). Having a standard set of addresses will greatly speed up testing and therefore deployment. Future modifications are also easier when all PCs use the same memory address configurations.

6. *Memory boards.* Major PC vendors will always supply whatever quantity of RAM is requested. Usually this RAM is more expensive than what can be purchased from computer parts vendors,

sometimes two, three, or even four times as much. Thus, in many situations, it pays to buy RAM (i.e., SIMM strips, memory boards) from a separate vendor. However, before RAM from low-cost vendors is purchased, it should be tested. Like software vendors, these RAM suppliers are trying to support many dozens of PC makers. To avoid any unpleasant surprises take the time to make the following checks:

a. Check to see that the memory chips you are buying are as fast or faster than those in the PC already. A PC expecting 100 nanosecond chips can usually run with 70 nanosecond chips but not the other way around. The speed of these chips is usually the one- or two-digit rightmost number on the chip.

b. Check any memory boards you propose to buy by actually installing them in the computer. In addition to checking the speed of the chips, check that the board interface is correct. That is, if the computer expects 32-bit memory boards, you should not be using 16-bit memory boards.

c. Check that the price you are proposing to pay is in line with the going rate. Remember that chips are priced not only by size but also by speed. A good place to get this information is *Computer Shopper* magazine.

7. *Syntax compatibility.* When testing PC workstation compilers, debuggers, and syntax checkers, it is vital to consider the degree of compatibility between the PC tool and its mainframe counterpart. Offloading mainframe development to PC workstations cannot be accomplished without this compatibility. Two important things to consider are the following:

   a. ANSI vs. IBM support. Just because a PC tool supports the ANSI definition of a language does not mean it can be used to emulate a mainframe tool that supports the same ANSI definition. The major problem here is IBM's extensions to the ANSI definition. Programmers in the field who use a certain compiler every day don't care if the code they are writing is strictly ANSI compatible or contains extensions beyond the ANSI definition. They usually don't know what is ANSI and what is an extension. One thing that is certain is that if a programmer who is used to some nice time-saving IBM extensions suddenly has to do without them she is going to be very unhappy. Therefore, when testing, make sure that the PC emulates the mainframe tool, not just adheres to the ANSI standard.

b. SQL variations. When SQL was being introduced, it was hailed as a way to reduce the number of database languages and to allow customers to write DBMS independent applications. While the former has happened, the latter, of course, has not. While some SQL commands are the same from DBMS to DBMS, many SQL commands are not.

Figure 8-1 shows a sample test plan worksheet.

Test Case Description	Result	OK	Not OK
		(Check one.)	
I. Workstation Tests			
1. RAM Cram (After moving all possible programs to high DOS memory, measure low DOS RAM requirements of all packages and compare results to the amount of low DOS RAM available.)			
SPF/PC	______	___	___
Micro Focus COBOL Wkbch	______	___	___
XDB DB2 Workbench	______	___	___
Emulation Software	______	___	___
Menuing Software	______	___	___
LAN Software	______	___	___
2. XM (Check that Micro Focus XM memory manager supports the selected hardware.)	______	___	___
3. Hardware Interrupts (Check that uses of all hardware interrupts are unique and that all components function together.)	______	___	___

Figure 8-1. Example of test plan worksheet.

Test Case Description	Result	OK	Not OK
		(Check one.)	
4. Memory Boards (Check that selected memory boards and chips used are functional; make sure that entire workstation RAM is accessible.)			
5. Memory Addresses (Check that use of all hardware memory addresses are unique and that all components function together; memory managers should be made aware of occupied address space.)			
II. Software Tests			
1. Highwater Mark (Test all subcomponents of workbench tools.)			
Micro Focus COBOL Workbench			
A. Editor			
B. Syntax Checker			
C. Animator			
D. Advanced Animator			
E. Diff (file compare)			
F. Hex Editor			
G. Session Recorder			
H. Batch File Facility			
XDB DB2 Workbench			
A. Create/Alter			
B. Data Entry			
C. Interactive SQL			
D. Reports			
E. Graphs			
F. Forms			
G. Menus			
H. Procedures			
I. Select Database			
J. Utilities			

Figure 8-1. Example of test plan worksheet. (cont'd)

Test Case Description		Result	OK	Not OK
			(Check one.)	
2. Syntax Compatibility (Run several existing representative programs through Micro Focus/XDB syntax checker, precompiler, and compiler.)				
Program #1		______	___	___
Program #2		______	___	___
Program #3		______	___	___
Program #4		______	___	___
Program #5		______	___	___
3. Runtime Compatibility (Check that representative programs give the same results as on the mainframe.)				
Program #1	Animator	______	___	___
"	Runtime	______	___	___
Program #2	Animator	______	___	___
"	Runtime	______	___	___
Program #3	Animator	______	___	___
"	Runtime	______	___	___
Program #4	Animator	______	___	___
"	Runtime	______	___	___
Program #5	Animator	______	___	___
"	Runtime	______	___	___
4. MS-DOS version 5.0 (Check that proposed PC operating system is compatible with other system software.)				
LAN Software		______	___	___
Menuing Software		______	___	___
Emulation Software		______	___	___
Micro Focus Workbench		______	___	___
XDB DB2 Workbench		______	___	___
SPF/PC		______	___	___

Figure 8-1. Example of test plan worksheet. (cont'd)

ORDERING COMPONENTS

After selecting and testing the components for the offloaded development environment, they must then be ordered from the appropriate vendors. This section addresses the issues connected with ordering, including licensing, pricing, and delivery.

Licensing Considerations

Software licensing varies depending on the vendor, the type of machine the software will run on, and the number of users the machine will support. The license allows the customer to use the software. Ownership is retained by the vendor, which usually means the customer cannot sell or redistribute the software to others.

With PC workstation and server software, the license is usually on the box and comes into effect when the customer removes the package's shrink-wrap or breaks a seal. Most licenses allow the software to be installed on only one CPU or allow copies on multiple CPUs but for only one user at a time. The latter is sometimes enforced with a block, otherwise known as dongle, that comes with the software package. The dongle is attached to a particular port on the PC and without the dongle a user cannot execute the software. Loading a single package onto a server and having all LAN users access the one copy is usually a no-no, unless the license is a network license. For network licenses the number of concurrent users will be specified (e.g., 3, 10, unlimited).

One of the most important things to look for on license agreements is what maintenance is to be provided. Maintenance can include training, a support hotline, on-site assistance, and/or the supplying of bug fixes/updates. The time frame for this assistance can vary greatly, usually from 60 days to 1 year. Beyond the initial support period, maintenance plans are available usually at a cost of 12% to 18% of the initial purchase price per year. If a maintenance plan is not purchased, or is not available, update packages can usually be purchased. The main rule is to buy only what is needed. If you get support from a central support group at your company, there may be little need for vendor maintenance plans. If an update comes out that does not have new fixes or features that you need, then don't buy it.

If the software package that is being purchased is not "off the shelf," but is being custom developed for a particular customer or set of customers, then the licensing agreement should address other areas. These include compliance with specifications, warranties, delivery schedules, and rights to the source code.

Pricing Considerations

You don't need to buy this book to know that hardware and software prices vary considerably. Significant discounts can be obtained from both the maker of the product and discount vendors. For software, the usual discount can range anywhere from 25% to 75%. For hardware the range is 10% to 40%.

Some things to watch out for with regard to pricing include the following:

1. *Customer sites being turned into warehouses.* Some vendors, in order to give the customer the largest discount possible, want the customer to buy large quantities of a product and then have the customer redistribute the product internally. This can be dangerous, unless the customer has buyers ready to receive and pay for the product. If this is not the case, then the customer will have to warehouse the purchase and risk the possibility of being stuck with outdated products. This is especially the case with software.

2. *Large customers getting "carved up."* In most large companies, individual groups are responsible for their own budgets and purchases of desktop and LAN equipment. So while the company as a whole may purchase enough equipment to be entitled to a significant discount, this discount may never be realized because the equipment will be ordered in dribs and drabs. Thus, some central organization within the large company needs to negotiate a company-wide discount that reflects the quantity of products that the company as a whole will be purchasing; otherwise the individual groups will not receive the discounts to which they are entitled.

3. *Vaporware.* The first rule in software buying is never, never, never pay in advance for software that will be delivered in the distant future (more than a few months). Once the vendor has the customer's money, most of the customer's influence is gone. Even if there is a high degree of trust between the customer and the vendor and the customer believes that the software will be delivered as promised, there is the problem of shifting allegiances. For example, even though a vendor may currently be devoted to

a customer and his needs, the vendor may be subject to a takeover, equity purchase, or alliance with another vendor that is not interested in that customer's needs.

Delivery Considerations

When placing orders for equipment, it is important to note when the items will be delivered. Why pay for an expensive software package if it is going to sit around for a couple of months because the equipment that it runs on is currently out of stock? In general, offloaded development environment equipment should be ordered in the following sequence:

1. *Network/communication wiring and gens.* Most mainframe data centers and networks that an offloaded development environment will need to interface with will require several months' notice before their services can be delivered. This delay can be due to many things including the time needed to design/engineer the required wiring changes, long intervals between scheduled mainframe gen changes, and strict work rules governing communication technicians.

2. *Hardware.* Once a specific set of hardware (PCs, LAN, server) is selected and tested, the situation may arise that some components are in short supply. Shortages come about because the equipment is new and exciting and demand is outstripping supply, or because the factory where the equipment is made is not scheduling production runs very often and the current inventory is not adequate to meet demand. A way to avoid these problems is to select more "established" components that are not subject to shortages and are still produced in large quantities on a regular basis. Another way to get around these kinds of problems is to go to a VAR (Value Added Reseller). VARs maintain inventories of products and can usually arrange for immediate delivery. VARs, however, may charge more than the manufacturers.

3. *Software.* Normally software should be ordered last. This is because delivery schedules for software are usually very short, often one or two weeks. As software is usually a large part of the cost of an offloaded development environment, it is not a good idea to order it too soon and have it sit around while the network and hardware orders are being processed. This may result in an expired maintenance agreement.

LAYING OUT THE HARDWARE (FLOOR PLAN)

Before the hardware is delivered its location should be determined. The PC workstations are easy. Since they are single-user workstations, they should be placed on the users' desks. Servers are a little bit more difficult. Their location will depend on the following considerations:

1. *Location of printers.* The printers that are attached to the server need to be located near the users. If the users are spread out over a large area or are in clusters, several printers may be needed. These printers must be within a certain distance of the server to avoid the need for signal repeaters or PC-based print spoolers.
2. *LAN distance limitations.* All LANs have distance limitations. The server, as a computer on the LAN, cannot be any farther away from the user's workstation than the LAN's distance limitation will permit.
3. *Security.* As discussed in Chapter 9, the server needs to be in a secure location. Optimally, this means a locked room, but a locked cabinet may suffice.
4. *Location of communication networks.* If possible, place the server close enough to the necessary communication networks so that modems are not required. These communication networks include any WANs that are used at the location and the mainframe (i.e., 3270) network. Since these connections are not as critical as the others (i.e., LAN and printers), modems can be used if required. But, whenever possible, avoid adding another potential point of failure by choosing a location that does not require them.
5. *Location of the local administrator.* For the sake of convenience it is nice to have the server located near the administrator's desk. This way when she walks by the server she can keep an eye on it (i.e., make sure the right modem and LAN LEDs are flashing, make sure there aren't any unauthorized people hanging around).

Once the locations of the PCs and servers have been determined, the hardware components must be connected together. The main options for these connections include fiber optic cable, coaxial cable (various sizes), and twisted pair (i.e., telephone wire). What you select depends on what you can use. Twisted pair is usually the cheapest and easiest to work with. It bends every which way, crimping is not a big problem, and it is already widely available in most buildings. It also can support the bandwidths needed for most offloaded development environments (1 Mb to 16 Mb/second).

The only major problem with twisted pair is distance. If users are scattered over an area greater than 100 meters square there may be problems. Generally though, 10 Mb/second networks can be expected to sustain distances of 100 meters. Longer distances may be possible depending on the configuration. Slow speed LANs (i.e., 1 Mb/second) should be able to go up to 500 meters.

Fiber and coaxial cabling are normally reserved for backbone networks (networks between servers). Those networks are normally the ones that need distance as well as large bandwidth.

Before going to the trouble of putting in new wiring, it is always a good idea to explore the possibility of using existing wiring. The main area of concern, of course, is the wiring between PC workstations and the server. If your LAN wiring uses a star configuration then there are the following possibilities:

1. *3270 lines.*
2. *WAN lines (e.g., ISN or DataKit).*
3. *Telephone lines.*
4. *Spare lines.* In some buildings there may have been someone with the foresight to have extra lines installed.

If your LAN uses a ring configuration there may be fewer possibilities.

Because offloaded development environments generally only need small bandwidth LANs, wireless LANs also may be suitable. As with wire LANs, there are restrictions, including distance, radio interference, and line of sight considerations. As with all other equipment, it should be tested before purchased. Suitability may vary from location to location.

LAYING OUT THE HARDWARE (CUBICAL LAYOUT)

Ideally, when the PC workstations are installed in the user's cubicles the terminals that are already there are removed. This very act forces the users into the offloaded development environment. Sometimes, however, this is not practical for technical reasons (the PC workstations aren't fully operational when deployed), political reasons (the implementors lack the clout to remove the old terminals), or psychological reasons (the users are too scared to give up their old terminals right away).

At this point PC workstation positioning becomes important. When the PC is installed it must be put in the most prominent position in the user's cubicle. Dumping it on the side won't do because the users will forget about it or ignore it. Figures 8-2 and 8-3 show some examples.

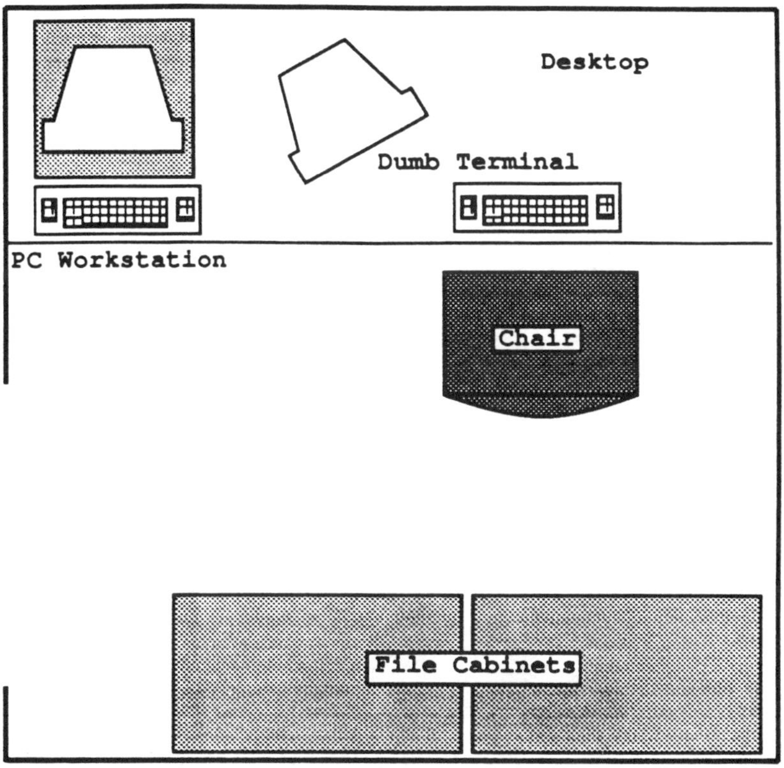

Figure 8-2. Improper positioning.

When we talk about PC positioning we are talking about the monitor and keyboard, not necessarily the CPU. Some PC workstations have CPUs that are no wider than the monitor. This will usually be the case because user PC workstations usually don't need a large number of slots or multiple bays for floppy disk drives or tape drives. Just one floppy drive and three slots are sufficient for most.

However, some PC CPUs have footprints so large you can play handball against them if turned on their sides. If desktop space is scarce (less than 20 square feet), then a small CPU or a floor-mounted CPU is needed. Most desktop CPUs can be turned sideways and put on the floor. Use a floor mount rack if the CPU is particularly tall.

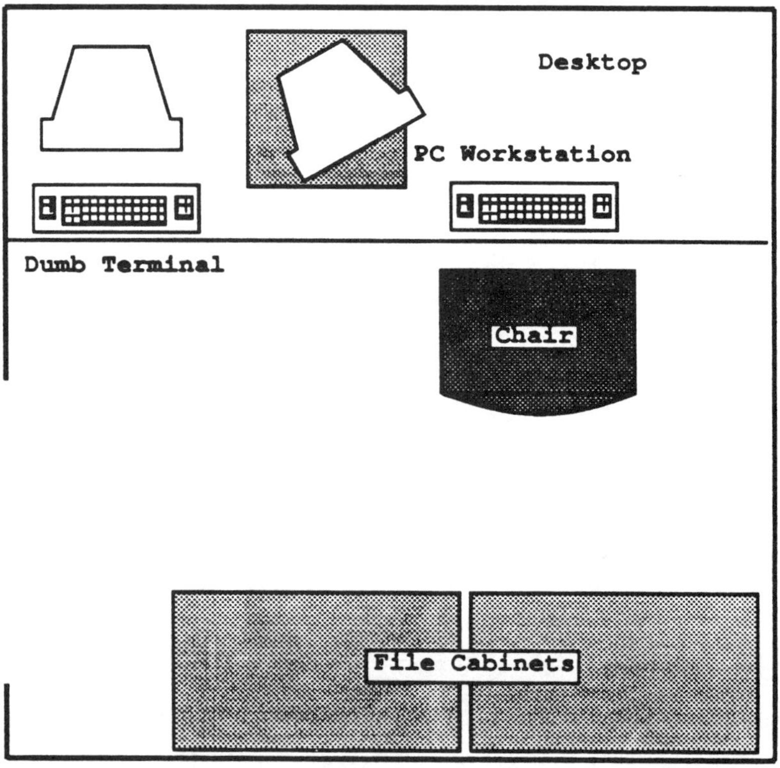

Figure 8-3. Proper positioning.

INSTALLATION

Installation is the stage when the local administrators really start to get some dirt on their hands. The first part of this section talks about hardware and software installation (the "dirt"). The second part deals with installation of communication links (less dirt, more hocus-pocus).

Hardware and Software

An option offered to most buyers of hardware, and sometimes software, is vendor installation. In most cases this should be turned down because local administrators need to "know their equipment." Offloaded development environments are multi-user computer systems. They are complex and always break at some point. In order to fix problems and make system modifications, local administrators need to have a good working knowledge of their equipment and how it was set up. Thus, local administrators should follow two rules with regard to hardware and software.

1. If you can install it yourself, do so.
2. If you can't install it yourself, you probably don't want it.

The above, of course, does not mean that all help should be refused. On-site "hand holding" by the vendor is extremely useful and greatly speeds up the installation process. The important thing is for the local administrators to do the actual work so they know exactly what is going on during the installation.

Another important source of information during installation, and later during operations, is other local administrators with similar systems. While they usually can't provide the same degree of assistance as the vendor's hand holders (they do have their own jobs to do), they can be a good source of advice and spare parts. Their value should not be underestimated.

Communication Links

The hairiest part of most installations is communications. This is because they take the most time to plan, order, and set up, and they are usually not conducive to hands-on involvement by the local administrator. This is for the best because most sites don't want too many people making changes in their telephone closets or their wiring trenches.

When placing orders for communications links between the offloaded development environment and the mainframe, a specific set of gen parameters is usually required. These should be obtained from the vendor of the emulation packages being used. Modem settings should also be specified. Once installed, new communications links are difficult to test since some components, such as 3270 links, need load testing to determine if they are functioning properly. Good information and planning, along with helpful communication technicians, can make this part of the installation fairly painless. Poor information and planning or apathetic technicians, on the other hand, can make this phase a long, drawn-out nightmare.

ROLLOUT PLANS

Before starting all the work activities required to bring in an offloaded development environment, a rollout plan with milestones should be drawn up. Not only is such a plan a management necessity, it will help keep observers informed as to what progress is being made.

The activities that should be included in all rollout plans are as follows:

1. *Select the environment.* In this step the candidates for an offloaded development environment are examined. The candidates work type (e.g., new development, maintenance), function, tools, and tool usage levels are determined via interviews and/or surveys (see Chapter 4 for more detailed information). The time required for this step is about two weeks.
2. *Select hardware and software packages.* After determining that offloaded development is appropriate, the right tools (editors, compilers, DBMS, CASE tools, PCs, LAN) need to be selected (see Chapter 5 for criteria) and a representative sample ordered. When delivered the equipment is set up and tested as described earlier in this chapter. Training probably will be required. The time required for this step will vary depending on the complexity of the environment and delivery times of the equipment. In most cases this step should take at least two months.
3. *Order communication links.* After the tools are selected and verified to be applicable to the user's situation, the needed communication links should be ordered. At this time links to the appropriate mainframe(s), usually via 3270 and RJE, should be ordered, and the LAN should be designed. The LAN design can be quite complicated depending upon the layout of the users. If the users are spread out over a large area (many hundreds of feet), the design of the LAN may be critical to the success of the offloaded development environment. LANs serving users over a small area are usually much simpler to design. Depending on the complexity of the LAN, this step can take up to two weeks. The reason this activity is number 3 on the rollout plan is because 3270, RJE, and LAN installation usually involves a lot of planning and lead time. At some sites this lead time may be as long as three months.

4. *Order hardware.* Between ordering the communication links and the software, the hardware (PCs, LAN hardware, servers) is ordered. Because of the large number of different components (cabling, memory chips, UPSs, printers) and the variety of vendors involved, ordering hardware can take from one week to one month, depending on the amount of comparison shopping that is done.
5. *Order software.* Because of the short delivery times needed for software packages, usually two weeks maximum, software is the last thing to be ordered. Ordering software last is important because of the short warranty periods associated with many packages, some as short as 60 days. This step should only take a few days.
6. *Make baseline measurements.* One activity that can be performed concurrent with the ordering process is making baseline measurements. This can include surveying future offloaded development environment users on their current levels of productivity and satisfaction, in addition to studying current mainframe chargeback bills. See Chapter 11 for more information. Depending on the complexity of measurements required, this step can take just a few days or up to three weeks.
7. *Take delivery of hardware/software.* When the hardware and software arrive, hopefully at roughly the same time, the components should be stored away in a secure area until needed. When the items are delivered they should, of course, be inspected to make sure they are in working order. Assembly can begin when all the critical components are available. The LAN and server, along with a couple of PCs, should be made operational. Some tuning of the environment can take place at this time. This period will usually last at least a month.
8. *Take delivery of communication links.* After the hardware is assembled and the software loaded, the communication links will be installed. For the LAN this means the wiring at a lot of different locations (mostly users' cubicles) has to be checked by the local administrator. For the mainframe links, this step usually means modem settings have to be tested along with the links themselves. The gen parameters for the links also have to be checked to ensure they were set correctly. Depending on the problems found and the responsiveness of the personnel installing the links, this stage can last a few days or a few weeks. Since this step is one of the last before becoming operational, the installation instructions need to be exact. Giving communication technicians leeway in the setup of the links will almost always result in delays due to inoperable links.

9. *Setup training.* Concurrent with the delivery of hardware, software, and communications, training is scheduled. This training can be done on site or off site at a training center. Training for offloaded development usually involves setting up a fully functional offloaded development environment. This can take some time to set up and test. If this option is chosen, be prepared to take a week to set up.
10. *Deploy workstations and start.* Immediately after training is concluded, the offloaded development environment should be made operational. This way the users can apply what they have learned before they have a chance to forget it. The downloading of user files (e.g., specifications, source code, copy members, test data) just prior to becoming operational is an important part of this step. The last-minute downloading ensures that the files are current. This step should last only a day or two.
11. *Measure results.* Measuring the impact of the offloaded development environment can begin from the first day of operation. This can include LAN, server, and mainframe usage reports. Surveys, while very useful, should be done no more than once every two months. The most important measurement, though, is the user's progression through the four stages of user involvement detailed in the next section.

An example of a rollout plan can be found in Appendix A.

THE FOUR STAGES OF USER INVOLVEMENT

Once the offloaded development environment is installed and made operational, the four stages of user involvement come into play. These stages are the steps or phases that users usually go through on their way to having a cost-saving offloaded development environment. The four stages are as follows:

1. *Dumb terminal usage.* Before the user enters the offloaded development environment he will have been using dumb terminals to do most of his work. In some offloaded development environments, especially when they are starting up, the dumb terminal and PC workstation may sit side by side in the user's cubicle. If, after the PC workstation is installed, the user is still using the dumb terminal, extra encouragement and support will be needed to help the user make the transition.

2. *Terminal emulation.* Terminal emulation is the first stage of offloaded development environment usage. It involves only a little investment on the user's part to reach this point (i.e., time to learn a few unusual keyboard changes). While this first step is important, it provides the user with no real benefits except that the user's dumb terminal can be removed from her cubicle. This is the stage where many offloaded development environments stall!!!
3. *Offloaded editing.* Offloaded editing, usually with SPF/PC, is the first stage that significantly exploits some of the advantages of the offloaded development environment. This is because offloaded editing of source code gives the user the advantage of subsecond response time (see Chapters 1 and 2 for more on the advantages of subsecond response time). Provided the offloaded development environment's upload and download facilities are fast and easy to use, and the users are doing significant amounts of editing, this stage should be easy to achieve, especially if the editor is a mainframe lookalike.
4. *Full environment emulation.* This is Nirvana — or as close to Nirvana as a mainframe programmer can get. This is the stage where the real benefits are obtained. Not only do users have subsecond response time for most commands, they get access to a wide variety of very powerful development tools that can greatly enhance productivity. This stage, however, should be viewed as containing several substages. For example, a COBOL-DB2 shop might first convert their COBOL-only work and, once that is stable, go onto COBOL-DB2. Lower CASE tools and upper CASE tools may be added later. The important thing is not to try to do too much too soon. Programmers can absorb only so many new tools at one time.

DEFINING LOCAL PROCEDURES

When preparing to operate an offloaded development environment, certain local procedures need to be defined in order to avoid time-consuming problems and to ensure smooth running operations. These procedures can be broken down into two groups, those for users and those for administrators.

User Procedures

User procedures are defined by the local administrator working in conjunction with the users. As in the mainframe-only environment, most of these procedures have to do with file handling, including file naming, access privileges for shared files, backups, file movement, and translation.

1. *File naming.* File naming, or adherence to naming conventions, is just as important in the offloaded development environment as it is on the mainframe. On the MS-DOS PC workstation a file name consists of an eight-character name followed by a period and a three-character extension. When a mainframe data set is located on the PC, the eight-character name should remain as close as possible to the data set name on the mainframe. For example, if the file is a PDS member, then the workstation name should be the PDS member name. If the file is a regular data set with a name with many qualifiers (e.g., R5041.TEST.DATA), then the key identifier should be the file name. The extensions, of course, also should follow a set convention. This is because many PC software packages use extensions to determine which set of defaults to use. For example, Micro Focus COBOL normally looks for a .CBL extension on files containing COBOL source code. With SPF/PC, separate sets of editing/browsing options are created for different types of files. The option selection is driven by the file name extension used.

   Table 8-2 is a partial list of file extensions that can be used as part of a naming convention.

   What MS-DOS lacks in file-naming flexibility, it makes up for in file organization. In MS-DOS, directories and subdirectories are easy to create. Each directory name can be up to eight characters and have subdirectories. Given that the number and depth of directories is practically limitless, we have an environment to emulate very complex mainframe data set names. For example, the MVS PDS member named

   ID001.PROJECT1.COBOL(PROGRAM1)

   could be named

   C:\ID001\PROJECT1\COBOL\PROGRAM1.CBL

   on the PC workstation. The key with naming conventions is to pick one that is simple enough for everyone to use and understand but robust enough to handle all file names in a nonambiguous way.

Table 8-2. PC workstation file extensions.

Extension	File Type
.CBL	COBOL source code
.CPY	Copy members; DB2 DCLGENs
.SQL	SQL statements; DB2 DDL
.MFS	MFS code
.TXT	Text file
.UND	EBCDIC data file
.COM	MS-DOS command file
.CFG	Configuration file
.BAK	Backup file
.BAT	MS-DOS batch file
.DAT	ASCII data file
.DIR	Micro Focus directives file
.EXE	MS-DOS executable file
.INC	Includable module
.JCL	JCL source code
.JES	JES message file
.LBR	Micro Focus library
.LST	Micro Focus source code listing
.SAS	SAS source code
.INT	Micro Focus intermediate code

2. *File access.* Unlike a standalone PC, where all files are usually in a read-write mode, a network of offloaded development environment PC workstations will need to access files in both read only and read-write modes. To start with, all files located on the PC's hard drive should be read-writeable with the possible exception of the AUTOEXEC.BAT and CONFIG.SYS files. In addition, all files on private (i.e., password protected) sections of the server hard disk should be read-writeable. The situation becomes more complex when dealing with directories of shared files. Most of these items, such as common code, copy members, test files/databases, should be read only, especially when the number of users who will have access is large or these users are geographically spread out. If the user group is very courteous, they may be able to leave shared directories of common code and copy members'

read-writeable provided they send warning messages when files are going to be changed or tied up. This may be a little difficult when it comes to test databases because once a user takes read-write control of a shared database nobody else will be able to access it until it is released.

3. *Backups.* One of the main ways a PC user can get into trouble is by failing to backup his or her files regularly. While a mainframe user would normally be appalled if the disk drive that he was using was not backed up each and every night, he is usually unconcerned about backing up equally valuable files that reside on a PC disk drive. One way to solve this problem is to encourage the use of private directories on the server, especially for important files such as source code that is being worked on every day. Even though this activity will generate extra LAN traffic, such traffic is useful because it gives the administrator a way to gauge the actual use of the offloaded development environment. This practice is also easier, faster, and cheaper for the users to perform than backing up files to PC-based floppy or tape drives.

4. *File movement.* Procedures for file movement between the mainframe and the offloaded development environment are required because of the complexity involved. This complexity results from the variety of file types that can be uploaded and downloaded and the different methods of transfer involved. The variety of file types that can be moved is the bigger problem. Procedures and methods are needed to move both source code, which involves translating EBCDIC to ASCII, and data files that should not be translated but may be of significant length (i.e., several million bytes versus 100,000 or 200,000 bytes for source code modules) and/or have unusual LRECLs (i.e., anything from 1 to 32K bytes versus 80 bytes for source code modules). In addition to moving individual files, the movement of whole PDSs has to be addressed.

   As for the method of transfer, most 2-tier and 2.5-tier offloaded development environments rely on 3270-based file transfers, some of which are accomplished by a process that runs in the background. This is okay for small environments with no more than half a dozen users, but it becomes a little messy on a large scale, mostly because 3270 environments are not set up for file transfers. A user of online 3270 applications is to be pitied if her terminal has to compete with a lot of PCs sending source code and data files up and down the interactive network. See Chapter 7 for more information.

The other main method is Remote Job Entry (RJE), which is made for file transfer. RJE's virtual reader is used for uploading source code and data and requesting downloads. The virtual printer is used for receiving downloaded source code, reports, and certain flat data files. The virtual punch is used to download packed data files. This division makes translation easy — the reader and printer are used for EBCDIC/ASCII translation, and the punch for no translation (remember that Micro Focus and certain other tools need to work in an EBCDIC mode on the PC). Some procedures, hopefully mechanized, are required for some of these activities, specifically the following:

a. JES message removal. When source code is downloaded through the virtual printer, there will be a bunch of JES messages and possibly banner pages surrounding the code. These, of course, must be stripped off.

b. File expansion/contraction (files with LRECLS ^= 80). When data files are downloaded through the virtual punch, they come through with an LRECL of 80. This is usually not the correct LRECL, so the file must be "reassembled" with its correct LRECL. This means chopping bytes off each record in the case of files with LRECLs less than 80 and joining records together to make up real records for files with LRECLs larger than 80. RJE header and trailer punch records also may be present and should be removed.

c. File padding. When data files are uploaded through the reader, they will have an LRECL of 80. This means the records of the uploaded data files need to be padded out to multiples of 80 and then "reassembled" with the correct LRECL when on the mainframe.

See Chapter 7 for more information.

5. *File translations.* In the previous section we mentioned briefly EBCDIC to ASCII translation. This, of course, alludes to the different character code representations, EBCDIC on the mainframe and ASCII on file servers and PC workstations. The mapping from one code set to the other is usually straightforward and automatically performed by the emulation package being used. However, glitches can occur in some cases. The best example is the "|" symbol (in some languages when used in a pair it represents concatenation). With some emulation packages it is

translated into the "!" symbol. Another example is the "¬" symbol, which sometimes is translated into the "^" symbol. Thus, 100% translation is not always possible.

Another concern in the area of translation is ASCII to ASCII conversion. In the UNIX operating system, one of the main operating systems used for file servers, the end of line symbol is "<ctrl> n". This is different from the end of line used by MS-DOS PCs. Thus, when handling source code, an additional UNIX ASCII to DOS ASCII conversion step is needed when downloading from the mainframe to the PC via a UNIX server.

Administrative Procedures

In addition to assisting users to establish and enforce user procedures, administrators have still another set of procedures they have to follow to accomplish their own activities successfully. Listed below are the administrator's main responsibilities for which procedures should be established and followed. Additional procedures may, of course, be necessary depending on the individual situation.

1. *Backing up the server and performing restores.* After encouraging users to put their source code or other important files on the server, the administrator needs to backup that server on a regular basis. This will usually involve a complete backup at least once a week and incremental backups (i.e., backups of files that have changed since the last backup) every day. See Chapter 9 for more information.

2. *Controlling PC workstation hard disks.* In order to keep users from making a mess of their hard disks, it is the administrator's job to identify ways to keep them organized. For example, the C: drive may be reserved for system software, with the D: drive available for user files. The administrator also may be the designated central point for ordering software packages, thus providing a check against incompatibilities or use of unapproved tools. When new tools are acquired, it also might be the administrator's job to customize the installation procedures so as to make sure that the package is installed the same way throughout the offloaded development environment.

3. *Organizing and maintaining server disk space.* When setting up an offloaded development environment, it is the administrator's job to calculate how much disk space the server will need. If

multiple groups will be using the server, there needs to be a division of the disk in order to limit contention to users within a single group (i.e., if a user takes up a lot of disk space, she will only impact users in her own group, so she has a considerable incentive not to overload the server). Once in operation, the amount of free space that each group has and the rate at which it is eaten up needs to be monitored. When these factors become critical, then the administrator will need to track down unused or very large files for deletion. If not enough files can be deleted, then a reorganization or expansion of the server's hard disk will be required.

4. *Maintaining printers.* Print serving is an important part of any LAN. The administrator will need to monitor the quality of the printer's outputs and change cartridges, ribbons, and so on as needed. In order to balance work loads, printer traffic levels may need to be monitored, with an eye toward rerouting traffic.
5. *Controlling the server.* It is the administrator's job to control all important server passwords and insure they do not leak out to the wrong people. It is also his job to insure that a backup administrator knows the passwords and all critical procedures in case the primary administrator is unavailable. The other main areas here include the adding or deleting of users and the granting of the appropriate privileges or access rights.
6. *Monitoring activity levels.* As with the server's disk space, the usage level of the server needs to be checked to ensure that its users are not experiencing significant delays. It also needs to be checked to see that the server, or offloaded development environment in general, is being used to its full extent. If an offloaded development environment is not being used, it is the administrator's job to find out why and take appropriate corrective actions.
7. *Tuning the server.* When monitoring the server's activity levels it is important to look at them from a system-tuning point of view. If users are approaching the limits on the number of possible client sessions or work with files that are exceptionally large, the administrator may have to change the system-tuning parameters.
8. *Setting up and maintaining server libraries and shared directories.* If the users are numerous or have a lot of modules, they may need a library and/or shared directory(s) on the server. The administrator will need to assess the need for such structures and track their usage levels just as she would for the entire server hard disk. See Chapter 9 for more information.

9. *Monitoring links.* Every day the first thing the administrator must do is check that all the links between the server and the outside world (mainframe, e-mail, other LANs) are working. If the links are down or "broken," it is the administrator's urgent requirement to bring them up again.
10. *Maintaining trouble logs.* It is always worthwhile to have a diary or log of reported system troubles. It is also prudent to have a log of enhancements that the users or the administrators have expressed a desire for. This is useful when reviewing activities with supporting organizations or suppliers. Log entries also demonstrate to users that their troubles are receiving serious consideration.
11. *Maintaining system-wide mailing lists.* Most e-mail systems allow for users to establish their own private mailing lists. However, for general lists it is a good idea for an administrator, or some other centrally located person, to establish and maintain such lists for the use of the entire user community.

"HAND HOLDING"

"Hand holding" is the term used to describe the level of technical support that offloaded development environment users will need from their local administrator when starting up. There are a number of effective methods for doing hand holding. These are the four main ones.

1. *Walk around support.* "Management by walking around" was popularized several years ago as an effective management technique. For technical support it is also very worthwhile. Because converting to an offloaded development environment involves absorbing a lot of new information on a lot of tools in a relatively short amount of time, it is important for the local administrator to make himself available to answer any and all questions at any time. One way to facilitate this dialog is for the administrator to "make rounds" by visiting her users on a regular, although informal, basis. Usually twice a week will suffice, although at the very beginning a daily visit may not be considered excessive.
2. *User meetings.* In addition to one on one walk around support, group meetings, chaired by the administrator, are also useful. They provide an easy way to discuss general needs and questions and give the administrator a better feel for what items need the most attention. They also provide a forum for users to exchange useful ideas. As with walk around support, the need for user meetings is greatest at the beginning of conversion and lessens

as users become more knowledgeable and comfortable with the offloaded development environment. Figure 8-4 is an example of minutes from a user meeting.

Folks,

Here are the items brought up at the last user meeting. If you have any questions or corrections please let me know.

Mark

1. SPF/PC UND Profile — Users who obtained their PCs prior to the training session may not have correct UND profiles in SPF/PC. To check or correct this situation go into SPF/PC option 3.5 and select UND by entering S UND on the command line. The information displayed should read (or be changed to):

Record Format	U
End of File Marker	N
File Tabs	0
Record Terminator	CRLF

2. Downloading Files — Remember that when downloading COBOL source code, text files or reports you need to run them through the UNIX to DOS conversion utility (in FILE AIDS). Do not use the TRIM utility!

Also, when downloading EBCDIC data files you need to run them through the TRIM utility (in FILE AIDS). Do not run them through the UNIX to DOS conversion utility! This will damage the file!!!

3. COBOL COMP Field Error — While running a COBOL program through the Micro Focus COBOL Workbench, Steve and I discovered that COMP fields were not being handled correctly (they were twice as big as they should have been). To correct this everyone needs to change the following entry in their c:\cobol\cobol.dir file:

Change: MS(2)

To: NOMS

4. Server Backups — Starting tonight the server will be backed up every business day. A complete backup will be done on Friday nights, with incremental backups done on Monday, Tuesday, Wednesday, and Thursday nights.

5. Server Availability — The server and LAN will be available for use 24 hours a day, 7 days a week. When modification or maintenance work needs to be performed by the administrators (i.e., when they need to take the server and LAN out of service) they will provide several hours' notice (at least). Most heavy maintenance work will be done after 5 PM on weekdays or on weekends.

6. Broken 3270 Link — Our support group has given us a trouble ticket number and has indicated that they have a good understanding of the problem and how to fix it. Stay tuned.

Figure 8-4. Minutes of user meeting.

3. *E-mail.* E-mail is an extremely useful tool in most office situations, and offloaded development environments are no exception. E-mail allows for the easy exchange of problem and status reports and the issuing of announcements, user meeting minutes, system changes, and user recognition. It is also a handy way to provide advice to geographically distant users or users who are difficult or unpleasant to visit in person.

4. *Use of monitoring software.* While it is difficult to monitor user activities that are entirely transacted on the PC workstation, it is quite easy to monitor the use of server resources. Depending on the operating system of the server and the software packages used, local administrators can and should collect all available usage statistics. This can include CPU usage reports (e.g., sar in UNIX), file transfer logs, server process reports (e.g., ps in UNIX), and LAN usage statistics. In addition, dynamic activity monitors that come with most LAN software packages should be used. All these items will help the administrator find out how much his offloaded development environment is really being used and where there may be problems.

SUMMARY

There are a significant number of steps that should be addressed when setting up an offloaded development environment. These include the following:

1. Creating a rollout plan.
2. Testing a representative sample of components.
3. Ordering the full set of components.
4. Laying out the hardware.
5. Installing the hardware, software, and communication links.
6. Monitoring "The Four Stages of User Involvement" (i.e., dumb terminal usage, terminal emulation, offloaded editing, and full environment emulation).
7. Defining local user procedures.
8. Defining local administrative procedures.
9. Defining user support methods (a.k.a. "hand holding").

9

Securing the Offloaded Development Environment

An important consideration when setting up any computer system for use by a large group is security. The issue of security includes system access, the physical security of the system itself, as well as file control and file integrity. The sections that follow outline the security concerns for the various platforms (i.e., PC workstation, LAN/server) of the offloaded development environment. A section on source code control issues can be found at the end of the chapter.

PC WORKSTATION SECURITY

The PC workstation has become an integral part of most office environments. Unfortunately, it has also become a source of many security woes, including unauthorized access, computer viruses, and hard disk malfunctions. Below is a list of guidelines for securing PC workstations in an offloaded development environment. As always, this list should be tailored or enhanced to meet individual needs.

1. *Use a surge suppressor.* Each PC should have a surge suppressor to protect it from power surges.

2. *Keep food, drink, and lit cigarettes away from the keyboard and CPU.* For obvious reasons.

3. *Use a private directory on the server to hold or backup important work files.* Very few PC users backup their critical files to tape or diskette. This lack of discipline in performing routine backup

is usually due to the fact that most users underestimate the probability of hard disk malfunctions or the consequences of data loss. Having users keep duplicates of their sensitive files (e.g., source code or current test data files) in private directories on the server and encouraging them to backup these files as often as necessary is an easy way to minimize data loss. An even better practice is the use of a server-based drive as the main repository for all work files. This way users will not have to take any action to make sure their files are backed up on a regular basis; the administrator will take care of it.

4. *Lock up all storage media when not in use.* Some people just cannot resist stealing unsecured diskettes and tapes.

5. *If your PC has a system password, use it.* A system password prevents the PC from booting unless the correct password is entered.

6. *If your PC has a keylock password, use it.* A keylock password utility locks the keyboard and mouse while the PC is on. This allows users to maintain security without having to turn off the PC every time they step away from their workstations. It is important to note that system passwords must be used in conjunction with keylock passwords to prevent an intruder from gaining access by rebooting. Users should turn off their PCs when they will be left unattended for a long period of time.

7. *Protect user passwords.*

   a. Establish a convention that forbids users to choose names, numbers, or dates that personally identify the passwords.

   b. Change the password(s) every 30 to 90 days. Of course, passwords should be changed immediately if they are suspected of being compromised.

   c. Do not post passwords on or near the computer. If passwords must be written down, they should be stored in a locked cabinet or locked desk.

   d. Do not hardcode passwords into programs or script files for automatic login to other systems.

8. *Protect against computer viruses.* The number and variety of PC viruses that can destroy hard disk resident files, and more, is

steadily increasing. According to Dataquest,[1] most virus incidents have been traced to the following sources:

a. Unauthorized software brought from home by employees. This is by far the leading source of viruses.

b. Shareware/freeware software downloaded from public bulletin boards.

c. Sales/demonstration diskettes.

d. Diskettes used by service/repair personnel.

The majority of viruses give no indication of their presence until after they have damaged files or contaminated other diskettes. The risk of contracting a PC virus can be reduced by following these guidelines:

a. Avoid using software from the sources listed above.

b. Only allow system bootable diskettes in the A: drive when the PC is being booted. Allowing nonsystem bootable diskettes in the A: drive when the PC is booting is an easy way to contract a computer virus.

c. Encourage file transfer via LAN, e-mail, or modem connections, never by "sneakernet."

d. Never load or run new software on PC workstations without first using virus detection software to scan the new package for viruses. In most situations, the local administrator should handle the installation of all software. Not only will this reduce the chance of unauthorized software being introduced on the PC workstations, it will help keep the number of different PC configurations to a minimum. A useful trick that helps administrators keep control is to make the user's AUTOEXEC.BAT and CONFIG.SYS files read-only. This won't fool the hardcore PC hackers, but it will stop some people.

e. Always check both used and new PCs for viruses before using them for the first time. This is particularly important if software has already been loaded by the distributor or manufacturer.

f. Scan hard disks and all associated floppies for viruses with a virus detection package on a periodic basis. Every month is recommended.

There are many virus detection software packages in the marketplace. Some of these include:

a. Central Point Anti-Virus. Produced by Central Point Software and recommended by PC Magazine[2] as an "Editor's Choice." This package has a list price of approximately $129. The vendor can be contacted at:

Central Point Software
15220 NW Greenbrier Parkway, #200
Beaverton, OR 97006
Phone: 800-445-4208

b. NORTON Anti-Virus. Produced by Symantec Corporation. This package also has a list price of approximately $129. The vendor can be contacted at:

Symantec Corporation
10201 Torre Avenue
Cupertino, CA 95014
Phone: 800-441-7234

c. Dr. Solomon's Anti-Virus Toolkit. Produced by Ontrack Computer Systems and also a PC Magazine "Editor's Choice." This package has a list price of approximately $149. The vendor can be contacted at:

Ontrack Computer Systems, Inc.
6321 Bury Drive
Eden Prairie, MN 55346
Phone: 800-752-1333

9. *Use PC workstation case locks.* Most PCs come with keys that lock the casing/cover of the PC to its chassis. This helps prevent tampering, but not all PCs have unique keys. A popular gag in some DP shops is to see how many PCs can be opened with a single key.

10. *Consider using a chassis lock.* Locks are available that can bolt a PC to a desktop or table. These should be used when there is a considerable risk that someone may steal the entire PC. One supplier of such devices is Anchor Pad International. They can be reached at 800-426-2467 (in California 800-626-2467).

11. *Consider using floppy locks.* If unauthorized or unsafe floppy usage is really a problem, consider using floppy locks that prevent users from inserting diskettes into floppy drives. Anchor Pad International also supplies these devices.

LAN/SERVER SECURITY

While PC workstation security is important, LAN and server security is essential because of the central role LANs and servers play in most offloaded development environments. Below is a list of guidelines for securing LANs and servers in an offloaded development environment. As always, this list should be tailored or enhanced to meet individual needs.

1. *Use an uninterruptable power supply (UPS).* Not only will a UPS give the administrator time to bring down the server gracefully in the event of a power outage, it also will protect the server from power surges.

2. *Keep food, drink, and lit cigarettes away from the keyboard and CPU.* As with PC workstations, spilled food or drink or smoke from burning cigarettes can foul up a CPU or keyboard. Do not allow the server room to become a hangout for people trying to evade restrictive smoking rules.

3. *Backup the server nightly.* All servers should be backed up at the end of every business day. Depending on the size of the server's hard disk(s), a complete backup can be performed nightly, or a complete backup can be performed once a week with incremental backups (a backup of all files that have changed since the last backup) performed every night in between.

4. *Keep a series of backups.* If complete backups are performed nightly, at least the last two complete backups should be kept. If complete backups are performed weekly, with incremental backups performed every night in between, at least the last two complete backups and the last two incremental backups should be kept. It is important to note that the above should be considered minimum requirements. Hopefully, a more thorough backup and restore procedure will be implemented.

5. *Establish a scheme for labeling the backup media.* A scheme that relieves the administrator from constantly having to relabel the storage media is best. An example of such a scheme is to keep five weeks of complete backups (performed every Friday night) and four days of incremental backups (performed every Monday through Thursday night). Label the storage tapes as Friday 1, Friday 2, Friday 3, Friday 4, Friday 5, Monday, Tuesday, Wednesday, and Thursday. The numbered Friday tapes contain a month's worth of complete backups. The daily tapes contain all

incremental backups performed since the last complete backup. This scheme allows the administrator to identify easily the tape or diskette to be used for a backup or restoration.

6. *Use write protect devices on backup media.* Write protect devices (e.g., tabs) should be used on all backup media to prevent accidental erasure or unintentional overwriting of the backup.
7. *Store completed backups separately, in a secure place.* A secure place is a locked cabinet or room that is separate from the storage location of the original tapes/diskettes used to load the server. Backups are worthless if they are destroyed along with the originals. Consider off-site storage if the files being backed up are extremely valuable.
8. *Test the restoration procedure.* After a set of backups has been created, test the restoration procedure to ensure that it does in fact restore the data properly. The first time that a user makes a restoration request is not the time to discover that the backup and restore procedures don't work.
9. *Safeguard server passwords.* To protect server passwords, follow the same guidelines outlined in the section on PC workstation password security above. In addition, make sure all system IDs have passwords. Administrators of UNIX servers should ensure that all IDs in the /etc/passwd file have associated passwords.
10. *Use password aging.* If the server has password aging facilities, use them.
11. *Disable all IDs of departing users.* All IDs belonging to employees that leave the company or institution should be disabled. Access privileges for employees transferring to other parts of the company also should be reviewed.
12. *Safeguard the server against viruses.* To keep the server virus-free, follow the same guidelines outlined in the section on PC workstation virus protection above.
13. *Position the server in a secure area.* Keeping the server behind a locked door is best because it keeps users and other people from tampering with the CPU or the console.
14. *Protect the reset button.* If your server is in a place that can be accessed by the users, the reset button needs to be protected. Rebooting servers that run certain operating systems (e.g., UNIX),

without first shutting them down properly, can result in damaged directories or files, which can be difficult to restore. A user may be inclined to reset a server when she experiences a problem (e.g., blocked LAN access, a hung-up 3270 gateway session, a sign-on problem) and she, correctly or incorrectly, perceives the server as the source of the problem. User-initiated resets are more prominent with Intel-based servers because many users think they have an inalienable right to reboot any 386- or 486-based computer. Two ways to fix this are to physically remove the reset button or, if this is not possible, to post a threatening sign (see Figure 9-1).

If you touch the reset button, you will be hunted down and KILLED!!!

Figure 9-1. User deterrence.

15. *Know where the nearest fire extinguisher is located.* Also know how to use it.
16. *Log off before leaving the server console.* Never leave the server console logged in and unattended.
17. *Attend a system administration course.* All administrators should attend a system administration course that covers the security issues, security methods, and security tools associated with the server and LAN operating systems.

SOURCE CODE CONTROL

A good source code control methodology should always be able to provide the answers to the following questions:

1. Where is the "real" source code?

2. Who, if anyone, is working on it?

In the mainframe development environment, these questions were usually easy to answer because all the code was located on a single computer. In a multiplatform development environment, things are a little more complicated. For this reason, a source code control methodology needs to be chosen and adhered to by the users. An example of a valid source code control methodology for the development of a new application follows:

1. Store all the source code as it is developed in a directory or library on the server.
2. When a programmer needs to work on a piece of existing source code he should copy or check out the code, make the required changes, test the modifications, and then restore the code to the server. Once a programmer is finished with a source code module it should be moved to the server, leaving no copy on the PC workstation.
3. When a system is ready to be cut to the mainframe for final integration and testing, all the source code should be moved or copied to the mainframe. A source code control methodology for the maintenance portion of the application's development life cycle would then be selected. Some examples are outlined below.

A valid source code control methodology for an existing application expecting low levels of enhancements or maintenance is as follows:

1. Once initial development is complete, all of the source code is moved to the target mainframe. No source code should remain on the server or individual workstations.
2. If trivial changes to a piece of source code are required (i.e., a few lines of code are changed, added, or deleted), the changes are performed using only mainframe resources (i.e., mainframe-based compilers and debuggers).
3. If unexpected major changes are required, the source code is downloaded to the PC workstation, changed, tested, then uploaded to the mainframe for final integration and testing. No copies of the source code should remain on the PC workstation or server.

For an existing application expecting high levels of enhancements and/or maintenance, a valid source code control methodology is:

1. Once initial development is complete, a copy of the source code is moved to the target mainframe for final integration and testing. The "real" copy of the source code remains on the server.

2. If a programmer needs to change a piece of source code, she would copy or check out the appropriate modules from the server resident directory or library to the PC workstation, make the required changes, test the modifications, and then copy or check in the code back to the server resident directory or library. After the server receives the modified source code, a copy is moved to the target mainframe for final integration and testing. The "real" source code remains on the server. No copies of the source code should remain on the PC workstation.

In most situations, a variation of one, and only one, of the above source code control methodologies should be in use at any given time. Of course, there may be factors other than the expected amount of enhancement work or development life cycle phase that determine which methodology to choose (e.g., only part of a programming group is working in an offloaded development environment, the extent of available source code control technology).

Once a source code control methodology is selected, supporting tools can be evaluated. Some of the questions that should be answered during any evaluation of a source code control tool include the following:

1. *Does it support the selected architecture and platform?* If a server is being used, the selected tool probably should run on it. If a mainframe-based tool (e.g., CA-Librarian, CA-Panvalet) is being used, can the offloaded development environment-based tool interact with it?

2. *Does it provide automatic synchronization with the mainframe?* This is especially important if not all of the developers working on an application are working within the offloaded development environment. (For example, a developer working on the mainframe changes a copy member there. Is the changed copy member automatically moved to the server of the offloaded development environment?) Also of interest would be the need to purchase a mainframe-based component of the tool.

3. *Is a source code control tool really needed?* Many small projects may be able to get by just using server-based directories.

4. *Is enough security provided?* Can the checking out of sensitive modules be limited to certain programmers or can anybody check out anything?

5. *What versioning capabilities are needed?* Can the branching of releases be done (e.g., one set of developers work on release 1.31 of a product, while another set of developers work on release 2.0)?

6. *Does it collect the right historical information?* Can the tool collect and report on the reasons for changes, program metrics, testing history, and so on? Can audit trail reports be produced?

Some of the tools that meet the challenge of tracking and controlling source code across multiplatform environments include Intersolv's PVCS Version Manager, LEGENT Corporation's ENDEVOR Workstation, and Computer Associates' CA-PAN/LCM. All of these relatively new products were created to give PC-based developers the kind of source code control they had on the mainframe but lost when they moved to offloaded development environments. The main advantage of these tools is that they provide facilities to maintain synchronization between mainframe-based modules and server/PC-based modules. Contact information for the above-mentioned tools follows.

PVCS Version Manager is a product of Intersolv, Inc. Intersolv can be contacted at the following address:

Intersolv
3200 Tower Oaks Boulevard
Rockville, MD 20852
Phone: (301) 230-3200

The ENDEVOR product line of software management products for mainframes, LANs, and PCs is offered by LEGENT Corporation. LEGENT may be contacted at the following address:

LEGENT Corporation
Westboro Executive Park
114 Turnpike Road
Westborough, MA 01581
Phone: (508) 870-1900

Computer Associates products can, of course, be obtained through your regular CA representative.

SUMMARY

Multiplatform development environments can be extremely vulnerable from a security point of view. At the PC workstation level, important security considerations include the following:

1. Using a surge suppressor.
2. Keeping food, drink, and lit cigarettes away from the keyboard and CPU.
3. Using a private directory on the server to hold or backup important work files.
4. Locking up all storage media that is not in use.
5. Using system passwords.
6. Using keylock passwords.
7. Protecting user passwords.
8. Protecting against computer viruses.
9. Using PC workstation case locks.
10. Using chassis locks.
11. Using floppy locks.

For LAN/server security, important considerations include the following:

1. Using a UPS (uninterruptable power supply).
2. Keeping food, drink, and lit cigarettes away from the keyboard and CPU.
3. Backing up the server nightly.
4. Keeping a series of backups.
5. Establishing a scheme for labeling backup media.
6. Using write protect devices on backup media.
7. Storing completed backups in a secure place.
8. Testing the restoration procedure before it's needed.
9. Safeguarding server passwords.
10. Using password aging facilities.

11. Disabling all IDs of departing users.
12. Safeguarding the server against viruses.
13. Placing the server in a secure area.
14. Protecting the server's reset button.
15. Knowing where the nearest fire extinguisher is located.
16. Logging off before leaving the server console.
17. Attending a system administration course.

Apart from securing the physical environment, there is the matter of source code control. All groups of offloaded development environment users need a scheme for source code control, even if it's just a rule that says that all source code will be stored on the mainframe and downloaded every time a change is needed. Most groups, however, will require something more elaborate. Depending on what source code control methodology is adopted, a source code control tool may be necessary. Some of the major tools in this area include Intersolv's PVCS, LEGENT's ENDEVOR, and Computer Associates' CA-PAN/LCM.

REFERENCES

1. Dortch, Michael. Down With a Virus. *Communications Week.* December 2, 1991. 1–5.
2. Ellison, Carol. On Guard: 20 Utilities That Battle the Virus Threat. *PC Magazine.* October 29, 1991. 199–250.

10

Expanding an Offloaded Development Environment

Once an offloaded development environment has users that have reached the fourth stage of involvement (see Chapter 8) and are making good use of mainframe emulation tools, such as Micro Focus COBOL and XDB-Workbench for DB2, the environment can be expanded. Additional users can be added and existing users can take on more tools to further improve their productivity. In addition, physically separate offloaded development environments can be connected to each other to take advantage of economies of scale.

ADDING NEW TOOLS

As mentioned in Chapter 8, the final stage of user involvement is moving hardcore development activities (syntax checking, compiling, dynamic testing) from the mainframe to the PC workstation. This final stage also consists of multiple substages. Users should start out with a single language tool set without a DBMS tool set, if possible. This way users are not trying to learn multiple complex tool sets simultaneously. Once the initial tool set is learned, additional tool sets can be added until the users are emulating the bulk of the mainframe environment in the offloaded development environment (i.e., 3GL and DBMS). At this point it is time to look for additional improvements.

For programmers, these improvements normally include a lower CASE tool, such as a code generator, preferably one that has a useful interface to the language/DBMS tool sets being used. A good example of this would be Intersolv's APS/PC or Computer Associates' TELON/PWS, generating code for the Micro Focus COBOL and XDB DB2 workbenches.

When extending an existing offloaded development environment, it is important to keep a final goal in mind. For most DP shops, the ultimate goal will be a forward and reverse engineering environment. That is an environment where specifications and designs can be turned into a 4GL, which in turn can be turned into a 3GL and vice-versa. All this would be accomplished with a minimum of human intervention. Implementing this, however, requires tight integration between tool sets, along with a fair amount of cooperation between vendors. Thus, expanding an offloaded development environment with additional tools is mostly a question of giving users the right amount of time and support to absorb the new tools and selecting the right vendor(s) to deliver tools that can talk to each other effectively.

ADDING NEW USERS

When considering the addition of more users to an offloaded development environment, the same selection criteria used to choose the initial group should be applied (see Chapter 1). Present mainframe tool usage, work type, and function are all part of user selection. Some potential users, however, may never be good candidates for an offloaded development environment. Still, once an environment is made operational, these people may benefit from being connected to it. For example, while a COBOL-DB2 programmer doing a large, new development project may need Micro Focus COBOL, XDB DB2, and APS/PC on a 486/SX PC workstation, an SPSS programmer doing repair maintenance may benefit from having a word processor, a spreadsheet, and an e-mail package on a 286 PC workstation. He would still be connected to the same offloaded development environment server, via the same LAN, but the justification here is based on improved office automation, not improved application development.

JOINING FORCES: CONNECTING TO OTHER GROUPS

Once multiple offloaded development environments start to crop up, the question of whether to connect them together into a larger network arises. There are reasons for and against such a consolidation.

Reasons for Linking Offloaded Development Environments

1. *Consolidation of administration.* Once established offloaded development environments start to come together, the need for local backup administrators is reduced. This is because administrators can be replaced by other primary administrators that run other offloaded development environments. This consolidation not only saves on the training and deployment of local backup administrators, it also should lead to better support as the other primary administrator will usually have more knowledge and experience than a backup administrator.

2. *Movement of users.* When offloaded development environments, or LANs in general, are initially set up, they usually serve a single group. Many times these groups consist of subgroups that work on different projects. If this is the case, there is a possibility that a subgroup may be broken off organizationally and assigned to another group. When this happens, one question that arises is what happens to their offloaded development environment (i.e., they might be able to take their PCs, but they cannot move the LAN or the server). Having offloaded development environments of different organizations linked together may allow these kinds of organizational changes to take place without changing LAN wiring. Even if the above situation is not the case, the movement of individuals (i.e., transfers) will still occur and need to be addressed in the same way.

3. *Reduced software costs.* When offloaded development environments are outfitted with software, some of the packages will be located at the server level rather than at the individual workstation level. When this happens, it may make sense to centrally locate all users of a particular package(s) to one server and move the other users to a different server instead of purchasing multiple copies of a package for multiple servers. Not only does this save money, it makes server set up and administration easier because fewer packages will need to be made to coexist with each other.

4. *Cheaper communications.* Most offloaded development environments will have an e-mail system that can communicate with other environments by going through an intermediate service (e.g., ATTMail). Unfortunately, these services cost money. Having separate offloaded development environments capable of contacting each other directly will save on these kinds of charges.

5. *Faster communications.* While it is possible to connect offloaded development environments with dial-up modems or WANs (e.g., AT&T ISN, AT&T DataKit), these options are usually nowhere near as fast as being directly connected. Linking multiple offloaded development environments together with bridges or brouters (see the next section for more information) will speed up communication significantly.

Reasons Against Linking Offloaded Development Environments

1. *Security.* While an administrator may know and trust all the users on her offloaded development environment, linking to other environments allows a lot of strangers to have access. Some of the concerns here involve password security — are all server logins password protected?, and will the new users put a strain on an otherwise well-balanced system? This means a great deal of trust must exist between the various administrators before their offloaded development environments can be linked together.

2. *More complicated administration.* When new links to other offloaded development environments are added, the job of the administrator becomes more complicated. This is because of the security issues listed above and the greater range of possible problems that may crop up. For example, if a user on System A plugs his LAN connection into the wrong port on his PC workstation, he may wipe out some or all of the users on System A. If, however, System A is linked to System B, the consequences of the error may spread there as well. So not only does an administrator have to be concerned about his own users, he has to consider the actions of other users he is not even aware of.

3. *Increased hardware costs.* While linked offloaded development environments may be able to save money by eliminating or consolidating redundant software packages, the equipment to link the environments costs money. A single bridge between two environments may cost $5,000, while a brouter that can link multiple systems may cost $10,000 or more. In addition to the hardware to create a multi-LAN environment, extra money may be needed for sophisticated multi-LAN management tools. Therefore, when linking multiple environments, it is important to have some knowledge of the various methods available (see below).

HOW TO LINK OFFLOADED DEVELOPMENT ENVIRONMENTS

Once a decision to link up separate offloaded development environments is made, the question becomes what kind of link should be established. This will depend on several factors, including traffic levels, type of access required, and the locations and number of groups being linked together. Here are the main types of links.

1. *Direct links.* Simply combining LANs by directly wiring them together is often the simplest and cheapest in terms of preparation and equipment. However, simply plugging two or more LANs together is not as easy as it sounds. One thing that has to be considered is security. As mentioned before, a local administrator might know and trust all the users on her LAN, but what about the users of the other LAN(s)? The inhibitions of users that prevent them from abusing a LAN in a small environment, where everyone is well known, might break down when super-LANs are created with many users. Another issue is segmentation. When LANs are large, traffic levels on the LAN tend to be high. This can slow down the LAN's response time. Therefore, large numbers of users on a single LAN must be closely monitored.

2. *Bridges.* Bridges are combinations of hardware and firmware that provide a permanent high-speed link between two co-located LANs. The main function of bridges is to restrict traffic between two LANs to only that traffic that needs to go from one LAN to the other. For example, if LAN A and LAN B were linked with a bridge, LAN A would only receive the traffic that was specifically addressed to devices on LAN A. This means that LAN B could have severe usage level problems and LAN A would be insulated against them. Thus, bridges provide a high degree of security and can operate at the same speed as a direct link. In addition to providing security, bridges are used to do speed conversion. For example, a 1 Mb LAN can be linked to a 10 Mb LAN or backbone network with a 1 Mb to 10 Mb bridge.

3. *Routers.* Routers are combinations of hardware and software that allow users on one LAN to establish temporary communication links with other LANs. Prior to establishing a session, however, routing information will have been stored in the router's database. When a session is requested, the router uses the information in the database to establish the link, and when the session

is over the link is terminated. Normally routers are used between remote locations and work at speeds that are slower than those found between LANs using bridges. They do, however, provide security similar to that of a bridge.

4. *Brouters.* Brouters are bridges and routers combined. They provide links between multiple LANs in two ways. When a link request is made, the brouter first checks its permanent bridge links to see if it can complete the request. If it can't, it sets up a temporary session using its router capabilities. Brouters are usually used to link groups that reside at a number of different locations (i.e., some that are co-located and some that are remote).

5. *Dial-up links.* Dial-up links are one of the cheapest and easiest ways to link LANs. This method should usually be chosen if the amount of traffic and contact between LANs is low. Examples of this include e-mail and the occasional online dial-up session. Again, security is an issue here, because both LAN administrators will need to be able to trust that the other's group is not going to make excessive resource demands on his system.

SUMMARY

Expanding an offloaded development environment usually means adding new tools, adding new users, or linking existing offloaded development environments together. The adding of new tools for programmers will usually mean the installation of a lower CASE workbench, such as Intersolv's APS/PC or Computer Associates' TELON/PWS. These tools work on top of language, DBMS and TP monitor workbenches, such as Micro Focus COBOL/2 Workbench and XDB-Workbench for DB2. The important thing to keep in mind is that the ultimate goal is a forward and reverse engineering environment.

New users may need to be added depending on business needs. The selection criteria used to determine if a user should be added to an offloaded development environment that was described in Chapter 1 still applies.

Once multiple groups of offloaded development environment users start to crop up, they probably will need to be linked together. This can be accomplished with direct LAN links, bridges, routers, brouters, and/or dial up links.

11

Measuring the Effects of an Offloaded Development Environment

Once an offloaded development environment is established, its effect on application development should be measured to ensure that the development group is getting its money's worth. The main areas to be measured are productivity impact and changes in mainframe usage. Quality also should be measured, especially if upper CASE tools are part of the environment.

MEASURING EFFECTS ON PRODUCTIVITY

The largest portion of the offloaded development environment's benefit is its effect on productivity (see Chapter 2 for more information). However, measuring application development productivity is, and always has been, very difficult because of the subjectivity of the measurements (e.g., function points, surveys) or questions about the value of the measurements themselves (e.g., lines of code). Despite these problems, the above measurements are probably the best and most widely used methods of measuring productivity.

Function Points

Function points is a technique, devised by Albrecht of IBM[1] and expanded upon by Capers Jones[2,3] and others, that involves the counting of a system's inputs, outputs, inquiries, master files, and interfaces and then multiplying the results by different weights to determine a function point count. This count can then be adjusted up or down based on certain factors (e.g., programmer experience), but when the development hours are divided by the function point count, a useful productivity indicator results.

When measuring changes in anything a baseline is always needed. With function points, it is always best that the baseline be local in origin. Of course, this may not be possible or practical in all situations. If this is the case, use of company-wide function point findings as a baseline may be possible. The key is to find enough sample numbers to make a valid baseline. This may not be easy because valid samples need to satisfy the following criteria:

1. *Function point numbers must be current.* The samples should be recent, two years old or less. Samples older than this are usually not useful for measuring the impact of new tools against the current mainframe-based development environment, because the environment of several years ago, in most situations, does not resemble the current environment.
2. *Must be comparing apples to apples.* Development hours per function point vary tremendously between languages, DBMSs, TP monitors, and operating systems. Thus, it is necessary to have an exact match. Comparing DB2 development against an IMS(DB) baseline is pointless.

Even if the above criteria are satisfied, other problems may crop up from using function points from other than local sources. These include the following:

1. Function point counters that don't count function point components the same way as their colleagues.
2. Possible concerns about the subjectivity of certain function point measurement practices (e.g., whether master files always have the same weight).
3. Difficulty in taking individual application developer talent into account. This is because a really good programmer can produce 10 times the output of an average programmer.

So, if at all possible, use local baseline measurements when using function points to measure productivity changes.

Lines of Code

Lines of code is probably the oldest productivity measurement. The problem with lines of code is that if a programmer knows he is being measured in this way, it's easy for him to pad his outputs. Another problem is what to measure. Should it be all lines of code, noncommented lines of code, number of verbs, or something else? Whatever is chosen, lines of code productivity measurements need to be balanced with lines of code per module quality measurements as a check (see section on quality scores below). This will prevent programmers from excessively padding modules to get high-productivity results, because only small modules can yield positive lines of code per module quality measurements.

Some tools that are helpful with lines of code measurements include PATHVU and Q/AUDITOR. Both of these tools are available in mainframe and PC formats.

Surveys

The simplest way to collect useful statistical information is to simply ask for it. This is best accomplished by using a questionnaire or survey. In most cases, if you have enough respondents and the surveys are designed correctly, survey numbers can be just as good as function points or lines of code. Here are few rules to follow when using the survey method.

1. Keep essay questions to a minimum. If possible, word questions so that quantifiable answers must be given.
2. If possible, give respondents a selection of answers. For example:

Excellent	Good	Fair	Poor
4	3	2	1

3. When giving respondents a set of possible answers, make sure the number of responses is an even number. This will force respondents to think more about the question and commit one way or the other, rather than taking a middle-of-the-road answer. For example, the following selection is, in most cases, poorly structured:

Very Positive	Positive	Neutral	Negative	Very Negative
5	4	3	2	1

Whereas this is much better:

Very Positive	Positive	Negative	Very Negative
4	3	2	1

4. Number all questions and use numbers in the quantifiable responses. This will make tallying the results easier.
5. If the survey is complex, always have the person collecting the survey information assist the respondent when she is answering the questions. This will ensure that all questions are being interpreted correctly by all the respondents.
6. If the survey is complex, test it out on a few users and analyze the results. Performing a field test will ensure that the right questions are being asked.

Another thing to remember when surveying offloaded development environment users is to collect information not only from the hardcore application developers but also from the project leaders and MIS. Their opinions will carry a lot of weight when it comes time to review the success of the offloaded development environment (see the end of this chapter for examples of surveys for application development users and project leaders/MIS).

MEASURING EFFECTS ON MAINFRAME USAGE

While the impact of offloaded development environments on mainframe usage is not as important as the impact on application development productivity, it is still a very significant part of the overall cost effectiveness of the environment. Measuring the effect can be done several ways, including examining and comparing mainframe chargeback reports, examining and comparing file server usage statistics, and surveys.

Mainframe Chargeback Reports

Obviously, the first place to look for information on mainframe usage is the chargeback reports that are produced by most mainframes. Depending on how charges are calculated, bills can be derived from CPU usage, diskspace usage, I/O activity, and/or connect time. All these numbers are useful, especially when broken down to their individual components. But before any comparison can be done, a baseline must be established. The baseline should consist of information produced by the same set of users that are now using the offloaded development environment. However, for any comparison to be truly accurate, all major influencing factors need to be taken into account. These include the following:

1. *Work cycle changes.* If there are large swings in the level of development activity this must be taken into account. For example, if a project implements large-scale updates to a system every spring, it would be important to compare non-spring offloaded development environment numbers against non-spring baseline numbers and spring offloaded development environment numbers against spring baseline numbers.
2. *Work type changes.* Just as work levels can vary, the type of work (i.e., new development, enhancement maintenance, repair maintenance) can vary. This, of course, can affect CPU chargeback, especially in the area of CPU usage attributable to compiles and dynamic testing (new development and enhancement maintenance usually use more CPU time than repair maintenance).
3. *Tool set changes.* Because we are trying to measure the effect of an offloaded development environment against the current mainframe-based development environment, it's important to know if the tool set used in the baseline is reasonably similar to the current mainframe tool set. Changes can occur for two reasons. The first is changes to the mainframe tools themselves, either upgrades or additions. The second is changes in tool usage because the users are using different tools to do their work (e.g., users may have started a project by only using COBOL but are now using a combination of COBOL and EASYTRIEVE PLUS). Both can significantly affect the baseline.

Other considerations when comparing mainframe chargeback bills include making sure that only application development activities are part of the bill (i.e., no production activities) and that non-offloaded development environment users are not included in the bill comparison. Finally, it's worthwhile to measure mainframe chargeback from the beginning of offloaded development environment usage. But it should be remembered that the learning curve for the PC workstation tool set may be lengthy. Thus, the offloaded development environment's effect on mainframe chargeback will be gradual.

File Server Usage Statistics

Usually it will not be possible to measure PC workstation usage, at least not in a mechanized way. However, file servers and LANs are different. So, just as mainframe usage reports should be studied to make a bottom line comparison of mainframe chargeback savings, file server usage also should be studied to determine if the change in mainframe usage is real and not just a coincidental shift in demand for mainframe resources. Thus, file server/LAN usage statistics provide a good indicator of the usage level of the whole offloaded development environment.

In normal circumstances, mainframe usage should be an inverse ratio of file server usage (see Figure 11-1).

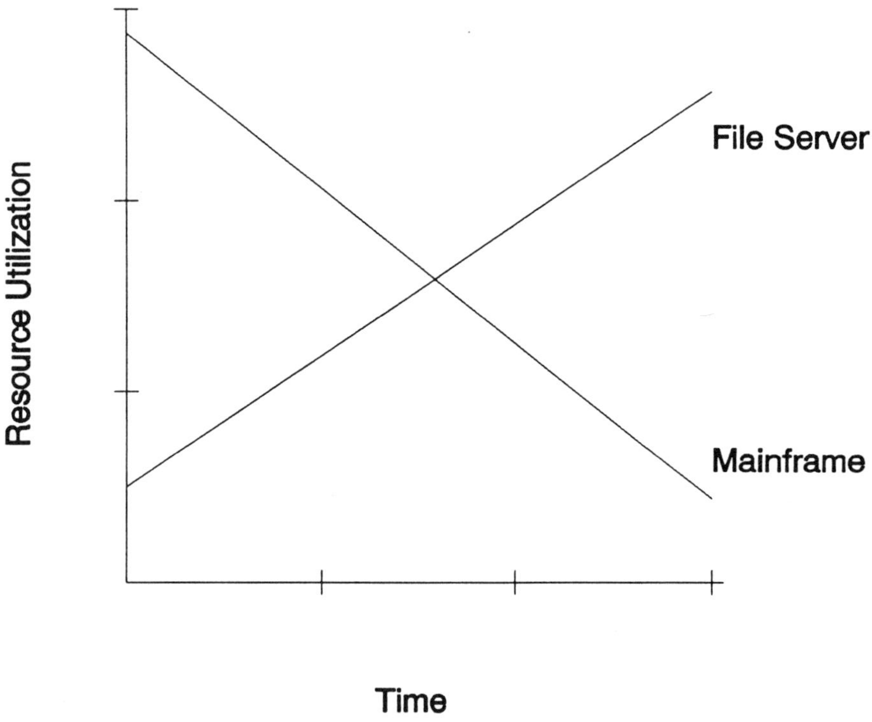

Figure 11-1. File server utilizations vs. mainframe utilization.

The information that makes up the file server utilization figures can come from a number of sources, including the following:

1. *CPU usage.* In multitasking operating systems it is easy to have a usage meter measure the level of CPU utilization. For example, in UNIX this is done with the **sar** command. By having **sar** reports saved away every day, via use of the UNIX **cron** facility, a picture of file server usage patterns can be drawn.

2. *File transfer logs.* If the offloaded development environment is routing file transfers through the file server there is usually a log showing who moved what. This is extremely useful, not only in measuring general offloaded development environment usage but individual usage as well.

3. *LAN statistics.* Many LAN software packages produce statistics for the LAN administrators to help them tune their system. These numbers, especially if they record the number of files accessed on the file server, are very useful in determining offloaded development environment usage.

4. *E-mail logs.* Most e-mail systems maintain some sort of log of e-mail traffic. In UNIX the log can be read with the **uulog** command. These logs are another indication of file server usage.

5. *Dynamic activity monitor.* Most LAN packages come with an activity monitor that shows who is linked to the LAN and what files or resources are being used. While these monitors may not accumulate the statistics for examination at a later time, they do give the administrator a way to get a feel for the LAN's usage level.

Surveys

Although surveys are usually subjective, they can provide some useful information when determining an offloaded development environment's impact on mainframe usage. This is because surveys can be turned around more quickly than, for example, a monthly or quarterly mainframe usage report.

Surveys also can provide a breakdown of mainframe and offloaded development environment usage activities that may not be normally available. For example, the following question could appear on the survey:

1. Break down, by platform, where the following activities are performed:

	PC Workstation		Mainframe		Total
Editing	___%	+	___%	=	100%
Compiling	___%	+	___%	=	100%
Debugging/Unit Testing	___%	+	___%	=	100%
System Testing	___%	+	___%	=	100%
Documentation	___%	+	___%	=	100%

MEASURING EFFECTS ON QUALITY

With the current emphasis on quality, a question that is always asked when any change is proposed is "What will be the effect on quality?" This will especially be the situation when upper CASE tools or sophisticated testing tools are included in the offloaded development environment.

Quality measurements come in numerous shapes and sizes. The ones dealt with here are quality scores/rating, error counts, and downtime.

Quality Scores/Ratings

Quality scores can be composed of almost anything. The quality scores that are most widely used are McCabe's Cyclomatic Complexity metric[4,5] and lines of code per module. McCabe's metric provides a single number score that reflects the complexity of a module. The lower the score, the more maintainable the module. Lines of code per module refers to the number of procedure lines of code in a module. One hundred or two hundred lines is usually regarded as a good number. As with McCabe's metric, the lower the number, the more maintainable the module. Both of these metrics are supported by the PATHVU and Q/AUDITOR packages mentioned earlier in this chapter.

Error Counts

Error counts are another type of quality measurement. They can be broken down into logic errors and execution errors. Logic and execution errors can, in turn, be identified and categorized by source and weighted by severity. For logic errors the possible sources would normally include the following:

- Requirements
- Specifications
- Design
- Coding/Testing
- System Software (offloaded development environment related)
- System Software (non-offloaded development environment related)

Execution errors can be expressed in the mainframe world in terms of executions per abend. As with logic errors, they should be identified by source using the same list as logic errors, along with a category for operations errors (e.g., incorrect tape mounts). Also, as with logic errors, the severity of errors would be a part of any report on execution errors.

Downtime

In addition to quality scores and error counts, application downtime is an important measure of quality. As with error counts, downtime, in order to be meaningfully measured, must be broken down by source. This can consist of the same list of error sources associated with execution error counts.

CONCLUSION

The measurements identified in this chapter are very useful in justifying the existence of an offloaded development environment and identifying and monitoring problems with the environment. However, some of the measurements can be expensive to implement, especially if elaborate baselines have to be assembled in order to do the comparison, which is usually the case. Others, such as the surveys, are cheap and should always be done. The important thing to remember, however, is that whatever set of measurements is chosen, the audience for the measurements must believe they are accurate and sound. Assembling reports of measurements that the audience is unfamiliar with, or does not believe in, is pointless.

Sample Survey for Offloaded Development Environment Users

Name: ______________________________

1. How long have you been doing work in the offloaded development environment?

   ___ months

2. Before the conversion to the offloaded development environment how much time, on average, did you spend in these environments to do your work?

   PC Workstation ___%

   Mainframe ___%

   ———

   100%

3. How much time do you currently spend in these environments to do your work?

   PC Workstation ___%

   Mainframe ___%

   ———

   100%

4. Break down, by platform, where the following activities are currently performed:

	PC Workstation		Mainframe		Total
Editing/coding	___%	+	___%	=	100%
Compiling/syntax checking	___%	+	___%	=	100%
Debugging/unit testing	___%	+	___%	=	100%
System testing	___%	+	___%	=	100%
Documentation	___%	+	___%	=	100%

5. How many file transfers (i.e., uploads and downloads) between the mainframe to the offloaded development environment did you perform since the environment was deployed? Break down the numbers by file type and direction.

	Number of Downloads	**Number of Uploads**
COBOL source programs:	____	____
COBOL copy members:	____	____
EBCDIC data files:	____	____
Documentation files:	____	____
Other (specify:________):	____	____
Other (specify:________):	____	____

6. How much time are you saving by using the offloaded development environment rather than your previous mainframe environment? Please indicate the savings as a percentage of your previous mainframe environment.

Activity	**Savings**
Coding, editing, and compiling/syntax checking	____%
Unit testing	____%
String testing	____%
Debugging (maintenance only)	____%

7. Overall, how much time are you saving by using the offloaded development environment rather than your previous mainframe environment? Please indicate the savings as a percentage of your previous mainframe environment.

   Overall savings ____%

8. Has the quality of your outputs been affected by the use of the offloaded development environment (check one)?

   Yes ____ No ____

   If yes, has the change been (circle one):

Very Positive	Positive	Negative	Very Negative
4	3	2	1

9. Is there anything else the survey coordinators should know?

Sample Survey for Project Leaders/MIS of Offloaded Development Environment Users

Name: ____

1. How long has your group been doing work in the offloaded development environment?

   ___ months

2. Currently, what percentage of your group's work is performed with the offloaded development environment?

   ___%

3. Please describe the work that is NOT performed in the offloaded development environment.

4. How much time is your group saving by using the offloaded development environment rather than your previous mainframe environment? Please indicate the savings as a percentage of your previous mainframe environment.

   ___%

5. Please estimate your mainframe chargeback savings.

   ___%

   How did you derive this estimate (check all that apply)?

   Mainframe usage bill ___

   Observation ___

   Other (specify: ___________) ___

6. What are your organization's plans for expanding the usage of the offloaded development environment? Please specify group size.

7. Has the quality of your group's outputs been affected by the use of the offloaded development environment (check one)?

   Yes ____ No ____

   If yes, has the change been (circle one):

Very Positive	Positive	Negative	Very Negative
4	3	2	1

8. Is there anything else the survey coordinators should know?

SUMMARY

Measurements need to be made to ensure that the offloaded development environment users and their management are getting their money's worth. What will be measured is the impact of offloaded development on productivity, quality, and mainframe usage. Possible productivity measurements include the following:

1. Function points.
2. Lines of code.
3. User surveys.

Possible quality measurements include the following:

1. Quality scores.
2. Error counts.
3. Downtime.
4. User surveys.

Possible mainframe usage measurements include the following:

1. Mainframe chargeback bills.
2. Server usage statistics.
3. User surveys.

An important thing to note in any study of mainframe usage is that the cyclical nature of some application development activities needs to be taken into account. In addition, any changes in the type of work (e.g., a shift from new development to repair maintenance) or tool usage (e.g., shifting from COBOL to EASYTRIEVE PLUS) will need to be noted.

REFERENCES

1. Albrecht, A.J. Measuring Application Development Productivity. Proceedings of the Joint IBM/SHARE/GUIDE Application Development Symposium. October 1979. 83–92.
2. Jones, Capers. 1986. *Programming Productivity*. New York: McGraw-Hill.
3. Leibs, S. Innovation Through Integration. *Information Week*. January 15, 1990. 60.
4. McCabe, T.J. A Complexity Measure. *IEEE Transactions on Software Engineering*, Vol. SE-2. December 1976. 308–320.
5. Weiss, R. Soon Integration Across Three Levels: CASE Moves Up. *Electronic Engineering Times*. April 3, 1989. 1.

12

The Future

It is futile to try to predict what impact events in the distant future (around the year 2000) will have on the developers of mainframe applications. Developments in the areas of hardware and software occur far too rapidly to make this kind of prophecy possible. As an example, most people (including the author) would never have believed in 1985 that they would be able to unit test COBOL-IMS programs on PCs in 1989. Thus, this chapter will only attempt to speculate on the impact that certain current events and trends will have on offloaded mainframe development in the next two to three years. These predictions fall into three main categories: PC hardware, software tools, and PC workstation operating systems.

PC HARDWARE

In the area of PC hardware, there is little doubt that Intel will continue to set the standard with faster and more powerful 80X86 CPU chips. This will ensure that today's PC software tools will not only run on future generations of 80X86-based PCs but will run better, since some of the current software tools (e.g., CASE tools) offer relatively poor performance on today's 386- and 486-based PCs.

SOFTWARE TOOLS

In the area of software tools (compilers, debuggers, DBMS emulators, TP monitor emulators, CASE tools) there probably will continue to be more consolidation among the vendors. In 1990 and 1991 we have seen the following activity:

1. Sage Software (vendors of APS/PC and PVCS Version Manager) merged with Index Technology (vendors of Excelerator) to become Intersolv.
2. Stingray Software (vendors of IMSVS86) and Innovative Solutions (vendors of CICSVS86) were bought out by Micro Focus (vendors of Micro Focus COBOL/2 Workbench).
3. Realia (vendors of Realia COBOL, RealCICS and RealIMS) was bought out by Pansophic Systems (vendors of TELON/PWS and PAN/LCM). Pansophic, in turn, was purchased by Computer Associates (vendors of CA-IDMS/PC, CA-ADS/PC, CA-DATACOM/PC, and CA-IDEAL/PC).

This trend probably will continue as the larger vendors attempt to expand their range of offerings by acquiring smaller companies with strategically important products. The one wild card in all this is IBM. With the 1991 announcement that the monolith would be restructured into a number of smaller businesses, the emerging IBM unit responsible for PC software may become a lot more aggressive in terms of developing mainframe emulation tools and in acquiring existing software tool vendors than it had been in its previous incarnation.

The implications of all this for the buyers and users of software tools probably will be the following:

1. *More competition for Micro Focus.* As of 1991, Micro Focus had approximately 90% of the offloaded COBOL tool market, with Realia holding most of the remainder. However, a Realia with the deep pockets of Computer Associates may be able to compete more effectively with Micro Focus than it could previously.
2. *Better integration of tools.* If a vendor owns a range of software tools (compiler, DBMS emulator, TP monitor emulator, and CASE tool) he will be able to sell more products if the tools are closely integrated. For example, close integration can mean the use of common libraries and dictionaries, seamless switching between tools, and a common presentation. These capabilities can encourage a buyer of a vendor's compiler and DBMS emulation tools to also purchase the same vendor's lower and upper CASE tools.
3. *Higher prices.* Buyouts and mergers cost money. This money, in the end, comes from the customers.

4. *Decreased levels of support and service.* In most situations, the levels of support and service decrease when a small company is acquired by a larger one. This is because the larger company usually has to provide support for a larger range of tools than did the smaller company. Consequently, when you have a problem with a particular tool, it is more difficult to find the right person to contact in the larger organization than it was in the smaller one.

PC WORKSTATION OPERATING SYSTEMS

In the arena of PC workstation operating systems, the battle of the Titans is expected to continue. Microsoft and IBM will slug it out to determine whether Windows NT or OS/2 will become the standard operating system for PC workstations within the world of offloaded development. As of the beginning of 1992, Microsoft has the early lead with Windows 3.X, but if IBM can actually deliver on all the promises it has made with OS/2 2.0, it may still emerge with the standard. These are the implications for offloaded development environment users:

1. *Easier systems integration and setup.* Offloaded development environment implementors will no longer have to fool around with memory managers and other "hocus pocus" that is now required with MS-DOS-based PC workstations.
2. *Effective multitasking.* Heavy-duty compilations and dynamic tests can be processed in the background without sacrificing foreground performance.
3. *More seamless presentation.* Switching between tools will become faster and easier.

Hopefully by 1993 or 1994 a standard will emerge so that everyone can enjoy offloaded development with far fewer hassles than is possible today.

SUMMARY

Over the next two or three years the main changes that will directly affect offloaded development environment users probably will be the following:

1. *Futher consolidation of software tool vendors.* This will lead to improved integration between software tools but at the expense of higher prices.

2. *Emergence of a standard PC workstation operating system.* With a little luck, something better than MS-DOS will emerge as a standard operating system for offloaded development environment PC workstations.

Appendix A: Sample Rollout Plan

Before starting all the work activities required to implement an offloaded development environment, a rollout plan with milestones should be drawn up. Not only is such a plan a management necessity, it will help keep observers informed as to what progress is being made. An example of a rollout plan follows. Please note that not all the activities/milestones are in sequential order. Some are concurrent with other activities.

	Activity/Milestone	Date
1.	Interview/survey potential users and issue report (collect information on work type, function, tools, and tool usage levels).	1/1 to 1/14
2.	Select and test hardware and software packages and issue report (hardware and software will include editors, compilers, DBMS emulator, TP monitor emulator, PCs, LAN; obtain training as required).	1/15 to 3/31
3.	Design and order communication links (communication links will include 3270, RJE, and LAN; identify gen parameters and design LAN; consult with LAN specialists if necessary).	4/1 to 4/14
4.	Order hardware (hardware will include PCs, LAN hardware, servers, cabling, memory chips, UPSs, and printers).	4/15 to 5/7

	Activity/Milestone	Date
5.	Order software (software will include editors, compilers, DBMS emulator, TP monitor emulator, operating systems, LAN software).	5/8 to 5/15
6.	Make baseline measurements (normally includes surveying future offloaded development environment users on their current levels of productivity and satisfaction and studying current mainframe chargeback bills).	4/1 to 5/15
7.	Take delivery of hardware/software and assemble a working model environment (assembly can begin when all the critical components are available; the LAN and server, along with a couple of PCs, should be made operational; some tuning of the environment can take place at this time). This period will usually last at least a month.	5/15 to 6/15
8.	Take delivery and test communication links (for the LAN this means wiring at a lot of different locations, mostly user's cubicles, has to be checked; for the mainframe links, this step usually means modem settings have to be tested, along with the links themselves; the gen parameters for the links also have to be checked).	6/15 to 6/30
9.	Deploy equipment to users (deploy hardware and load software on user's PC workstations; double check that all components are fully operational).	7/1 to 7/7
10.	Schedule training (after all components are deemed fully operational, training is scheduled; this sequence is important because users will need to have a fully operational environment to return to after training, or they might forget what they learned).	7/8
11.	Download user files and databases (identify which files and databases — specifications, source code, copy members, test data — will be loaded on the server and how they will be organized; just prior to becoming operational, move the identified files and databases to the server).	7/9 to 7/31
12.	Train users.	8/1 to 8/7

	Activity/Milestone	Date
13.	Users start using offloaded development environment.	8/8
14.	Measure results (measuring the impact of the offloaded development environment begins from the first day of operation. This can include LAN, server, and mainframe usage reports. Surveys, while very useful, should be done no more than once every two months. The most important measurement, though, is the user's progression through the four stages of users' involvement as detailed in Chapter 8).	8/8 & onwards

Appendix B: Glossary

ANSI — American National Standards Institute. An organization whose purpose is the establishing of voluntary industry standards in the area of computers and business equipment.

ASCII — American National Standard Code for Information Interchange. The standard code used for interchange of information on PCs and servers.

AUTOEXEC.BAT — Initial program executed when an MS-DOS or OS/2 PC is (re)booted.

BMS — Basic Mapping Support. Screen definition language used by CICS.

Bridge — Device that allows computers on one LAN to communicate with computers on another LAN using the same protocol.

Brouter — Device that has the function of a bridge and router.

BSC — Binary Synchronous Communication protocol. Usually associated with IBM mainframes.

Channel attached — Referring to the attaching of devices directly to the I/O channels of a computer.

CICS — Customer Information Control System. An IBM TP monitor.

CONFIG.SYS — Initial configuration program executed when an MS-DOS or OS/2 PC is (re)booted.

Controller — Device that can control the I/O operations of multiple connected devices.

DBMS workbench — A set of PC-based software tools that work in conjunction with a language workbench to emulate a mainframe DBMS development environment (e.g., XDB-Workbench for DB2).

DDNAME — Data definition name.

EBCDIC — Extended Binary-Coded Decision Interchange Code. The standard code used for interchange of information on mainframes.

Extended memory — Normally the RAM on PCs or servers above the 1MB line.

Flat file — A readable file made up of one- or two-dimensional arrays.

Gen — A system generation. The process of creating an operating system tailored to the specifications of a particular installation.

High DOS memory — Normally the RAM on an MS-DOS PC between the 640KB and 1MB lines.

Language workbench — A set of PC-based software tools that emulate a mainframe language development environment (e.g., Micro Focus COBOL/2 Workbench).

Low DOS memory — Normally the first 640KB of RAM on an MS-DOS PC.

MFS — Message Format Service. Screen definition language used by IMS(DC).

OA&M — Operations, administration, and maintenance.

Offloaded development environment — The collection of software and hardware (e.g., Micro Focus COBOL/2 Workbench, XDB-Workbench for DB2, PC workstations, file servers, LAN) that are used by an application developer to build applications that will run on the mainframe.

Packed data file — File that contains data in packed decimal format.

PC workstation — High-powered PC that normally has an 80386/SX CPU or higher.

RAM cram — The condition found on MS-DOS PCs when too many packages want the same chunk of RAM, usually the first 640KB.

RJE — Remote Job Entry. Normally associated with mainframe printers, punches, and readers.

Router — Device that allows computers on one LAN to communicate with computers on another LAN using different protocols. Sometimes used to connect LANs that are infrequently accessed or geographically dispersed.

SAA — IBM's Systems Applications Architecture.

SDLC — Synchronous Data Link Control. Usually associated with IBM mainframes.

Server — Micro- or minicomputer used to provide shareable services to PC-based users connected via a LAN. Some of these services include 3270 emulation, RJE emulation, e-mail, source code control, printer access, and access to shared directories/files.

SNA — Systems Network Architecture. Usually associated with IBM mainframes.

Sneaker net — The practice of using floppy diskettes to share information among PC users.

3270 — Communications protocol used by terminals to talk to mainframe networks.

TP monitor workbench — A set of PC-based software tools that work in conjunction with a language workbench to emulate a mainframe TP monitor development environment (e.g., Micro Focus CICS Option).

UPS — Uninterruptable power supply. Usually used with servers.

Vaporware — Software that does not yet exist.

WAN — Wide Area Network. A collection of network and telecommunications facilities used to link a large number of devices of a large physical area.

Appendix C: Trademarks

3+Open is a trademark or registered trademark of 3COM Corporation.

386MAX is a trademark or registered trademark of Qualitas.

3Com is a trademark or registered trademark of 3COM Corporation.

i286 is a trademark or registered trademark of Intel Corporation.

i386 is a trademark or registered trademark of Intel Corporation.

i486 is a trademark or registered trademark of Intel Corporation.

Access Plus is a trademark or registered trademark of American Telephone and Telegraph Company.

ADS/O is a trademark or registered trademark of Computer Associates, Inc.

ADSA is a trademark or registered trademark of Computer Associates, Inc.

ADW is a trademark or registered trademark of KnowledgeWare.

ADW/COBOL is a trademark or registered trademark of American Telephone and Telegraph Company.

AIX is a trademark or registered trademark of International Business Machines Corporation.

AM386 is a trademark or registered trademark of American Micro Devices.

Animator is a trademark or registered trademark of Micro Focus Limited.

Apple is a trademark or registered trademark of Apple Computer, Inc.

APS/PC is a trademark or registered trademark of INTERSOLV, Inc.

APS/MVS is a trademark or registered trademark of INTERSOLV, Inc.

AST is a trademark or registered trademark of AST Research, Inc.

AT&T is a trademark or registered trademark of American Telephone and Telegraph Company.

Attachmate is a trademark or registered trademark of Attachmate Corporation.

ATTMail is a trademark or registered trademark of American Telephone and Telegraph Company.

Bachman\Analyst is a trademark or registered trademark of Bachman Information Systems.

Banyan is a trademark or registered trademark of Banyan Systems, Inc.

BTS is a trademark or registered trademark of International Business Machines Corporation.

Central Point is a trademark or registered trademark of Central Point Software.

CICS is a trademark or registered trademark of International Business Machines Corporation.

CICS OS/2 is a trademark or registered trademark of International Business Machines Corporation.

CICSVS86 is a trademark or registered trademark of Micro Focus Limited.

Cleo is a trademark or registered trademark of Cleo Communications.

CO-MFS is a trademark or registered trademark of Micro Focus Limited.

COMPAQ is a trademark or registered trademark of COMPAQ Computer Corporation.

COMPAREX is a trademark or registered trademark of Sterling Software.

Cooperation is a trademark or registered trademark of American Telephone and Telegraph Company.

DATA-XPERT is a trademark or registered trademark of COMPUWARE.

DATACOM is a trademark or registered trademark of Computer Associates, Inc.

DataKit is a trademark or registered trademark of American Telephone and Telegraph Company.

DB2 is a trademark or registered trademark of International Business Machines Corporation.

DBASE is a trademark or registered trademark of Ashton-Tate.

DEC is a trademark or registered trademark of Digital Equipment Corporation.

DML/O is a trademark or registered trademark of Computer Associates, Inc.

DOS/16M is a trademark or registered trademark of Rational Systems.

Dr. Solomon is a trademark or registered trademark of Ontrack Computer Systems, Inc.

Easylink is a trademark or registered trademark of American Telephone and Telegraph Company.

Easytrieve Plus is a trademark or registered trademark of Computer Associates, Inc.

ENDEVOR is a trademark or registered trademark of LEGENT Corporation.

ESCORT is a trademark or registered trademark of American Telephone and Telegraph Company.

Etherlink is a trademark or registered trademark of 3COM Corporation.

Excelerator is a trademark or registered trademark of INTERSOLV, Inc.

File-AID is a trademark or registered trademark of COMPUWARE.

FOCUS is a trademark or registered trademark of Information Builders, Inc.

GroupSystems is a trademark or registered trademark of Ventana Corporation.

IBM is a trademark or registered trademark of International Business Machines Corporation.

IBM Token Ring is a trademark or registered trademark of International Business Machines Corporation.

IDD is a trademark or registered trademark of Computer Associates, Inc.

IDEAL is a trademark or registered trademark of Computer Associates, Inc.

IDMS is a trademark or registered trademark of Computer Associates, Inc.

IEW is a trademark or registered trademark of KnowledgeWare.

IMS is a trademark or registered trademark of International Business Machines Corporation.

IMSVS86 is a trademark or registered trademark of Micro Focus Limited.

Informix is a trademark or registered trademark of Informix Software, Inc.

Intersolv is a trademark or registered trademark of INTERSOLV, Inc.

IRMA is a trademark or registered trademark of Digital Communications Associates, Inc.

ISN is a trademark or registered trademark of American Telephone and Telegraph Company.

ISPF is a trademark or registered trademark of International Business Machines Corporation.

KEDIT is a trademark or registered trademark of Mansfield Software Group.

KnowledgeWare is a trademark or registered trademark of KnowledgeWare.

LAN Manager is a trademark or registered trademark of Microsoft Corporation.

Librarian is a trademark or registered trademark of Computer Associates, Inc.

Lotus 123 is a trademark or registered trademark of Lotus Development Corporation.

LPI-PL/I is a trademark or registered trademark of Liant Software Corporation.

MCIMail is a trademark or registered trademark of MCI.

Micro Focus is a trademark or registered trademark of Micro Focus Limited.

Micro Focus 370 Assembler is a trademark or registered trademark of Micro Focus Limited.

Micro Focus CICS Option is a trademark or registered trademark of Micro Focus Limited.

Micro Focus COBOL/2 is a trademark or registered trademark of Micro Focus Limited.

Micro Focus COBOL/2 Workbench is a trademark or registered trademark of Micro Focus Limited.

Micro Focus IMS Option is a trademark or registered trademark of Micro Focus Limited.

Microsoft is a trademark or registered trademark of Microsoft Corporation.

Model 204 is a trademark or registered trademark of Computer Corporation of America.

MS-DOS is a trademark or registered trademark of Microsoft Corporation.

MS-EXCEL is a trademark or registered trademark of Microsoft Corporation.

MS-Windows is a trademark or registered trademark of Microsoft Corporation.

MS-Word is a trademark or registered trademark of Microsoft Corporation.

MVS is a trademark or registered trademark of International Business Machines Corporation.

NCR is a trademark or registered trademark of American Telephone and Telegraph Company.

NetWare is a trademark or registered trademark of Novell, Inc.

NewWave is a trademark or registered trademark of Hewlett-Packard Corporation.

Norton is a trademark or registered trademark of Symantec Corporation.

OLM is a trademark or registered trademark of Computer Associates, Inc.

Oracle is a trademark or registered trademark of Oracle Corporation.

OS/2 is a trademark or registered trademark of International Business Machines Corporation.

OS/2 Database Manager is a trademark or registered trademark of International Business Machines Corporation.

Pansophic Systems is a trademark or registered trademark of Computer Associates, Inc.

Panvalet is a trademark or registered trademark of Computer Associates, Inc.

PATHVU is a trademark or registered trademark of COMPUWARE Corporation.

PFS Professional Write is a trademark or registered trademark of Software Publishing Corporation.

PMX/StarMAIL is a trademark or registered trademark of American Telephone and Telegraph Company.

Presentation Manager is a trademark or registered trademark of International Business Machines Corporation.

Portable NetWare is a trademark or registered trademark of Novell.

Proximity Software is a trademark or registered trademark of Proximity Software, Inc.

ProxMvs is a trademark or registered trademark of Proximity Software, Inc.

ProxSort is a trademark or registered trademark of Proximity Software, Inc.

PVCS is a trademark or registered trademark of INTERSOLV, Inc.

Q/AUDITOR is a trademark or registered trademark of Eden Systems.

QEMM is a trademark or registered trademark of Quarterdeck.

QMF is a trademark or registered trademark of International Business Machines Corporation.

Rabbit is a trademark or registered trademark of Rabbit Software.

RAMIS is a trademark or registered trademark of Computer Associates, Inc.

Real370 is a trademark or registered trademark of Computer Associates, Inc.

RealCICS is a trademark or registered trademark of Computer Associates, Inc.

RealDBUG is a trademark or registered trademark of Computer Associates, Inc.

RealDL/I is a trademark or registered trademark of Computer Associates, Inc.

Realia is a trademark or registered trademark of Computer Associates, Inc.

Realia COBOL is a trademark or registered trademark of Computer Associates, Inc.

RealIMS is a trademark or registered trademark of Computer Associates, Inc.

RED is a trademark or registered trademark of Computer Associates, Inc.

Relay Gold is a trademark or registered trademark of Microcom Software Division.

REXX is a trademark or registered trademark of International Business Machines Corporation.

Rhapsody is a trademark or registered trademark of American Telephone and Telegraph Company.

RM-COBOL is a trademark or registered trademark of Liant Software Corporation.

S-COBOL is a trademark or registered trademark of INTERSOLV, Inc.

SAA is a trademark or registered trademark of International Business Machines Corporation.

Sage Software is a trademark or registered trademark of INTERSOLV, Inc.

SAS is a trademark or registered trademark of SAS Institute.

SORTMVS is a trademark or registered trademark of Micro Focus Limited.

SPF/2 is a trademark or registered trademark of Command Technology Corporation.

SPF/PC is a trademark or registered trademark of Command Technology Corporation.

SPSS is a trademark or registered trademark of SPSS, Inc.

SPUFI is a trademark or registered trademark of International Business Machines Corporation.

StarGROUP is a trademark or registered trademark of American Telephone and Telegraph Company.

Stingray Software is a trademark or registered trademark of Micro Focus Limited.

SyncSort is a trademark or registered trademark of SyncSort, Inc.

System Strategies is a trademark or registered trademark of NYNEX.

TELON/PWS is a trademark or registered trademark of Computer Associates, Inc.

TESTCOB is a trademark or registered trademark of International Business Machines Corporation.

Time Line is a trademark or registered trademark of Symantec Corporation.

TransJCL is a trademark or registered trademark of Miller-Fairchild.

TRAPS is a trademark or registered trademark of Computer Associates, Inc.

Tritus is a trademark or registered trademark of Tritus, Inc.

Tritus SPF is a trademark or registered trademark of Tritus, Inc.

TSO is a trademark or registered trademark of International Business Machines Corporation.

UNIX is a trademark or registered trademark of UNIX System Laboratories.

VAX is a trademark or registered trademark of Digital Equipment Corporation.

Ventura is a trademark or registered trademark of XEROX Corporation.

Viewpoint is a trademark or registered trademark of Computer Aided Management.

VINES is a trademark or registered trademark of Banyan Systems, Inc.

VM is a trademark or registered trademark of International Business Machines Corporation.

WordPerfect is a trademark or registered trademark of WordPerfect Corporation.

XDB is a trademark or registered trademark of XDB Systems.

XDB-Workbench for DB2 is a trademark or registered trademark of XDB Systems.

XENIX is a trademark or registered trademark of Microsoft Corporation.

XM is a trademark or registered trademark of Micro Focus Limited.

XEROX is a trademark or registered trademark of XEROX Corporation.

XPEDITER is a trademark or registered trademark of COMPUWARE Corporation.

Index

3+Open LAN Manager, 157
3B2, 28
3Com Etherlink, 157
286 PC, 224
386- or 486-, 156
386, 48, 217, 243
386MAX, 123
486/SX PC, 224
486, 48, 217, 243
3270, 67, 159, 160, 164, 165, 168, 169, 170, 194, 197, 198, 204, 217
  controller, 150
  emulation, 62
3274/6 emulation, 160
80286, 44, 128
80386, 120, 128, 158
  /SX, 44, 128, 129
80486, 44, 158
  /SX, 44

A
Administrative procedures, 206
Administrator(s), 62, 63, 64, 66, 193, 52, 197, 201, 217
  training, 67
ADW/COBOL, 178
Albrecht, A. J., 229, 241
AM386, 44
American Micro Devices, 44
Analysts, 15
Anchor Pad International, 214
Animator, 12, 29, 91, 95, 96, 106, 110, 111, 112
ANSI, 96, 101, 186
Application Development Workgroup/ COBOL, 28, 176
APS/PC, 49, 84, 114, 115, 116, 117, 129, 143, 244
Architecture, 47, 133, 136
ASCII, 68, 76, 88, 95, 96, 105, 108, 111, 119, 169, 172, 204, 206
Assembler, 61
AST, 155
AT&T, 27, 28, 29, 29, 30, 46, 49, 155, 177, 226
  6500, 160, 164
  Application Development Solutions
  Application Development Workgroup/COBOL, 51, 177
  Easylink, 33, 153
  ESCORT, 95
  Mail, 33
  LAN Manager, 157
  NCR, 120, 174
  StarGROUP, 151
  StarGROUP/StarLAN, 48

StarLAN, 47
Attachmate, 141, 150, 174
ATTMail, 153, 174, 225

B
Bachman, 117
Analyst, 129
Back up, 135, 138, 139, 144, 204, 211, 215, 216
administrator, 225
Banyan VINES, 158
Bell South, 34
Benefits, 25, 36, 37
BMS, 110
Borland, 33
Bridges, 227
Brouters, 228
BSC, 160, 169, 172, 108

C
CA
ADS/PC, 109, 244
DATACOM, 103, 109
/PC, 244
IDEAL/PC, 109, 244
IDMS/PC, 244
LIBRARIAN, 77, 138, 141
PANVALET, 77, 138, 141
TELON/PWS, 84, 95, 117, 118
TRAPS, 16, 95, 120
Case locks, 214
CASE, 15, 20, 30, 49, 71, 76, 77, 78, 79, 81, 82, 84, 113, 118, 128, 134, 150, 152, 169, 177, 198, 201, 223, 243, 244
Central Point Anti-Virus, 214
Change Management, 4
Channel-attached, 12
Charandon Group, 111
Chassis lock, 214
Checker, 12, 29, 91, 95
CICS, 106, 109, 110, 111, 112, 114, 116
BMS, 78
IMS(DC), 84
DL/I, 108
VS86, 244
Cleo Communications, 174
Client-server, 32, 80, 171
CO-MFS, 108
Coaxial cable, 193, 194
COBOL, 12, 15, 28, 32, 61, 78, 84, 87, 88, 91, 95, 96, 96, 101, 102, 103, 104, 108, 114, 177, 233, 244
II, 61
code generators, 49
DB2, 67, 68, 201
IMS, 243
COBOL to Easytrieve Plus, 241
2 Workbench, 115
Code Generators, 4, 15, 71, 72
Command Technology Corporation, 84, 87
Common modules, 5
Communication links, 197
COMPAQ, 155
COMPAREX, 4, 16
Compatibility, 186
Compiler(s), 12, 95, 133, 244, 198, 243
Compilers/Run Time Environments, 4
Computer Associate's, 49, 96, 116, 120, 244
CA-IDMS(DB), 103
CA-TELON/PWS, 113, 116, 224
CA-IDMS, 109
CA-PAN/LCM, 220, 220
TELON, 49
Computer viruses, 212
COMPUWARE's
File-AID, 95
XPEDITER, 91
Costs, 13, 45
CSI, 95
Cubical layout, 194
Cumulative contracts, 50

D
Data handlers, 118
tools, 71
DATA-XPERT, 95
DATACOM, 84
DataKit, 194, 226
DB2, 61, 78, 81, 84, 103, 104, 105, 106, 114, 116, 183, 230
SQL, 110

DBA(s), 13, 81, 107
DBMS, 4, 5, 76, 77, 81, 133, 198
  Emulator, 71, 72, 79, 84, 125, 243, 244
  workbench, 103
DDNAME, 80
Debuggers, 4, 133, 243
DEC, 158, 174
Delivery considerations, 192
Development Cycle, 11
Dial-up links, 228
Digital, 155
  Communications Associates (DCA), 174
  VMS Services for PCs, 158
Direct links, 227
Discounts, 50
DLT0, 81, 108
DML, 106
DML/O, 81
Documentation, 80, 83, 104, 115, 117, 170, 172
Doherty, W. J, 23, 25, 40
DOS/16M, 97
Downtime, 237
Dr. Solomon's Anti-Virus Toolkit, 214
DRAM chips, 45
Dumb terminal usage, 200
Dynamic activity monitor, 235

E
E-mail, 17, 18, 33, 34, 136, 150, 153, 208, 210, 225, 235
EASYTRIEVE PLUS, 233
EBCDIC, 68, 76, 88, 95, 96, 105, , 108, 111, 119, 169, 172, 204
  /ASCII, 205
Editor(s), 14, 2, 79, 88, 91, 198
Education levels, 20
Electronic
  mail, 33, 174
  meetings, 34
Error counts, 237
ESCORT, 16, 120
EXCELERATOR, 115, 117, 120, 244
Exec Language Interpreter (JCL), 4
Expectations, 21

F
FEP, 160, 164, 165
Fiber, 194
  optic cable, 193
File
  access, 203
  -AID/PC, 120
  movement, 204
  transfer logs, 235
  translations, 205
Fire extinguisher, 217
Flash cutting, 61
Floor plan, 193
Floppy locks, 214
Freedom of Information Act, 50
Full environment emulation, 201
Function point(s), 229, 230

G
Gens, 192
Gradual approach, 62
Graphics, 34
GroupSystems, 34
Groupware, 18, 33, 40, 175

H
Hand holding, 208
Hard disk space, 158
Hardware interrupts, 185
Hawthorne effect, 29
Hewlett Packard's NewWave, 33
Highwater marks, 185

I
I/O, 159
IBM, 105, 12, 25, 26, 27, 29, 34, 37, 88, 112, 124, 155, 158, 173, 186, 229, 244, 245
  370 Assembler, 87
  3274/6, 160, 164
  Assembler, 84, 102
  DFSORT, 119
  OS/VS COBOL, 4, 76, 88, 91, 97, 110, 116
  PL/I, 116
  VS COBOL, 97

VS COBOL II, 76, 88, 91, 110, 114
IBM's CICS OS/2, 109, 111, 112
DB2, 103
IMS, 106
ISPF, 79, 84
Token Ring, 46, 47
XEDIT, 87
IDMS, 61, 84
(DB), 114
(DC), 84
/PC, 49
IEW/ADW, 117
IMS, 28, 61, 81, 84, 114
(DB), 106
(DB/DC), 78
DL/I, 110
MFS, 78
(DB), 103, 116, 230
(DB/DC), 108
(DC), 114, 116
VS86, 108, 108, 244
Incompatibilities, 182, 183
Index Technology, 244
Innovative Solutions, 110, 244
Installation, 196
Intel, 122, 128, 243
80X86, 43, 44
Interlanguage calls, 5, 6
Intersolv's APS/PC, 49, 113, 224
Intersolv, 116, 244
PVCS, 220, 222
IRMA, 141, 143, 150
ISMS, 81
ISN, 194, 226
ISPF, 12, 87, 88, 114

J

Jackson, 78
JCL, 31
emulators, 71, 118, 1198
JES, 173, 205
Job satisfaction, 7
Jonathan Sayles, 105
Jones, Capers, 41, 241

K

KEDIT, 87
Kelisky, 25
Keyboard mapping, 169
Keylock password, 212
Knowledge levels, 7
KnowledgeWare's
Application Development Workbench (ADW), 176
IEW/ADW, 115

L

Lambert, G. N., 23, 40
Lambert(s), 25, 28, 29
LAN, 17
gateware, 164
Manager, 157
statistics, 235
Language Workbench, 71, 79, 87, 134
Languages, 5
Learning Curve, 54, 138, 139, 147, 150
LEGENT Corporation's ENDEVOR, 220, 222
Liant, 88, 101
Libraries, 207
Licensing Considerations, 190
Lines of code, 229, 230, 231
Lower CASE, 4, 72
LPI, 102
PL/I, 101
LRECL, 82, 205, 173, 204
LU 6.2, 159

M

Mainframe charges, 7
Mainframe Usage, 30, 40, 229, 232
Maintenance, 14
plans, 190
Management, 3, 18, 19, 20, 22, 62, 65
Managers, 21
Mansfield, Software Group, 87
Mao Tse-tung, 61
Martin, 78
McCabe, T. J., 241

McCabe's Cyclomatic Complexity metric, 236
MCI Mail, 33, 153
Measurements, 199
Memory
  addresses, 185
  boards, 185
Metrics, 175
MFS, 108
Micro Focus, 28, 31, 46, 48, 88, 96, 104, 110, 115, 119, 143, 244
  370 Assembler, 102
  CICS Option, 95, 105, 109, 111, 112, 115, 129
  CO-MFS, 107
  COBOL, 223, 224
  COBOL Workbench, 49, 182, 185
  COBOL/2 Workbench, 68, 88, 91, 106, 108, 111, 127, 129
  IMS Option, 95, 105, 106, 107, 115, 129, 182
  XM, 6, 122, 123
Microsoft, 33, 88, 157, 245
Model 204, 4
Modems, 67
Morgan Stanley, 35
MS-Windows, 121, 122, 124, 125, 126, 128, 129, 135, 138, 143, 145
MVS, 12
  TSO, 13
  SORT, 31

N

Naming conventions, 202
NCR's Cooperation, 33
  WaveLAN, 46
NetWare, 158
New Development, 11
NFS, 107
NORTON Anti-Virus, 214
Novell NetWare, 46, 157
NYNEX, 174

O

OA&M, 54
OA, 35
  groupware, 34
Object Oriented Programming, 96
Office Automation (OA), 33, 35, 40
Offloaded editing, 201
Operation, Administration, and Maintenance (OA&M), 53
OS/2, 32, 67, 87, 88, 96, 105, 106, 108, 116, 121, 124, 125, 128, 129, 135, 143, 145, 147, 152, 155, 157, 158, 168, 245
  2.0, 177
  Database Manager, 105

P

PAN/LCM, 244
Panko, Raymond R., 41, 35
Pansophic Systems, 96, 116, 244
Password aging, 216
PATHVU, 231, 236
Pitfalls, 59, 60
PL/I, 5, 61, 84, 87, 101
Playback Test Tools, 4
PLI, 102
POTS lines, 176
Pricing considerations, 191
Printers, 156, 199, 207
Production, 16
Productivity, 11, 20, 40, 229, 230
Programmer(s), 15, 31
Project
  leaders, 18
  management, 17
Protocol converters, 160
Prototyping, 81
PROXMVS, 31, 119
PROXSORT, 119
PVCS Version Manager, 244

Q

Q/AUDITOR, 231, 236
QEMM, 123
QMF, 81
Qualitas' 386MAX, 122, 126
Quality, 12, 20, 29, 40, 229, 236

Quarterdeck's QEMM, 122, 126

R

R. P. Kelisky, 23, 40
Rabbit Software, 174
RAM cram, 183, 184
Rational Systems', 97
    DOS/16M, 127
Real
    370, 102
    CICS, 108, 109, 111, 112, 129, 244
    DBUG, 97
    DL/I, 111
    FED, 97
    IMS, 106
    IMS, 108
    IMS, 129
    IMS, 244
Realia, 48, 49, 88, 97, , 101, 104, 108, 111, 244
    COBOL, 96, 127, 129, 244
RED, 97
Regression testing tools, 71
Release Management, 4
Report painter, 81
Report Writers, 4
Reset button, 216
Response time, 12
Restoration procedures, 216
REXX, 87
RISC, 43, 44, 156
RJE(s), 67, 159, 164, 165, 171, 173, 198, 205
    file transfer, 168
RM-COBOL, 88, 101
Roach, S. S., 35, 41
Rollout Plan, 198, 247
Routers, 227
Runtime environment, 95
Ryan McFarland, 88, 101

S

S-COBOL, 114, 115
SAA, 105
Sage Software, 244
Sales representatives, 182
Sayles, Jonathan, 120
SDLC/SNA, 169, 172
Security, 135, 138, 139, 144, 154, 170, 193, 211, 226
Server 47
Shareware/freeware, 213
SNA/SDLC, 160
Sneakernet, 213
SORTMVS, 119
Source code control, 217, 218, 219
    (library), 135, 138, 144
SPF
    2, 87
    PC, 28, 84, 201
Spreadsheets, 4, 17, 34
SPSS, 224
SPUFI, 81, 103
SQL, 103, 104, 105, 187
StarGROUP, 49
StarLAN, 28, 46, 157, 158
Statistical packages, 4
Stingray, 108
    Software Company, 106
    Software, 244
Stockpiling, 50
Strategy, 19

Subsecond response time, 12, 25, 32, 77, 139, 145, 148
Surge suppressor, 211
Survey(s), 5, 200, 229, 231, 235
SyncSort, 4, 31
System
- analysis, 20
- password, 212
- Strategies, 174
- testers, 16

T

TELON/
- PC, 129
- PWS, 49, 244

Terminal emulation, 201
Test Data Generation, 4
TESTCOB, 12, 29
Testing, 14, 15, 31, 181, 183, 237
Thadhani, A. J., 23, 25, 27, 40
TIMELINE, 17
Token Ring, 157, 158
TP Monitor(s), 4, 5, 13, 71, 72, 76, 77, 84
- Emulator, 79, 125, 105, 244, 133, 243
- Workbenches, 109

Training, 52, 53, 66, 79, 82, 115, 118, 200
TransJCL, 119
Tritus, 87
- SPF, 87

Trouble logs, 208
TSO, 7, 14, 30
Twister pair, 193

U

UniSoft, 125
UNIX, 16, 32, 32, 67, 101, 121, 124, 125, 135, 145, 147, 151, 155, 157, 158, 168, 177, 206, 210, 216, 235
Upper CASE, 72
- Tools, 4

UPS, 153, 156, 199, 215
User
- meetings, 208
- procedures, 201

Utilities, 4

V

Vaporware, 191
VARs, 45, 49, 50, 192
VAX, 155
Ventana Corporation, 34
VIEWPOINT, 17
Viruses, 216
VSAM, 114, 116

W

WAN(s), 67, 175, 176, 194, 226
Windows NT, 245
Word processing, 4, 17, 33

X

XDB DB2
- Workbench, 95, 104, 115, 129, 182, 224
- Systems, 103, 104, 105

XDB-Workbench for DB2, 68, 103, 223
XM, 95, 96, 127
XPEDITER, 77

Y

Yourdon, 78